STAYING IN LOVE
explains how to work your way through the different emotional realities that are a part of any relationship, to a mutually satisfying partnership. It also discusses new patterns of relating that have been emerging in recent years and new lifestyles that have become widespread.

Most important, it tells how to create a partnership that is appropriate for you and your partner as individuals, with your own special ways of experiencing life.

—DR. NORTON F. KRISTY
in the Introduction

STAYING IN LOVE:
Reinventing Marriage And Other Love Relationships

STAYING IN LOVE

REINVENTING MARRIAGE AND OTHER LOVE RELATIONSHIPS

DR. NORTON F. KRISTY
WITH MARION MAUK

A JOVE BOOK

Copyright © 1980 by Norton F. Kristy and Marion Mauk

All rights reserved. No part of this publication may be reproduced or transmitted in any form or by any means, electronic or mechanical, including photocopy, recording, or any information storage and retrieval system, without permission in writing from the publisher.

Requests for permission to make copies of any part of the work should be mailed to: Permissions, Jove Publications, Inc., 200 Madison Avenue, New York, NY 10016

First Jove edition published October 1980

10 9 8 7 6 5 4 3 2 1

Printed in the United States of America

Jove books are published by Jove Publications, Inc.,
200 Madison Avenue, New York, NY 10016

To Davida, Brickton and April, and to those special friends who have so enriched my life.

Contents

Introduction		1
Chapter 1	A Successful Marriage is a Personal Invention	5
Chapter 2	How to Design a Loving Relationship	15
Chapter 3	Inventing a Loving Sexual Partnership	36
Chapter 4	Extramarital Sex in Modern Marriage	61
Chapter 5	Swinging, Swapping and Sexual Freedom	75
Chapter 6	Great Expectations and Other Problems	87
Chapter 7	Dealing With Anger	96
Chapter 8	No-Win Marital Games	110
Chapter 9	When Sex Turns Sour	122
Chapter 10	Jealousy is an Awful Pain	145
Chapter 11	Reinventing a Failing Marriage	162
Chapter 12	Radical Alternatives for Reinventing a Marriage	177
Chapter 13	Will History Repeat Itself?	188
Chapter 14	Live-in Arrangements	202
Chapter 15	Improving Your Chances for a Successful Marriage	220
"The State of Your Union" Questionnaire		227
Answers to the Questionnaire		238

Introduction

Creating an emotional partnership is different today from what it was a mere twenty-five years ago. We have new options and possibilities in our pairings, and new pressures and problems. We are confronted with a smorgasbord of possible choices in lifestyle and ways of relating. But in gaining this freedom to shape our relationships in new ways, we have lost the securities and stabilities, traditions, beliefs and myths that helped our grandparents know themselves and live accordingly. We have been thrown back on ourselves to identify who we are and what kinds of connections with others will make us feel safe, comfortable and pleased with ourselves.

In these circumstances, millions of couples have marriages and other pairings that are less satisfying than they could be. Some have partnerships that are rewarding in some ways but lack the closeness and intimacy or the sexual satisfaction they want. Others are stuck in relationships that contain a great deal of anger and unhappiness. Many feel locked into traditional marital roles that frustrate their desire and capacity for personal growth. Some in experimental lifestyles find aspects of their experience troubling.

It isn't necessary for two people to remain in painful or unrewarding ways of relating. A partnership can be reinvented if partners learn how to go about making this kind of change.

I use the word *reinvent* for this process of recreating a marriage that is disappointing in some way, because it conveys a concrete image of what two people must do to achieve the kind of relationship they want. There is no precise marital pattern to follow; there is no one model of marriage that is appropriate for everyone—or even for the majority of human personalities. And no two couples face exactly the same problems. Every marriage has its special constellation of difficult issues carrying some degree of pain, anger, fear or doubt associated with the partners' earlier experiences in life. These issues, which become the foci of pain and disillusionment between partners, are as varied as human experience and personality.

Staying In Love explains how to work your way through the different emotional realities that are a part of any relationship, to a mutually satisfying partnership. It also discusses new patterns of relating that have been emerging in marriage in recent years, and talks about new lifestyles that have become widespread (living together without marriage, open marriage, swinging and mate-swapping), pointing out the advantages some persons find in these lifestyles and the difficulties encountered by many others. Most important, it tells how to create a partnership that is appropriate for you and your partner as individuals, with your own special ways of experiencing life.

As a psychotherapist and marriage counselor, I have discussed aspects of this subject (and others) for more than ten years on radio call-in programs. I do not do marriage counseling or psychotherapy on the radio, but give short informational talks and converse with people who call in about their marital problems. In this setting, I have talked to thousands of men and women about their emotional partnerships. Their experiences have run the gamut from traditional marriage to new, experimental lifestyles. They reflect what is happening in intimate relationships between men and women in our society.

Most of the many experiences that are discussed in this book were selected from the radio conversations that I participated in on the popular "Bill Ballance Show," which originated in Los Angeles and San Diego, and was syndicated in more than seventy cities across the United States and Canada.* The

---

*Bill Ballance currently broadcasts on the West Coast from KFMB, San Diego.

names of callers are fictitious, of course.

What I have attempted to do in these discussions of personal experiences is to lay open the emotional realities of human relationships. I talk in terms of the feelings we have about ourselves, of how we use ourselves to get what we want, how we protect ourselves, and how, in protecting ourselves, we sometimes effectively block getting what we want. In specific situations important feelings behind what a person says, feelings the caller may not have been fully aware of, are discussed. I don't always try to create a rational understanding; rather, I attempt to trigger emotional awareness of feelings in relationships, an "Aha!" sense of the connection of this feeling with that feeling, or this behavior with that set of feelings.

Many people operate on the premise that we are rational beings. We think that if we can understand with our heads, we can then solve any kind of problem. But the reality is that by far the greater part of our behavior is determined by our feelings, sensitivities and sentimentalities. We're very complex amalgams of past, present and future feelings, hopes, dreams and fears.

Frequently radio listeners from around the country have written or called to say that my comment to a particular caller on a question has triggered a realization about their own lives and that, as a result, they have made certain changes in their relationships. I believe that *Staying In Love* can be even more helpful. In writing a book, I have been able to expand my comments on the individual experiences that are presented in the various chapters, and discuss what I have sensed about the life situation of the caller through intensely tuning in on this individual, hearing what really was said—and what was not said, which can be just as important.

I have also been able to provide much more extensive discussion of emotional partnerships and the psychological aspects of our lives than is possible on a radio program. I have tried to give specific guidelines for creating intimacy, negotiating differences, and coping with sexual problems, anger and jealousy. Also included is a "State of Your Union" questionnaire, which can be useful not only for evaluation of the state of a partnership but as a tool for opening the kind of communication needed to improve it. Chapter discussions spell out what might be done to turn a marriage with a great amount of anger in it into a rewarding one. They include an explanation of the concept of marriage partners as "roommates," which I developed as a therapeutic technique for use with couples whose anger at one another and hostile patterns of relating are too deeply entrenched for ordinary marriage-counseling techniques to be effective, yet who, at some fairly deep level, don't want to break up the marriage. This concept, which I first described publicly in a speech at the annual meeting of the American Association of Marriage Counselors in 1971, is now being used by many marriage counselors throughout the country.

The book also makes clear when reinventing a marriage probably is impossible and tells how to handle a divorce, when that is the only workable answer, so that one can avoid repeating past mistakes in any new partnership.

Chapter 1

A Successful Marriage is a Personal Invention

We live in a time when to have a successful marriage (or important pairing without marriage) you have to invent your own model. You can no longer follow the model of your parents, for their relationship, typically, was not one that meets present expectations of marriage or of life.

If a partnership is to remain successful, the inventive process must continue over a lifetime. We all change as we pass through the various stages of life. Ways of relating that work in one period of a partnership may not work as the attitudes and desires of partners change. So a successful marriage needs not only to be invented but periodically *reinvented*. Whenever there are nagging frustrations, some reinventing of the marriage is needed.

Profound changes in society over the last half-century have thrust us into this new era in marital relationships. But the key element in present requirements for successful matrimony is simple and personal. *We expect a partnership to make us happy*.

In the past, when a marriage brought more pain than pleasure, people generally accepted it as the way life was. Today, people feel that they deserve better than the pain and frustration of a bad marriage, and won't endure them. Out of the affluence and mobility of our society, the freedom of choice in style of living, the concept has evolved in our thinking that the individual really has a right to happiness. This dramatic rise in our expectations of life is largely responsible for our divorce rate, twelve times that of fifty years ago. It is also a significant factor in the present rapid change in the ways men and women relate in marriage.

Today millions of persons, pursuing their personal notions of a rewarding partnership, have marriages that differ markedly from those typical in the relatively recent past. A sizable minority of the population is experimenting with lifestyles radically different from traditional patterns. Some two million persons are estimated to live with persons of the opposite sex in semi-spousal relationships without marriage. "Open marriage" (with both partners free to have relationships individually with members of the opposite sex) is being tried by a small but increasing minority. Mate-swapping parties for couples seeking varied sexual experience have sprung up in cities around the country.

Millions of other persons are struggling to make some accommodation between traditional marital attitudes and newer social attitudes—attitudes toward male and female roles, sex, child-raising, family, and marriage itself.

Inevitably, there is great variety in the ways particular couples relate. We human beings are not all alike in our predilections. We vary in the way we view the world around us and in our conception of what constitutes a rewarding life. We vary in the ways we go about getting what we want out of life. Nevertheless, there are factors in modern life and marriage with which every couple must deal. Definite trends have emerged in new ways of relating successfully in marriage.

The Trend Toward Coequal Relationships

One major factor in what is happening, of course, is our changed and still changing perception of women. In the past in this country, marriage was usually viewed as dominated by men in terms of control and decision-making. It often happened that a dependent man married a strong woman and the situation was somewhat reversed, but they more or less had to hide this from society and, in a way, from each other.

Today the dominant-dependent kind of marriage is fading out. The trend for some years has been toward coequal relationships.

An important outgrowth of this has been a diminishing of role differentiation between the sexes. More and more, men are not saddled with the sole responsibility of making a living, and women with the sole responsibility of homemaking and child-rearing.

With our relatively new affluence, combined with the breakdown of old role definitions, we now have the freedom to invent whatever kind of marriage roles we want. The variety of lifestyles that has evolved out of this freedom in the last few years is almost infinite. In some marriages, traditional emphasis on the man's career has been replaced by similar emphasis on the advancement of the woman's career. In other two-career marriages, a man concentrates on the pursuit of his career for five or six years, then gives priority to his wife's for the next five or six years. Also beginning to be seriously considered as acceptable is an almost complete reversal of traditional roles, with the wife making the living and the husband staying home to rear children and care for the home. Less extreme departures from tradition are commonplace.

There is no reason why these variations from tradition in marital roles cannot work out well. In recent decades there has been more and more evidence that the old concepts of masculinity and femininity, which played a strong part in traditional marital role definitions, were more a product of cultural influences than of inherent biological makeup. When young people grow up with both sexes having similar experiences, there are few profound emotional and psychological differences between them. The similarities are much greater than the remaining differences. Individuals of both sexes reflect the entire spectrum of human traits.

For instance, studies show that the proportion of men possessing a high natural aptitude for child-rearing, an aptitude long assumed to be predominantly female, is nearly as large as the proportion of women with the same high aptitude. And the proportion of women who are very low in this aptitude is almost as great as the proportion of men.

The Confusion of Changing Relationships

However, this transitional period is confusing and upsetting for many people. Most of us have been indoctrinated with rigid ideas of masculine and feminine roles. Letting go of these familiar attitudes and adjusting to new ones does not come easily, even when we have recognized that old roles are no longer desirable.

This was apparent in the marriage of twenty-one-year-old Ann, who had a warm relationship with her husband, Lou, but was distressed by the lingering influence of traditional marital stereotypes in her life.

She had lived with Lou for three months before their marriage, and during that time had felt herself an independent individual, "a really liberated person," admired by others.

"People seemed to think I was very dynamic and intelligent," she said. "Now they refer to me as 'just a housewife.' I find myself unable to cope with this housewife image. You know there's a stereotype society places on married women—that they go to bed with cold cream and curlers in their hair and nag their husbands. These things just aren't true. How an individual is varies with the person. But with this kind of demeaning image, just being in a state of marriage makes me feel guilty and mad at myself for letting myself get into this trap."

The most disturbing aspect of this situation, to Ann, was that she frequently suspected that her husband shared this stereotyped image of a wife, and that perhaps in some way she herself had changed.

"For example, he likes to buy me little gifts," she recounted. "We don't have a lot of money and sometimes I warn him he shouldn't spend the money. I think maybe he thinks I'm nagging at him and starting to sound like the stereotype and that I don't realize it. And sometimes when other men joke about marriage in a way that puts down wives, he laughs along with them and may even add a crack of his own. Yet he apologizes when I mention it and is usually very understanding and considerate."

Ann's problem was that Lou, like most men, had been taught by our society, both directly and indirectly, that men are more important than women and that a wife is somehow merely an extension of her husband. In fact, he had grown up in a subculture in which the concept of male supremacy is particularly important. Part of the baggage that has accumulated around this concept are demeaning caricatures such as those mentioned by her.

Ann believed that Lou had changed his attitudes toward women since knowing her, and had come to share her belief in the equality of men and women. But a more accurate view would be that his attitudes *were changing* rather than that they *had changed*. When you are conditioned to any kind of bias or stereotype, you can have an intense experience that convinces you that one person escapes your preconceived view of a particular group, but that doesn't break down the earlier conditioning. You still have to go through a long learning process.

The Need to Change the Ways We See Ourselves

Much of the confusion that Ann and others experience in trying to give up old attitudes in marriage occurs because creating new ways of relating with the opposite sex involves changing the ways in which you see yourself.

The experience of twenty-nine-year-old Ron shows this from a man's point of view. His traditional attitudes about masculinity had prevented him from having a close relationship with his wife. In the distress and upset of divorce, he had come to understand this, and had begun to let go of those attitudes.

"I was only twenty-two when I was married and I guess I had a limited idea of what a man should be like," he told me. "I'm a policeman and I felt I had to be pretty hard-shelled on the job. My wife complained that I was that way at home, too. It got to be a habit, keeping my emotions down and not showing them. She said it made her feel like she wasn't doing enough. After five years she left me. She said she wanted a man who was more open and loving."

The divorce shook Ron up badly, and in trying to figure out what had happened to his marriage, he learned a great deal about himself.

"I eventually realized that I had been trying so hard to be a tough, courageous cop that I hardly knew I had any feelings," he explained. "I didn't know how to go about being open about them and relating to her the way she wanted. It didn't fit into my idea of a man then. But I sure had feelings when she left."

When he called the radio program, Ron was dating another woman. With his new self-knowledge, he found his old inflexibility in a man's role dropping away. The idea of being tender with someone didn't scare him as much as it had with his wife. He was able to be much more open and affectionate.

A Married Couple is Two Separate Persons

In addition to such changing attitudes toward sex roles, frequently an element in the thinking of couples working out nontraditional partnerships is the recognition, uncommon in the fairly recent past, that when two people marry, they are still two separate persons with their own identities and preferences. This is a useful insight. To perceive oneself as simply part of a couple, as many of us have been conditioned to do, is to deny the reality of our individuality and separateness as persons, and is usually undesirable. One result of this new perception has been a trend toward partners having separate interests, activities and friends (and in less frequent cases, lovers) as well as interests, activities and friends in common.

One of the many persons who called the radio program reflecting this kind of thinking was twenty-eight-year-old Dan. He had gone into marriage with some traditional ideas about the relationship and the male role, but he had not liked the consequences of these. He hadn't liked having a woman psychologically dependent on him, and he hadn't liked the supertogetherness created by ideas about marriage that come down to us from the forties and fifties.

"I know that I had a traditional view of a woman as being dependent, but this was a drag on me," he said. "My wife, Lisa, thought we should do everything together. I felt stifled. I felt I needed some time to do things on my own. As a result, we almost broke up."

But rather than give up the relationship or remain stuck in the situation, Dan had decided that marriage didn't need to be so confining—that it could give more room for each person's individuality. He had proceeded to work this out with his wife, who also realized she had lost something after marriage.

"She had been quite an independent person earlier," he said. "But once married, she had begun to think of herself mostly as just part of a twosome. And I was inclined to expect her to go along with my ideas on how things should be. We both decided that we had to change our attitudes toward marriage. Since then, she too has begun to fight for her independence. I didn't care for her friends but she insisted on seeing them anyhow. It worked out well because now I like them. And I've begun to be more ready to listen to her point of view. Also, we take a week of separate vacations. When we get back together, we have a lot of things to talk about. At first I spent more time away from home than she did. When I came home, I'd find notes from her all over the house—like, 'I'll meet you in the bathroom.' I got a kick out of it and I let her know I'd missed her when I was away. Now I find I have the urge to get away less and less."

The Mythology of Marriage

As can be seen in each of the preceding marriages, part of the difficulties young couples have in creating new-style relationships relates to the fact that most of us carry into marriage some of the expectations of earlier generations that don't quite fit our modern expectations of life. In fact, by far the majority of young persons go into marriage with quite traditional expectations and then find that the roles they adopt do not give them what they want.

A great many of these attitudes and expectations come from the myth in our culture that marriage is for women. The mythology is basically nonsense that tends to create distorted values and attitudes which account for a great deal of stress in teenage marriage.

One part of the myth is that men are naturally reluctant to make emotional commitments, and allow themselves to be dragged into marriage primarily because they want easy and regular access to sex. The myth has partial validity in the case of very young men, who generally experience sexual desire more intensely than women of the same age, and sometimes do marry for sexual availability and regularity. But research has shown that men have as strong a need for tenderness, for the feeling of being loved, and for affectionate companionship as women do.

The other side of the myth is that marriage makes a woman happy and complete, and that the woman who isn't married is an inadequate, unfulfilled person. Women generally have been brought up with this idea and the related implication that females are less valuable than males. It is an attitude unlikely to create self-esteem, and the majority of young women still view themselves as dependent persons unable to cope with life independently.

Despite the high rate of divorce and the fact that half of all married mothers are now in the work force, three out of four female high school seniors surveyed by the California Commission on the Status of Women in 1970/71 considered marriage their primary future occupation, and did not see themselves as requiring preparation for another vocation. As a result, very young women often accept or even grab at the first minimally reasonable offer of marriage without testing their options or possibilities.

Typically, they go into marriage expecting to fill the traditional dependent female role, and implicitly give control and direction of their persons to their husbands, essentially sending out the message, "Take care of me. Make me happy." Even young women who have fought for independence from their parents, going through tempestuous teenage years when they felt great resentment at parental control, in the early stages of marriage will turn over their persons to their husbands, making the husband a surrogate parent.

A few women find this kind of relationship comfortable enough, but the great majority come to resent their unequal position more and more. A marriage suffers from this resentment in many indirect ways. This is true even in societies such as those of the Middle East, in which the tradition of considering women much less valuable than men is especially strong. A woman who feels powerless usually fights back indirectly, and Moslem women have ways of getting back at their men. They "zap" a husband through control of the children, or by denying sexual contact and closeness, or by becoming ill, even seriously ill, with real diseases that often have a psychosomatic basis.

In our own society this issue of male dominance is a more frequent cause of problems in marriage than any other.

Twenty-three-year-old Janet, married to a man ten years older than herself, was one of the many women troubled by this kind of problem.

"He never asks me what I want before he gets me something," she complained. "When I needed a new sewing machine, he picked it out and brought it home, and it wasn't the kind I wanted. When he bought me a new car, he just drove it up to the house. I didn't even know he was going to buy one. And it's too big for me. I have to sit on a cushion to drive it. I don't even like the color.

"In many ways he's the perfect husband," she went on. "But I don't feel I'm number one with him. I'm playing second fiddle to his sister, his mother—anybody. When we were on vacation, he invited his sister out to dinner with us. I was looking forward to a lobster dinner, but we didn't even go to a restaurant that had one. He's always saying what perfect housekeepers they are. I make most of his clothes for him. I learned to cook Italian food. But somehow he never thinks I measure up to them. In his eyes they're perfect."

If Janet discussed the marriage in greater detail, I suspect it would be apparent that her husband doesn't talk to her about his inner feelings. He doesn't communicate to her the anxieties and insecurities and pressures arising from his work, for instance. Basically, a great deal of what she is saying is that she feels terribly lonely. She doesn't exactly know how to articulate it, but she feels left out. There isn't warm companionship in the marriage. If there were, the relationship would have such momentum that his family would begin to recede into the background in terms of their significance to him.

She describes a husband still seeking a good deal of parenting from his family, in the sense of looking to them for approval and disapproval, rather than getting this from himself. At the same time, he attempts to play a parent role with Janet. He undoubtedly has a complicated set of relationships with his family, involving guilt and anger as well as love. He has brought into the marriage attitudes toward women and family shaped by those earlier associations, and is acting out with Janet much of the mixed feelings he has towards members of his family. He may have been dominated by his mother in childhood and had to fight aggressively for independence. This would explain his disinclination to allow Janet to have power in the marriage. He acts out historical unwillingness to be controlled by a woman and his fears of losing control if he becomes a coequal partner.

At the beginning of their marriage, Janet probably wanted a "daddy" figure in her husband. She admitted that she had started out feeling that he should know how things should be because of his being older than she. But, like so many women in similar situations, as she has gained a better sense of herself as an individual, she has come to see her husband's attitudes and peremptory behavior as disrespectful of her wishes and desires. She is becoming more and more offended by this, and is beginning to recognize that the relationship she originally bargained for isn't what she wants to live with for the rest of her life.

It has become important for her to become a stronger partner by saying what she wants and feels. If her anger and conflict with her husband are not to increase, eventually destroying the marriage, changes must be made in the ways the two relate. The marriage must be reinvented. Their dominant-dependent style of partnership needs to be converted to a more equalitarian model so that Janet can function as a competent adult, rather than as a dependent, subservient person.

The specific areas in which any two people might make this kind of change and the ways of relating they might develop will vary with the individuals involved. Creating a successful marriage is an inventive process in which two unique individuals over a period of time work out ways of interacting that are rewarding to both persons. The result, which reflects many facets of both personalities, is as idiosyncratic as any single human personality.

How two people go about inventing a unique partnership tailored to themselves is described in the next chapter.

Chapter 2

How to Design a Loving Relationship

Most of us go into marriage assuming that we know how to be a loving person in this very complex, involved relationship that brings us close to another person. But this is not necessarily true. Most people have to learn how to be intimate. We have to learn how to reach out to one another and how to give and take in working out our differences. Even long-term marriage partners often have not mastered the art.

Creating a close, loving partnership is not an elusive, inexplicable process discoverable only through lucky accident, however. Psychological knowledge includes an increasingly clear understanding of the way in which two people achieve emotional intimacy. Although each couple includes two unique personalities with their own sets of attitudes, feelings, personal histories and individual ways of viewing reality, the methods that may be used are essentially the same for all.

The basic situation with which every couple must deal, whatever the surface problems, can be seen in what was happening between twenty-five-year-old Kitty and her fiance, Paul, when she called the radio program.

Kitty, the mother of a three-year-old daughter by her ex-husband, was distressed by the fact that Paul, a stockbroker, repeatedly expressed doubts about his ability to support them. Bringing such anxieties out in the open is desirable in a partnership, but to Kitty, his expression of this fear suggested possible rejection of her.

"He never seems to want to call the wedding off," she reported, "but he keeps bringing this up. I've waited two years already and I don't want to say, 'Hey, we'll either get married or forget it.' Why doesn't he say, 'Let's wait a year'? He has this hangup about making a ton of money. I've told him I'm not worried at all."

It may well be that Paul wants very much to marry Kitty. He may want the comfort, the security, the closeness of a partnership. And perhaps he wants the emotional support that he may sense he will get from her once they are married. But the economic issue could be very important to him. He may have seen his own father struggling for a long time. His mother might have been a materialistic woman for whom affluence was very important. Other feelings may also be involved. At twenty-five he has never been married and is about to take on not only a wife but a three-year-old daughter. He may worry about his own capacity for fatherhood, or he may have ambivalent feelings about being a daddy to another man's daughter.

The point is that Paul has a personal history and undoubtedly a complicated set of feelings associated with his expectations of life, with marrying a divorced woman with a child, and with a lot of other issues that need to be talked about between the two of them. If Kitty responds only to the overt message he has given her, she will miss the rich background of his feelings and they will go around and around on the problem. If she wants to know Paul, if it is her intention for him to feel that she cares for him, then somehow she has to draw forth from him that whole background of feelings.

On the other hand, Kitty has a whole range of feelings, too. She has feelings about having had a marriage failure and about whether she is worth enough to Paul for him to take on a woman with a small child. She has feelings about marriage and family and personal relationships that are connected to her father, to how her father and mother related, to siblings and to her first husband. And she has feelings of rejection when Paul raises the economic issue.

Both of them need to draw each other out and risk revealing some of their inner feelings and inner attitudes to the other.

"I get the feeling that this bothers you. Do you want to talk about it?" one might say. Or: "Hey, I've been feeling lonely and I want to tell you what I feel." If two people reach out to each other in this way, each gains a greater sense of involvement, an empathetic understanding of the other. Access to another's inner life brings an appreciation of the joys, hopes, fears, pain and inhibitions of the other. You feel closer and very special to the other person in being admitted to these private feelings. And when you know another's inner life and accept it and respond to it, you create in that person a feeling that you care, that he or she is very special to you.

When, through testing and trying, two people gain the confidence to risk telling each other their innermost feelings, the relationship gains momentum in a self-reinforcing cycle that builds up a special trust and love between them.

What most married people who find a problem in loving lack is this kind of access to the deep feelings, emotional sensitivities, fears, frustrations and historical images that each of us has. Two people marry with the idea that they will really know each other, love each other and be close to each other. But too often they avoid the kind of communication necessary to achieve genuine intimacy.

Negotiating Differences

The second thing two people must do to create a loving partnership is to begin at least a partial accommodation of differences. No two people have exactly the same style of emotional life or identical feelings about family, friends and other kinds of relationships, much less identical feelings about what constitutes a rewarding life. No two human beings have exactly the same way of looking at events. We tend to think that if two people are married, they are sharing the same experience, but in fact they are not. Each of us has a reality that is the total of our experiences in life as filtered through our basic biological personality and the experiential personality that is the product of our nurturing—childhood and all the rest.

Differences on many issues come up in a marriage: styles of social, recreational and sexual life; money problems; relationships with in-laws; the question of whether or not a couple is to have children, and child-rearing attitudes if they do have them.

Even if two people are not marrying, substantial temperamental differences or differences in style must be reconciled if they are to have an important relationship. There are sixteen primary personality factors on which two people can vary significantly. Any two people who live together must deal with some of these differences. One person may have a strong desire for constant companionship and the other may like a lot of time alone. One may be socially outgoing, the other shy. One generally cheerful, the other pessimistic and inclined to be depressed. One could be an independent, self-sufficient person and the other one who constantly seeks approval from everyone. These kinds of differences can cause a great deal of stress between two people. Partners need to recognize the disparities between them and find ways to be together in which both can be comfortable.

Without negotiation and a willingness to compromise and accommodate, a relationship becomes rigid. Unfortunately, the romantic myth associated with marriage often includes the idea that if two people fall in love, each automatically knows what the other wants, needs and feels. Nothing could be further from the truth. But according to the thinking in this romantic nonsense, if you don't sense intuitively how I feel about things and give me what I want, you don't love me. Nothing makes a person more deeply angry than the feeling of being unloved. So two people operating in this kind of logic soon begin to deal with one another as antagonists with expectations that the outcome of any confrontation on differences will be rejection and humiliation. Often each begins to see the other as deliberately frustrating or denying what one wants in the marriage. By then a good deal of determination and inventiveness is necessary to put a relationship back together.

That was the case with twenty-six-year-old Debbie and her racing-car-driver husband, who, like many young men, was tremendously motivated to achieve success in his chosen field. In the early years of their marriage Debbie hadn't taken his ambitions seriously. They had come to a crisis point where each had to give a great deal in order to effect what amounted to a compromise.

"I thought his plans to be a racing car driver were like those of a seven-year-old who says he wants to be a cowboy," she said as she looked back at that period. "I didn't have the slightest idea that he could do it. When he became so involved with trying to be successful that he seemed to want to spend all his waking hours trying to get ahead in racing and none at all with me or our son, I threatened to leave him and take our little boy back to my parents. I told him that there were tens of thousands of things that men in their early twenties could find to do for a living, and that he could choose either this racing career or me. For a period of weeks we sort of had an armed truce. I wasn't sure what I was going to do other than leave. Then he found the opportunity he was looking for and relaxed a bit with the family, because he wasn't trying so hard on the job. I realized he had a chance to be successful and said I'd hang on and see what happened. But I told him we'd have to sit down and discuss the whole situation and he'd have to spend more time with the family. He told me that I had taken virtually no interest in what he was doing and didn't go to the races, so there wasn't much we could talk about, because that was his life. I started to become more interested in his activities and now I'm there almost every time he's racing. And since he's become successful, he's more interested in the family and more relaxed. The only problem is that he's gone a lot."

By going back to school, Debbie has satisfactorily filled the empty hours a husband's absence often creates. She is happily working hard at her studies while waiting for the arrival of an expected second child. But with her husband's success, she also has found it necessary to make other adjustments to the realities of his occupation.

"Now I have to put up with a lot of baloney from other women who are attracted to him because of what he's doing for a living," she explained. "These women always hang around sports. It's a case of 'Am I attractive enough personally to compete with the women he meets when he races?' Many of them are very glamorous gals. For a while I was jealous. I had to realize that things will go on when he's on the road, but he will always come back to me."

For Debbie this was a tolerable situation, so apparently the marriage had been successfully renegotiated.

Respecting Each Other's Way of Being

To avoid marital crises such as Debbie and her husband faced and build a solid partnership, two people need to take the responsibility for telling their partners how they see life and what their desires are. But in doing this they must respect each other's way of being without either partner having a sense that one way is right and the other wrong. Each must be open to understanding the other's viewpoint and feelings, whatever they are, and be ready to negotiate differences.

When each has heard the other's feelings, attitudes and perhaps childhood images that are associated with an issue, if their desires differ, they should begin to consider possible ways for giving each at least part of what each one wants. Differences must be worked out in such a way that both partners feel they have been fairly treated and haven't given up too much. Otherwise one will feel victimized and become angry. The anger may not be directly expressed immediately, but over a period of time it will make itself felt in destructive ways. It may become internalized and end up as self-hatred. Many of us have self-destructive impulses such as compulsive eating, gambling or drinking. It may be turned against the outside world, with the angry person becoming hostile at work or in social exchanges, sadistically cruel to animals or mean to children in the family.

Even in largely happy partnerships, resolution of an issue in a way not truly tolerable to the inner feelings of both partners can cause difficulties. Thirty-one-year-old Gloria, married two years, was finding this out when she called.

"Richard is a very unusual person," she began. "In my mind he's just perfect and I respect him. I enjoy his company much more than I've ever enjoyed anyone's. And I don't just mean sexually, but as a person. We have a fantastic marriage, yet we find ourselves continuously struggling to become what we call financially mature. After we had been married awhile, we decided that in order to achieve our monetary goals, we would limit our spending. But sometimes when Rich says, 'You cannot charge any more,' I feel, 'Well, why can't I? I have an excellent income and so does he. Why do I have to give this up?' I run down to the store, then find myself with pangs of guilt thinking, 'How unfair can I be? If I really believe in our goals, why am I standing here with a charge-a-plate in my hand?' Usually I feel that I have it all together and know where I'm going. But sometimes I come home and think, 'Is it really always going to be like this? Are we never going to reach these goals?' I really am quite concerned about these feelings I have."

Gloria's problem seemed to be that she was demanding more of herself in a rational, logical, controlled fashion than most of us can provide. We humans are often emotional, irrational beings. We respond to inner impulses and compulsions. These are part of our own persons that we have to expect. She and Richard had negotiated this issue on a rational, logical level, but her inner feelings hadn't been taken fully into account. Apparently she had agreed to go too far in being financially responsible. I suggested to her that if she and Richard would agree to give one another freedom to save less, her impulses to spend would have more freedom, and there would be less likelihood of her being angry with herself and indirectly angry with him. When inner feelings are not taken into account, we suppress our anger and are likely to convert it into passive aggressive behavior toward the other person. In this situation we may have a mixture of feelings that are almost poles apart. Passive aggressive behavior characterizes the low-key personality whose anger, though largely hidden, can be harsh or even cruel.

Temperamental Differences

Temperamental differences between partners, or differences in capabilities in contacting another person, cannot always be adjusted to in terms of rational discussion or decision-making. Often we become confused about these differences, which can be as widely varied as differences in values, tastes, and the ability to tolerate criticism or to experience feelings. Often we transform them into conflict about more concrete matters—money or social engagements, perhaps—because these things can be negotiated more readily. It is important that partners identify each other's temperamental or emotional responses, recognize that important differences exist and begin to talk about the childhood memories and associations that lie behind each partner's way of being. Usually a tremendous amount of early conditioning has created a particular style of personality. Sharing recollections of early images and experiences builds recognition and appreciation of the basis for each other's attitudes toward life. This creates a tolerance that gives both persons freedom to be as they are. Once they feel this freedom, they become free to change. With ongoing communication over a period of time, partners often subtly recondition each other to become somewhat different persons, closer together in their styles.

Sharing the Whole Emotional Experience

Sometimes a partner not only doesn't share inner feelings with a spouse, but doesn't tell the other of important emotionally-charged experiences. Twenty-three-year-old Nancy took this course after being attacked in a parking lot one morning by a stranger who tried to rape her. The incident was embarrassing to her and perhaps, like many rape victims, she had a strange sense of guilt, as if she had somehow brought it on. She decided that telling her husband would only cause him unnecessary anguish.

"What good would it do?" she asked me. "It was over and there was nothing he could do about it. I thought it would be selfish to tell him. He is devoted and it would upset him greatly. It would cause him anxiety when he has to leave me to work nights."

Nevertheless, it would have been much better for Nancy to have told her husband. The attack had been a shattering experience for her.

"For a week after it happened I was such a wreck that I had nightmares and couldn't sleep," she reported. "I couldn't even look at a man. It was three months before I could again wear the dress I had on. In fact, I couldn't wear anything that was sexy. It was months before I could put on a short dress. I still have the feeling of someone coming up behind me."

Anything having such a powerful emotional impact on Nancy should be shared with the most important male in her life. It will probably be several years before an experience this powerful will fade out for her, and in some ways it will affect the relationship between the two of them. She will have unconscious fears of men that he is not privy to. On another level, she has cheated him out of sharing an important emotional experience and denied both of them the intimacy that can come from doing so.

My feeling about the emotional intimacy possible in marriage is that it is important for two people to share not just the good parts of life but the whole of the emotional experience. My spouse takes me as I am—lumps, warts and all. If I'm angry, that's part of me. When I'm frustrated, that's me, too. This is not to say that you're not alone and I'm not alone. But we do have the option of sharing our inner emotional life with people who are important to us.

Why We Avoid Intimacy

Opening up one's inner life to another person isn't easy. By the time most of us are adults, we have had so many inhibitory messages, so much control and socialization, that we do not feel free to express our feelings readily. For many people, habitual avoidance of sharing inner feelings with another begins in childhood. Sometimes it is because we are somewhat lost in a large family in which no one has the time to listen and respond to a child's experience of life. Since the child's feelings and fantasies are not expressed, this inner life is somewhat disconnected from outer life, and the individual doesn't learn that those feelings are important elements in family life. Keeping feelings to oneself becomes a habitual part of the growing child's personality. The problem for this person as an adult in relating to a partner may simply be unfamiliarity with having a close relationship with another person. It is not in the individual's established emotional repertoire to have feelings, identify them, and then communicate what is felt to another as part of the process of intimacy.

The most common reason for avoidance of intimacy, however, is habitual self-protection. If most of the emotional business that occurs in a person's early life is unhappy and hurtful, if parents are hostile and hateful to one another, a child tends to tune out that hostile, angry world, creating a different one— a world of books, sports or something else.

For people with this kind of experience it is hard to break through and open up inner feelings with another person. There is a powerful inner resistance to being so emotionally available and vulnerable.

The husband of forty-year-old Jane is an extreme example of a person with this problem. Terribly lonely, cut off from people, he has attempted suicide, then tried therapy, but, after becoming deeply upset by the conflicts within himself, has given it up. He is a man of serious mental instability, but fundamentally, his ways of interacting with Jane, and avoiding interacting with her, are similar to the ways many stable men deal with a spouse.

"My husband is the kind of person who, when he has to go anyplace, whether it be next door for a few minutes or somewhere for a few days, feels he has no obligation to tell me he is going; he just goes," she said in describing her marriage. "If I say, 'Where are you going?' or, 'Where have you been?' he says, 'None of your business.' Yet if I reason out if he is cheating, I decide not. One day he asked me if I trust him and I jokingly said no. Then the conversation turned to whether he trusts me. I am almost supertrustworthy. Infidelity is not in my vocabulary. Yet I can go to the neighbor's or anywhere wearing dirty slacks and no makeup and he doesn't know whether I'm trustworthy or not. If I come home twenty minutes late, he accuses me of picking somebody up on the street. It's an insult to me. He is just as mysterious to me as I am to him. I am a talker and he is not. If I ask him to explain to me what he means when he says something, he says, 'I haven't got the time. Forget it.' Yet he thinks the only thing in life worth having is marriage and a family. So how can he act that way?"

Jane's husband may think consciously that marriage is the most important thing in life, but in his behavior he is avoiding commitment to it and involvement in it. His unwillingness to be open with Jane about where he is and what he is doing says that he views marriage as locking him in, and that he wants freedom to be his own person. However, he is jealous of her and that indicates that he wants something important with her, so presumably he wants the marriage. But he doesn't want involvement in the intimacy of marriage. Any expression of feelings, any openness of communication apparently terrify him.

Many emotionally stable and successful people are also extremely protective of their inner feelings and emotions. They go through life wanting affection and closeness and active participation with family members, but never indicate that they want this except indirectly, through jealousy or angry withdrawal.

Unless you experience yourself in quite positive terms as a love-worthy person, it is painfully difficult to trust another with your affection and lovingness and to actively reach out and ask for what you want. This is the problem of the husband who is not free to be affectionate, but is aggressively sexual once the couple is in bed in the anonymity of the darkness. The woman who communicates, "Give me presents," because she cannot say, "Love me," in the sense of saying, "Let's spend time together; let's do fun things together," is another example. Many people create elaborate scenarios in their personal relationships to avoid asking for anything so they cannot be rejected. Some couples communicate their feelings through their children in order to keep from saying directly and openly, "This is how I feel. This is what I'd like you to do for me." Others say things to each other in a social setting, often by indirection, that they are unwilling to say to each other alone.

If You Don't Share Feelings

For almost everyone there is some feeling of risk in speaking openly of inner feelings. All of us have had a less-than-perfect childhood. Each of us lives with historical pain, guilt and fears.

We have a constellation of historical images and emotional sensitivities in our guts that can trigger childhood feelings of powerlessness, guilt and inadequacy. More often than not, when these feelings are triggered, couples feel the need to cover up and protect themselves emotionally from one another.

But in a marriage you have to make a commitment that the relationship is worth the risking and testing that are involved in the process of moving toward greater openness with another person. If, over a period of time, two people do not expose and experience inner feelings with one another, they are likely to engage in hostile behavior. The marriage will begin to cycle negatively, with both individuals anticipating not being listened to and being misunderstood. Both partners will begin to feel that they can't possibly be loved or treated well by the opposite sex, and will become rejective of the other.

This was happening in the marriage of twenty-one-year-old Sara. Feeling locked in her apartment by the care of a baby, and wanting a great deal more communication than she was able to get from her self-protective, taciturn husband, she felt powerfully frustrated and desperately alone when she called.

"I like Al to talk to me and I like to do things together," she said. "Even if it's going for a walk in the park. But when I want to talk, he doesn't want to. I keep asking him, 'Can we talk?' He gets mad and leaves. It's been like this since we married. When he doesn't pay any attention to me, I say things I don't mean. At night, if he doesn't want to talk and I do, I ruin his sleep and he has to go downstairs to sleep. Then I'll go downstairs—boiling mad, you know—and find a way to get back at him because he left me. I say something mean, then I feel better and can go back upstairs and sleep. But when things don't go right, either he or I take it out on the baby. I feel guilty about that.

"I love my husband and I still want to be married to him, but I feel I need to find someone else to keep me happy. Someone I can talk to and be with."

A man who acts like Sara's husband is uncomfortable with emotional communication and probably grew up in an environment where there was little. During his courtship of Sara, and in the early weeks or months of marriage, he was no doubt more outgoing, for in this period he would have been inclined to talk and share his feelings with her at his maximum level. But inevitably, he reverted closer to his normal level of communication. Sara's demands for more companionship make him feel inadequate and guilty about not giving her something she deeply wants. These feelings further decrease his communicativeness.

For Sara, her husband's avoidance of relating to her probably confirms doubts she has about her own worth as a desirable or lovable person. So it enrages her, and her rage amplifies his avoidance. He feels powerless to give her what she wants, and hears her demands not as, "It would feel good to have your companionship," but as, "You're a bad person; you're inadequate." As a way of protecting himself, he may see her as unkind and aggressive, and be very angry with her. This issue is poisoning the relationship, depriving both of them of the joy and pleasure they might have in sharing a marriage and a child.

I suggested to Sara that she seek out several other young mothers like herself and form an informal club. There are many young women in similar circumstances who are getting relatively little attention from their husbands, and feel locked in with the care of children. In such a club she could create important friendships and share child care. The members could take turns babysitting so that all would have time to become involved in creative or educational activities or just have fun together. Then Sara would not be so dependent on Al or so needful of his attention. If he felt less demand on him, this might make it easier for him to communicate.

I also suggested that she write a series of notes to him that would serve as invitations to a dialogue on this issue of communication, for these two badly need to gain some understanding of each other on the question of companionship. I proposed that, without blaming or criticizing him, she express the feelings that come from her lack of companionship—her loneliness, fears, doubts about herself—and state what she is seeking in the relationship.

If Sara can start a dialogue in which Al begins to understand how lonely, rejected and unloved she feels when he is at his normal level of taciturnity, he may be able to let her know how confusing and distressing he finds her demands. If they can begin to hear each other actively, each will become empathetic to the other's feelings. If this happens, they will begin to hear ways in which each can be helpful to the other and can contribute affirmatively to the relationship. However, it takes a good deal of courage for anyone as accustomed as Al is to using silence as a way of protecting himself to become more expressive of his feelings. Sara will have to be very persuasive in her invitations to dialogue, making it extremely clear how rewarding and fulfilling it is to her when he becomes more visible emotionally.

Dealing With Differences

Writing a series of letters expressing your feelings about an issue and proposing conditions that would make you comfortable, as I suggested to Sara, can be an effective way to approach discussion of differences. Frequently a person can disclose more in writing than in facing someone eyeball-to-eyeball. There are other advantages to written communication. You can take your time in composition and rewrite your message until you are sure that you have said what you really mean. Also, a letter can be read a number of times by the other person, who can thereby better discern what is meant than in a single verbal encounter.

Written communication of your feelings may also be made through a personal journal that you keep for an extended period of time and then share with the other person.

Another effective way to approach an issue that involves deep sensitivities is for partners to agree to schedule several periods together for discussion of the issue. I recommended this to twenty-eight-year-old Wendy, mother of two, for discussing problems about her four stepchildren with her husband.

"My husband has guilt feelings about leaving the children and wants to spend a lot of time with them. He's devoted to them and I think that is wonderful," she said. "But he brings the children home on weekends, then locks himself in the garage and works on the car, leaving me with the kids. They like me very much and we're all good buddies, but we have a discipline problem. He doesn't recognize that and I don't know how to present it without it sounding bad."

There is no way Wendy can raise this issue without upsetting her husband. Any discussion of it will trigger his guilt and generate anger on his part. But if Wendy does not talk with him about it, she will become increasingly angry and the anger will come out in indirect or sneaky ways. She won't be able to control the ways in which anger is expressed if she allows it to build up. She's bound to get more and more angry with his kids.

Her husband is playing a game of "I'm a good father" when actually he is not. He has ambivalent feelings about his children. I suspect he does not really want to be with them. Probably he doesn't know how to relate to children and can't confront that feeling and the fact that he wants to play with his own toys. Somehow, having the children at his house relieves him of guilt. He is using Wendy to avoid his guilt and feelings of pressure from the demands being made on him for fatherhood. So it is a very touchy issue.

I suggested to Wendy that she tell her husband that the two of them have some gut-level emotional issues to deal with relating to the children, and make a date for four discussion sessions, each one to last an hour and a half. They should agree to be completely honest and open, and tell each other what they feel. At the first meeting, Wendy should touch on everything troubling her at a surface level. She can begin by telling him about the discipline problem and her feeling that he leaves her alone with the children. Then she can ask him to examine his own feelings about them. Basically, she says that she wants to listen to his inner feelings.

In the first session it will be very difficult for him to get through to those feelings. But with four sessions—if she doesn't indict him, if she doesn't say, in effect, "You really are a lousy father, you're dumping your damn kids on me"— step by step his feelings will become more and more clear to him. Then he will probably be able to move toward an accommodation.

He may find, as he gets in touch with his deeper feelings, that he does not want the children around every weekend, but that occasionally he could have a rewarding relationship with them. It would be more valuable for him to focus his attention on them for just one day a month, when he really wants to be with them, than for them to be around the house eight days a month, with him avoiding them all eight days.

However, if he and Wendy start a discussion on the basis of having it all out at once, they are not likely to get into his deeper feelings. They will probably put each other on the defensive, trigger each other's anger and verbally beat each other up.

How to Fight Through Differences

Negotiating differences is often difficult and touchy for a couple because so many issues trigger historical feelings of guilt, anger or unlovability. Compounding the difficulties is the fact that most of us are so intensely concerned with our problems being heard that we rarely listen actively to the other person.

To resolve differences successfully, partners need to listen carefully to one another to get a sense of what the other is experiencing and actually wants in the marriage. Each partner must have a turn expressing feelings and thoughts on an issue that is causing concern, and must take a turn listening actively to the other. Partners not accustomed to dealing with each other in this way should then check to determine whether both feel that they have been truly heard.

A second basic rule for fighting through differences constructively is that you must not so offend your partner that the partner stops listening. Specifically, you should not make charges so sweeping and overwhelming that the encounter has no place to go. Narrow down your complaint to the real or imagined offense. Then focus on the situation and what you are feeling. Do not indict the other as a bad person. For instance, if you are angry with me, concentrate on your anger. "I'm feeling angry," you might say. "I'm frustrated. I'm feeling as if something I really wanted has been taken away." Or, "I'm feeling hurt. I'm feeling an inner pain that I can't identify, but it's there."

Do not say that I undercut you or that I am a mean, miserable, unloving, ungiving person or a lousy spouse. The moment you identify me as a bad person, I stop listening and defend myself. My own ego strength requires that I respond to an attack on my person. My automatic impulse is to counterattack.

Similarly, issues should be dealt with *as issues*, without partners attacking each other. If a man doesn't like his wife's style of child-rearing and, by implication or directly, says she is a lousy mother, her response will be counteriadictment—"You don't know anything about being a father," or something similar—and no resolution of their differences is likely to be reached.

They will be in a better position to find some degree of conciliation if they approach their differences with the view: "We have a common task of being parents. Let's take a fresh look at it. Let's examine how each of us views parenthood. Let's look at the responses of the kids and let's read some of the information available about parenting."

These basic rules for constructively fighting through differences can be kept in mind if you think of them in terms of using "I" language ("I feel..." "I think..." "I want..." and finally, "I am willing to...") and avoiding "you" language ("You are..." "You want..." "You do...").

Any reference to your partner other than, "I would like to

hear from you what you feel (or think, or want)" is prohibited in "I" language, which concentrates on self-disclosure and self-identification of each person. Through this language of sharing, you can create a common base of knowledge of the inner life-responses of each of you to whatever issue is the cause of concern. In addition, a sense of having been truly heard—and heard in a kindly and receptive way—is likely to be triggered in each of you. This makes it easier for each to give the other some degree of fulfillment in regard to what the other is asking for, either explicitly or implicity. Not only are differences at least partially resolved in this way, but the sense of intimacy and communication that comes from inner life-sharing is reinforced. You learn that it has a direct payoff. You get more of what you want.

Making Changes in a Partnership

Building and reinforcing both this sense of intimacy and the ability to communicate inner life-feelings are essential to reinventing a marriage in a way that is satisfactory to both persons.

Over an extended period of time, a marriage often evolves in a way that causes one partner to be unhappy or uncomfortable, and a major change in the couple's style of relating may be required for a successful marriage. As mentioned earlier, very often today a woman with a subservient position in the relationship is asking for a fuller life or a greater sense of control of her own destiny.

Making a major change in marital roles cannot be quickly accomplished simply as an act of will. Usually, a good deal of negotiating must be done over an extended period of time to reinvent a satisfactory partnership. Self-learning and learning about the other person must take place in both partners for a successful outcome. A wife with this kind of concern needs to be listened to and responded to by her husband. On the other hand, the husband's feelings need to be heard and responded to by his wife, for he is likely to feel that his prerogatives are being undermined. If a woman is adequately heard, she may sense that her person is being respected and that some evolution of roles is possible. If a man has a full chance to ventilate his fears and doubts about changes in behavior, responsibilities and roles, he is likely to be far more free in negotiating in that direction. Then, a step at a time, old behaviors, feelings and ways of responding can be let go of and new ones taken on, until a major reintegration of the relationship is accomplished.

Any other major alteration in a partnership similarly takes active effort over a period of some duration.

Sometimes marriage partners have gone through the routine of married life for years, with little sharing of intimate feelings. In that situation, an extensive effort to share feelings and create mutual understanding of each other's experience of life is necessary before old attitudes and ways of responding to one another can be changed.

The twenty-six-year marriage of Joyce, which was foundering when she called, is an example of one in which there had been little sharing of intimate feelings through many years.

Three months before she called, her husband, Jack, had told her that he had been in love with another woman all of the years of their marriage—years in which she claimed to have been happy and to have thought him happy.

"I guess I was living in a dream world," she said. "I've finally come to accept the fact that there is no way that he will love me, and there is nothing for me to do but to let him go to the person he wants. She's divorced now and he wants to be free. She lives in another state and he says he must spend some time with her. He is so confident that he will relate to her. He says that every time he sees her there are electric feelings that have never subsided in all these years, and she has felt the same way. He's been very tender and understanding with me, and we have talked so much in these last few months that we are closer now than we ever have been, because we finally have been able to communicate. But it's such a problem. Our family situation with our children makes it impossible for him to leave right now."

Joyce had been a dependent, relatively powerless person through the years. But unlike many women, who become progressively angry in that position, she had been rather comfortable in the role. For women like her, life often holds surprises.

The responsibilities and feelings of obligation that descend on a man in the dominant role often squeeze all the fun out of the relationship for him, making the marriage a tiresome burden. That apparently is what has happened to Jack. Romantic idealization of another woman over many, many years is often an escape fantasy for a man who finds marriage more responsibility than pleasure.

His fantasy love affair over so many years also suggests avoidance of closeness and open communication about feelings between him and his wife.

It is a good deal easier for him to romantically idealize the other woman than it is for him to have the same feelings toward his wife, for he hasn't had to fight through all kinds of conflicting and confusing feelings and day-to-day issues with the other woman as he has with Joyce. But it is unlikely that he will engage in the hard work of creating a viable partnership with the other woman, especially since he has had years of practice in avoiding emotional closeness and the requisite exchange of confidences with his wife. Men don't often go off with women about whom they have had fantasies for years. When they do, both parties usually have a big letdown after they spend some time together.

If Jack leaves Joyce to spend time with his lady-love, he may discover in two weeks or less that his love is a myth of his own invention. But if he splits up the family to do this, even for a relatively brief period of time, he is likely to so fracture the feelings of trust and loyalty between him and his wife that he may not be able to put the marriage back together again if he wishes, even though he may badly want to regain the stability and solidity that he has experienced in a long-term marriage.

I suggested to Joyce that it would be valuable to both Jack and herself to expand the communication the two had begun about their relationship before any separation. If they clarify their feelings and the issues that have created disappointment in the marriage, they will come to new understandings. Then there will be a possibility of renegotiating the marriage, and Jack may be ready to do this without extreme defensiveness. In reality, his romantic fantasy is his special way of telling himself that he feels a powerful need for something he isn't getting in his marriage. If he attempts to communicate to Joyce his dream or ideal of a love relationship, he may hear his own feelings clearly enough to perceive what he wants so badly. With the greater emotional closeness that sharing feelings with Joyce would create, he may come to sense a new possibility for this kind of relationship with her, and give up pretending to himself that he is in love with someone he hardly knows. But even if, in the end, these two choose to live apart, partners who have invested so much in a marriage have much to gain by going through this process of sharing feelings about themselves and their partnership. Not only will they be able to continue to be important friends to one another, but each will become a better candidate for a loving pairing with someone else.

In this kind of dialogue, they need to talk about their inner life-feelings in a way that enables each one to get a clear sense of the other person. They need to share their hopes, joys, desires, doubts, fears, frustrations, and dreams of being appreciated and cared for by another—in sum, their feelings about living. It is a lack of this kind of sharing that has caused them to be so isolated from one another. I suggested they set a time every week for active communication about these feelings. First, one should try to identify and reveal his or her feelings without putting down or abusing the other, while the partner takes the role of active listener. Then the roles can be reversed.

Differences also need to be discussed. To facilitate the dialogue, they might keep separate personal journals, writing down how they have experienced the marriage in relation to the issues that play a part in any emotional partnership: the quality and character of sex; the use of money; social life; relations with extended families; child-rearing; religion or ethical systems. Each time one comes across an issue that creates some discomfort or pain, the person would write out as much as possible about the associated feelings. After assessing their own attitudes on these issues and what part these attitudes have played in the relationship, they would share these thoughts.

Being and Having a Friend Who Cares

No marriage partners, no matter how loving, are completely open and self-disclosing with one another. Getting a clear sense of another's inner feelings takes intense listening. We humans are a complex mixture of sentiments, images and associations that come out of the earliest years of our lives. Often we ourselves do not have a clear sense of what we are responding to.

When a spouse feels restless and dissatisfied, is it a concern about aging? About a drop-off of sexual interest? Or about not having achieved parental expectations in terms of education or financial status? There are many possible answers. The clues may be in expressions of irritation, frustration, sadness, depression or disappointment. You have to listen, ask questions and explore possible explanations.

An example that comes up frequently in family therapy involves the husband who travels in connection with his business. His absence for a week at a time triggers deep feelings of desertion or abandonment in his wife, who is angry with him every time he returns. It may be because her father did not pay attention to her when she was a child, or died when she was ten years old. There are many reasons why she may have such a sensitivity.

Usually she doesn't know how to tell her husband her feelings. She can't say, "Hey, when you take off, I feel deserted. It takes me back to when I was eleven or twelve years old and suddenly my loving dad was no longer a loving dad. He went fishing with my two older brothers and no girls were allowed. And he wouldn't hug me anymore because suddenly, when I reached puberty, hugging had sexual implications. I felt painfully deserted by my father, and now you're deserting me. It's tearing my guts out."

Usually she can't say that. She isn't clear about it. In a sense she doesn't understand it. But she feels it.

If the husband asks, "Why does my leaving trouble you so? Why do you have such painful feelings?" and listens carefully to her responses, he becomes aware that his leaving creates pain in her and that the pain has its own validity and reality in her earlier life. If she is listened to and responded to, her distressed feelings will diminish. Also, he may find that he can reduce the distress-causing occasions.

But if a husband feels he is being hassled unreasonably about what to him is a requirement of making a living, and responds with anger and irritation, their differences will be aggravated and there will be a profound change in her behavior. No longer the loving wife acting out a romantic fantasy, she will be the abandoned child, angry and resentful. Then she is likely to find something besides his travels to be bitterly dissatisfied and hostile about: his tendency to drink three bottles of beer in front of the television; his premature ejaculation; his not making enough money for them to buy a second car. The marriage will start to cycle negatively, with each upsetting element reinforcing every other such element until they have a very pained relationship.

When two people begin to reveal their inner lives to one another, each one listening attentively to the other, a complex interaction develops.

Many persons are not clear in their own minds about those primary things that have influenced them in their lifetimes. They haven't thought through how they want to live or what they want out of the experience of life. When you get into intimate emotional contact with someone and try to clarify these things for that person, you become more aware of what is going on in yourself, and gain a clearer sense of your own personal purposes.

For example, if you are feeling lonely, you may not know why you feel that way. If you feel free to say out loud what you are feeling, and your partner actively explores your feelings with you, then as you talk about your feelings, some image will arise inside your head. Perhaps a picture of your father when you were five or six. As you describe this picture, you find that he's an angry, disapproving father. There was a time when nothing seemed to please him, and you may recall that it was a time when his business failed. He went through a period of great anxiety and the whole family was subjected to his irritability. At that point you may say, "Oh my God. My boss's marriage is breaking up and he's chewing on me in an unfair way. It brings back historical feelings." Then you sense that you are dealing with stress in everyday life that connects to your own childhood and the feelings of powerlessness that you experienced then.

In this process in which one person ventilates and the other listens, probes and explores, two people create a sense of loving companionship, a sense that one has in one's spouse a friend who cares.

A special kind of trust develops. They trust each other to be there at moments when it is important. They trust that, no matter what they are feeling, any conflict will have a good outcome. They will be able to talk it through, even scream it through, and come out of the experience having solved some problems or accommodated to each other's emotional styles. And after the upsetting emotions pass, each one will be saying, "What can I give you to make your life more rewarding? What will make you feel good?"

This is not to be confused with, "I'll take responsibility for making you happy. I'll solve your problems." No person can do this for another. We all face adult life as single, separate, lone individuals. We can't take responsibility for the happiness of another, nor can we make anybody else responsible for making us happy. If we try to do so, and millions of people do try, we are doomed to failure. We cannot make life come out right for a spouse or anyone else; we cannot be parents to one another. But we can listen to each other with the ear of a caring friend. Within the limits of our own desires, feelings and personalities, we can give to one another what we are able of those things that are satisfying to the other's personal style. We can be good partners.

Chapter 3

Inventing a Loving Sexual Partnership

"I play a game so I don't have to go to bed and make love. My husband thinks I'm getting it somewhere else, but I'm not," twenty-seven-year-old Marie said dolefully.

"I have a fear of sex because it's hard for me to get into it enough to have an orgasm, and if it doesn't come out right my husband makes me feel guilty. It puts a damper on the whole thing. To him it's almost like a marathon, and if we don't reach orgasm every time..."

The image of sex that Marie's husband had was inaccurate and confusing. The notion of simultaneous orgasm, even the notion that either partner has to be orgasmic in any single sexual encounter, is undesirable.

In doggedly pursuing this goal, he had created fears in his young wife (or magnified those she may have had at the outset of marriage) in a way that denied both of them enthusiastic, joyful sexual contact. In effect, they had become spectators of their own lovemaking. They were judging and evaluating, rather than participating and enjoying. My guess is that he is an extremely achievement-oriented man who feels that his value depends upon excelling in everything he does. In sex, a concern with competence often denies pleasure.

Under ideal circumstances, sex involves two people with loving feelings for one another who are engaged in play. Two different human personalities are attempting to synchronize attitudes, physical responses, sensual awareness and tender feelings. If they are playful, experimental and spontaneous, they will never be able to do this the same way two times in a row, and the outcome of any specific encounter will be unpredictable.

Similarly, many persons have false expectations of sex. Much of the information that young people learn from both contemporaries and adults is only partial information or misinformation that diminishes or frustrates experiencing sexual feelings naturally and spontaneously. Even the advice about sex provided for years by supposed experts often has been no more accurate than the proverbial old wives' tales. The book about human sexuality that until the late fifties was the most popular ever written, Van Der Veld's *Ideal Marriage*, is a massive assemblage of misinformation. And as recently as the late sixties, an extensive survey of physicians, to whom people have traditionally turned for advice on sexual problems, indicated that doctors tended to have less accurate information about sex than did the average college graduate.

Over the past twenty-five years, many sex manuals have put an unfortunate emphasis on orgasm and made people disconcertingly anxious about it.

There are occasions when, because of psychological or physical cycles, a woman may be nonorgasmic no matter how long her partner persists in lovemaking. There are times, also, when a man is fatigued or hyper, that he is liable to have an orgasm after three or four minutes, even though he can usually control it for twenty to forty minutes, or even indefinitely.

It is important that partners see these happenings as perfectly acceptable and nothing that one must apologize for, any more than if two people set out on a picnic and one of them turns out to have a very limited appetite that day. They can still enjoy the scenery and each other's company.

Too often, we delude ourselves with the notion that a man or a woman ought to be turned on—or ready to be intensely sexually aroused—all the time. We're not. We vary in mood. We vary in relation to stress in terms of work, fatigue or illness. Sex is optimally a spontaneous act, and spontaneity can't be forced.

Sexual pleasure over an extended period of time between two people who care about each other is a process of getting in tune with each other's feelings, desires, inner timing and many other variables. If the process is approached with playfulness, spontaneity, sentimental tenderness between partners, and even a goodly amount of humor, no single sexual encounter is world-shaking. There are no guilt feelings.

When partners are caught up with concern about sexual performance and outcome, they preclude a spontaneous, loving emotional environment, which plays an important part in pleasurable sex. Often they neglect the many things they could do to create and enhance such an environment.

This kind of neglect was apparent in the three-months-old marriage of Becky, twenty-five, and her husband, Phil, who were having sex problems. Like many young men and women in the first years of marriage, they were embarrassed and awkward with each other concerning their desires in sex, and were not communicating intimately. Both also were avoiding taking responsibility for initiating or pursuing sexual contact—for saying, "Hey, love, come here. I want to play and cuddle." When this occurs in a partnership, two people may stop thinking and feeling sensuously and sexually to a considerable degree, but hidden anger builds up in both parties, making avoidance even more likely. Then they start punishing one another. Some of this was suggested by Becky's first statement: "We both work all day and come home tired and I get so used to not having sex that when he mentions it, I don't want it.

"Another problem we have is that we have to use a lubricant," she went on. "That petrifies me because right before we do anything we have to use this. I don't even look forward to it anymore. But he tells me he's always ready. Then I feel bad."

Becky's need to use a lubricant regularly indicates that something is wrong. Assuming nothing is wrong physically— and ninety-nine percent of the time nothing is—then it is a matter of her not becoming sufficiently sexually excited. This and her other comments indicated that she and her husband were not giving sex the time, playfulness and circumstances necessary for her to experience adequate sexual arousal.

With a little imagination, the two of them could create environments conducive to sensuality and sexuality. They could sit in the living room, with Becky dressed in her most attractive nightwear, and with music, a little wine, affectionate conversation, hugging and kissing, create attitudes of willingness and permissiveness, and trigger the desire to touch and play. They could take a shower together or be playful in the bathtub. They could go skinny-dipping in a favorite spot, or walk around the house the last hour or two before going to bed, dressed in whatever they wear or don't wear to bed, occasionally hugging or being playful with one another. There are many things that two people can do to trigger the desire to fondle and kiss and play.

Essentially, they are ways of acknowledging the importance of the other person to you, ways that say, "You're important to me and it pleases me to please you."

Too often in sex there is an overemphasis on foreplay in terms of clitoral stimulation at the expense of freely playful physical contact. Men often come into my office and talk about having followed the detailed instructions of sex manuals on sexual foreplay as if they had been constructing the foundation of a garage, and then wonder why their partners aren't satisfied. When I inquire as to whether an affectionate, sentimental feeling has been developed between the man and his partner, he looks blank. It has never occurred to him.

Yet sex without an environment of warm, affectionate feelings and mutual attitudes of willingness and lovingness can have a devastating effect on the sexual relationship of partners over a period of time.

Twenty-seven-year-old Bill was inviting this kind of disaster in his marriage at the time he called.

"I work long hours," he told me. "Our financial situation requires it right now. I go to bed late and get up early. Nevertheless, I have a high sexual appetite and manage to give sex enough time to satisfy me. But most of the time there is not enough time so that my wife, Gladys, can be sexually satisfied. I feel she should understand this situation, accept it and want to satisfy me. But the effect has been that her sexual appetite has decreased. She says she's more or less submitting herself, and not necessarily willingly. I feel that by the end of the year, which is pretty far away, I'll be able to cut down on my work and we'll have more time together. But she's afraid the effect on her before then will be more drastic than I can understand."

Bill and his wife are likely to end up paying a dreadful price for this situation. Any time two persons relate to one another in an intimate way and either party feels deprived, shortchanged or humiliated, there is a residue of anger and negativism that feeds back into the relationship. Gladys has been reacting negatively to what amounts to repudiation of her basic nature—her need to be loved, cuddled, and responded to fully as a person. If Bill continues to arouse that kind of negative response over an extended period of time, thus conditioning his wife negatively toward sex, when the time comes that he has more time and desires to create or recreate warm, tender passionate intimacy, the two of them probably will not be able to do it. For her, the wellsprings will have been poisoned by the negative conditioning. It will be just as difficult and painful for him, because he will be likely to discover that rather than relating to his wife with spontaneity, enthusiasm and excitement, he will feel he must perform. There is nothing as destructive to our sexuality as a demand for performance.

I suggested to Bill that he and his wife talk to each other about the situation in depth, scheduling three sessions of an hour and a half each, that they agree not to get angry or avoid the conversation, and that they say to each other what each really feels and wants. I would guess that if Bill becomes aware of his wife's real feelings, somehow he will find time for lovemaking that is not one person using the other, but true lovemaking.

Any two people who care enough about one another to be marital partners can and must create an environment of communication and confidence that enables either partner to say, "I feel" and "I want," or "I don't want," in sex as well as in other areas of life.

When a woman perceives sex as a duty, she initiates a very hurtful experience for both partners. The man is bound to feel somewhat deprived of warm, loving companionship. At worst he is likely to view himself with self-hatred as being some kind of animal. The woman is likely to feel abused and self-pitying. Frequently, this feeds back into the sexual relationship in a very painful fashion.

Part of Bill's problem in understanding his wife's situation was that, like many other persons, he had the false idea that women can always "perform" sexually. This is part of the considerable mythology concerning human sexuality. One element of the myth is that males can make love only when they really want to. Yet there are men who have sex frequently, dreading it, hating it, despising it. Some men have an erection very easily and are perfectly capable physiologically of engaging in the sex act, although psychologically they reject it and do not enjoy it. On the other hand, just as the blood rushes to the male penis causing an erection, the blood rushes to the genital areas of a woman when she is sexually aroused. Not only is the vagina lubricated, but it changes shape and the clitoris becomes substantially enlarged. A woman who participates in sex without having the female version of a full erection may experience physical as well as psychological pain. So men and women are not in as different a position as many people think.

Often it is overlooked that it is not necessary to have sexual intercourse to be tender, to cuddle, to play with one another, for the relationship to have sexual content. Many men and women are embarrassed and unenlightened about sensuality, so that they think physical contact is possible or okay only if it is followed by sexual intercourse. This is not true. If the only time that people have this tender contact is during sex, the relationship is deeply shortchanged.

Intimate Communication

An environment of trust and confidence, in which partners communicate what each feels and wants, is important in physical contact as well as in other phases of a partnership.

There is no one type of sexual contact that is universally pleasurable. A set of circumstances that is sexually stimulating for some people dampens the sexual enthusiasm of others. What is delightful to one person can be painful or uncomfortable, unpleasant or just plain unrewarding for another. Some people go into ecstasy if you rub their backs; others don't like to have their backs rubbed. Some people are intensely erotically aroused by a foot rub, and others couldn't care less. There are great differences among people in the responses of the erogenous zones of the body. The response to touching the nipples, for instance, varies in both men and women.

So two people need to check with each other and go through a learning process in which they become more and more in tune with each other's feelings and desires.

For most of us, this is painful and difficult. We find ourselves tongue-tied when it comes to saying, "I want this. This is what I feel. This is what pleasures me." Or, "I would like to try this." Or, "I have a fantasy of doing that." Telling someone what is pleasurable and rewarding in this intimate relationship makes us vulnerable to the deep inner fears of rejection that most people have. Saying "I want" is saying "I'm worth it," and this puts us in touch with powerful feelings about whether we are lovable and worthwhile people. If you had disapproval as a child, as many of us had, it is almost intolerable to run this kind of risk. Even many persons who are fairly aggressive in telling the world what they want in almost every other dimension of their lives, freeze up when it comes to communicating about sex. So whatever ideas a person has about what is appropriate in stimulating a partner, they are usually held for long periods of time without ever being checked out with the other person.

We do send each other many indirect messages about sexual feelings, however. Sometimes the fact that a message is being sent is quite apparent. In other instances it may only be sensed by a perceptive partner. But often it is difficult to decipher or deal with what is wanted without open communication. This was apparent in the case of thirty-one-year-old Vera.

"My husband has gone to a couple of places where there are bottomless dancers," she said. "I had never seen anything like that and I was curious, so I asked him to take me to one. When I went, my reaction was to get mad at him. I didn't get mad at anybody else in the place, just my husband. And he just sat there. I don't know what made me mad, because when we got home I had a good time. It turned me on."

When I asked her what she thought her husband wanted, she indicated some understanding of the message in his interest in bottomless dancers.

"Maybe he wants me to act that way a little bit," she said. "But that's not easy when you were raised a generation ago."

Although Vera discerned that her husband probably wanted her to become more adventuresome and freer sexually, she didn't understand clearly what kind of behavior was being sought from her, and experimenting with new ways of being sexual wasn't something she could easily do. So her husband's implicit demand made her angry. In his way he was as inhibited as she, for he was afraid to tell her what he wanted. If she talked to him about what he desired, as I suggested to her, it is likely that her anger would disappear and his sexual freedom might increase considerably.

Sexual Fantasies

Disclosing what you would like sexually from a partner often involves communicating your fantasy life. Most people find this particularly difficult to do. Generally, people think that their particular sexual fantasies are not only unique and weird, but bad—quite unacceptable socially. When people in a group compare fantasies—as more and more persons have been doing in recent years—they find that there are a great many common fantasies. They then tend to be more self-disclosing. But it is very unfamiliar to someone who has not experienced it.

Adding to the difficulty of self-disclosure with a partner is the fact that often just telling the other person you have a fantasy life is threatening to that person—or you feel that it may be. A woman's first reaction to this kind of disclosure is often, "There's something inadequate about me and our sex life. If he has to fantasize about breasts and thighs and pubic areas and buttocks, then I'm not enough."

This was the case with forty-five-year-old Doris when John, her husband for eighteen years, showed an interest in soft-core pornography.

"He is being unfaithful to me through pornographic magazines," she said. "To me it's a real hurt. Although he is still very affectionate, I feel he isn't desirous of me. I feel he's getting his sexual gratification through these magazines and not through me. He doesn't know that I know about them, and I just can't talk to him about it."

Doris is a sexually inhibited woman, and to some degree her husband is inhibited also. If he is embarrassed by his fantasy of sex with the sweet young things that pose for the girlie magazines, I suspect he feels guilt or embarrassment about other aspects of his sexuality also.

It is likely that sex between the two of them has become somewhat stale. The sexual stimulation he is undoubtedly getting from the sex magazines could be rewarding for both of them, unless he is simply using the magazines as a way of avoiding Doris sexually through some form of autoeroticism. If he could bring the subject out in the open, it could become part of their sexual activity—of the teasing, joking and playing between them. Or if Doris could just say, "Hey, let's share our fantasy life" when she picks up these messages from him, in experiencing his fantasies she would gain greater and greater freedom to communicate and to fantasize in this area, and probably would amplify her own fantasy life, which may be very limited. At first, exploring their fantasies together would be scary, but getting into things that are new and risky can be exciting, and the two would begin to feel very close to one another in being able to do it.

At the time she called, however, this would have been extremely difficult for Doris to do. She had gained considerable weight and was very afraid of being rejected sexually. She was not really willing to open up with her husband the question of sexual fantasies or how sexually attractive she wanted to be.

I suggested that she and her husband talk about initiating an active program for revitalizing their sexual relationship, and that she begin this with a ninety-day plan to lose the weight she needed to lose and get into top physical condition. I proposed that they plan a holiday in a new place as a second honeymoon, point their expectations toward it and do whatever they need to do in order to recreate the sexual life between them. Reading books on sensual awareness would help them become active participants in such a re-creation of their sexual life. They could also bring this pornographic literature of his, as well as other erotic materials, into the relationship. This might involve reading sexy novels at the same time or seeing X-rated movies together in order to incorporate his fantasy life and hers.

The Value of Erotica

For many people, erotic materials, such as movies, books or the magazines Doris's husband reads, are useful aids to gaining more spontaneous and free access to their own sexual feelings. Erotica can stimulate and expand sexual fantasies, thus heightening sexual excitement. Fantasy begins to feed into reality, and we can become freer in experimenting sexually and in creating new sexual environments. Many people need this kind of encouragement to get into their own fantasies, which are an important dimension of our capacity to respond to another. For instance, if a thirty-five-year-old woman does not allow herself sexual fantasies—if her image of a man she finds intensely attractive involves no more than the romantic whisperings of a fourteen- or fifteen-year-old girl, and she cannot allow herself to imagine the two of them swimming nude or holding each other in bed—her sexual excitement will be somewhat inhibited and she may be nonorgasmic. If she begins to experience sexual fantasies, her capacity for arousal and intensity of feeling is likely to be heightened.

Erotic materials also provide a way for partners to communicate with one another about sexual issues that seem too awkward to talk about directly. As a tool for desensitizing sexual fears and inhibitions, they are widely used in sex therapy. Many people use them similarly on their own.

Often a man and a woman progress through various stages, starting with the mildest erotic materials—perhaps a love story with a sexual episode that is arousing to them—and proceed to more explicit sexual scenes, until they find their appropriate level. For some, it is novels that are very sex-oriented. For others, R-rated movies. For some, hard-core pornography.

This was the case with thirty-two-year-old Frank.

"I love hard-core pornographic books," he told me. "Reading dirty books helped my sex life. Until I read some, I was very inhibited. I started practicing some of the things I learned in one of these books and it changed our marriage completely. I was surprised how naive I'd been.

"A lot of times my wife and I buy a pornographic book and go to bed and read it together. It turns us on. I think all women should read these books."

While erotic materials can be useful to many people, Frank's assumption that all women should read hard-core pornography is mistaken. What is suitable for particular individuals in erotica depends on the person's sensitivities and background. Some women would find Frank's hard-core books offensive and deeply troubling to their sense of self and to their moral and personal values. They would respond with emotional shock and withdrawal, rather than with greater freedom and spontaneity. There are many women who are sexually free and spontaneous, whose personal attitude is that eroticism ought to be associated with deep emotional feelings. External stimuli turn them off or diminish their spontaneity. However, the social changes of the last twenty years have made an enormous difference in the numbers of women who feel free to experience erotic feelings through visual means. Kinsey, in the late forties, found that eighty-three percent of all women had no interest in erotic pictures and were offended by them. Yet recent sexual research has shown that more than half of all women now say that they get erotic stimulation from seeing erotic films and pictures.

Unfortunately, until recently the quality of most erotic films has been pretty dreadful, suggesting that the attitude of the producers toward their clientele is that they are into something socially unacceptable and dirty. But in a few years we may see more eroticism in good films tastefully made. Erotic materials have been part of the human experience for thousands of years, and many of those from the past show us that erotica can be aesthetically pleasing. For example, the early illustrations of Omar Khayyam, drawn seven or eight hundred years ago, were beautifully but very erotically done.

The value of erotica wanes for most of us when we give ourselves full freedom to experience a wide range of sexual fantasy and gain full access to our sexual feelings. Then these feelings are adequately generated in sexual encounter with a real person. As the Danes discovered when they eliminated curbs on pornography, erotic materials eventually become repetitive and boring to an individual.

Seeking Love in Sex

Not all sexual messages between partners concern the character of physical contact. Many persons are asking for love in seeking sex. They don't know that they are asking for love. They don't know how to ask for love.

In an incident twenty-four-year-old Pat discussed with me, the man she had been living with for three months, forty-nine-year-old George, probably was seeking in sex reassurance about his lovability far more than he was seeking sexual and sensual pleasure.

"We went to a birthday party for a friend Saturday night and I started feeling sick, like I was coming down with something," she recounted. "He took me home. Then he got very amorous. All I wanted was to be left alone to go to sleep. But he bugged me and bugged me until finally I said, 'If you don't leave me alone I'm going to stay at my parents' house. I just want to get some sleep.' He became very irritated with me. Sunday I got up late and he was gone. I called his office this morning and left a message to let him know that I didn't go to work today. When he called back, he said, 'You really are sick.' And I said, 'No, the whole thing was just a big farce. Of course I'm sick.' I don't know what's gotten into him. He isn't usually like this."

The age difference between Pat and George, plus some other elements of self-doubt in his personality, probably had combined to create a desertion or rejection anxiety in him. His first wife had left him, and he may have had other experiences with women, starting in childhood, in which he had had a feeling of rejection. It is not a question of whether or not he was actually rejected, but that he *felt* rejected. He almost certainly has a suppressed fear of rejection by a woman. All it takes is a mild pushing of that emotional button for him to overreact and go through what amounts to a low-key temper tantrum.

What he was probably saying to Pat that particular evening was, "Is this the beginning of your no longer loving me?"

"But he knows I love him," Pat protested, when I explained

this to her. It may well be that George knows rationally that Pat loves him, but he can still have a painful overreaction based on gut-level anxiety.

If Pat can learn to recognize that this is happening, she can say, "Look, George, this has nothing to do with my loving you. It has to do with my feeling physically ill now. I'm truly not rejecting you."

Every human being has sensitivities like George's—emotional buttons that can be pushed—and these sometimes create incredible pain. Since everyone has a complicated history of being loved or not loved, or of being loved in certain kinds of ways as a child, most people send out very complex messages about what they expect and what they fear, what kinds of rejection they're avoiding, what areas of sensitivity they have, what freedom to experience intense emotions they allow themselves, or, more frequently, what feelings they do not allow themselves. The message anyone receives from another person is very complicated. So it is not surprising that sex is frequently burdened by needs for communication, or by frustration, anger, disappointment and confused feelings. Often a very unsatisfactory sexual relationship is related to feelings of being unloved.

This may well have been the case with the husband of Susan. He was sending her strong messages of frustration in their sexual life when she called.

Rewarding Sex is Mutual

"When my husband comes home from work, he talks about sex constantly—what other women would be like," she said. "I listen for a while, but pretty soon he starts repeating himself and I just get up and walk away. I don't know what to do. I don't know if it's something I'm doing to him or what. It upsets me. I've tried to tell him what it does to me and he stopped for a while, but all of a sudden he starts up again. We're going somewhere with the children and the same subject comes up again."

Apparently, Susan's husband did not have the ego strength to say outright to his wife, "Look, there's something unrewarding about our sexual life and I'd like to do something about it," but there is a clear message in his conversation that he feels sexually inadequate or unrewarded or not free and spontaneous sexually. Or that some frustration or inhibition bothers him. Their sexual relations were not very rewarding for Susan, she said, but she felt sure that they were for her husband. This is unlikely. Unless he is not very bright or is an emotionally shallow man, he is aware that she is not satisfied in sex and this awareness troubles him. You cannot successfully fake sexual satisfaction over a period of years with a person. It is rare that a man feels deeply emotionally rewarded in sex with a wife who is not also deeply rewarded. Many women find it hard to understand that a powerful element of sexual reward for a man is his feeling that he has truly delighted and created a joy and ecstasy in his wife. If this does not occur, many men translate that into a sense of inadequacy. They feel ego-diminished. However, most men find it hard to say what they're missing and what they're feeling.

If sex continues to be unrewarding for Susan, sex between her and her husband will decline prematurely because it won't be worth it to him. It will be boring and dull. He will feel slightly guilty about it and have less and less impulse to initiate it or participate in it. By the time he is forty-five or fifty, two or three months may go by between sexual contacts. Sex may be perpetuated over many years into a couple's seventies or even into their eighties when it is joyful and intensely pleasurable for both persons, who express to one another a warm outflow of affection as a result of the sexual experience. But otherwise it is likely to slip into decline much earlier. If Susan and her husband would agree to talk to each other about their sexual feelings, they could become more at ease in their sexual relations. If they had the determination to share all of their impressions of sex, going all the way back to their early lives, there would be a great amount of intimate communication between them. They would get over the idea that men and women are completely different in sexual feelings, attitudes and responses, and would begin to feel more comfortable with one another. The section of "The State of Your Union" Questionnaire (pp. 227–237) that deals with sex could be helpful in stimulating this kind of communication.

After that, a two-month program of nude cuddling could substantially improve their sexual life. In such a program, every night for sixty days, partners spend ten or fifteen minutes holding and caressing each other in the nude without expecting intercourse. One night one caresses the other in pleasurable ways; the next night the roles of pleasurer and pleasured are reversed. The one being pleasured describes what is being experienced as it is experienced.

Such a program would create a great deal more warmth and understanding between Susan and her husband, and would very likely provide a substantial increase in the intensity and pleasure of sex. However, if they cannot open up communication about their sexual feelings, they will need the help of a professional therapist who has appropriate training and specializes in the sexual area.

The Powerful Effect of Early Conditioning

Much of what Susan's husband was experiencing in sex may have had little to do with her. Often only a relatively small part of the total sexual transaction between a man and a woman concerns what goes on between them in the here-and-now. Most likely, her husband was responding primarily to his inner imagery and feelings of self-worth and his biological and psychological cycles. His sexual responses probably had much to do with his personal history, both ancient and recent, and with the personality he brought into the marriage—with his attitudes toward the opposite sex and his expectations of himself.

Susan reacted to his messages of sexual dissatisfaction by feeling that she was inadequate or unlovable, however. Most of us constantly make this kind of self-reference about the responses of a partner. If the other person is passionate one night, we feel, "I must be sexy and exciting." If a partner is passive when we're interested in sex, we feel we must be duds.

In reality, Susan's husband may have been feeling sexually unrewarded primarily because he *expected* to be sexually unrewarded. He may expect that that is how he is going to be with a woman. If you have strong failure expectations, it is hard to achieve a successful relationship in any dimension of life.

The large role played by our early histories and early cultural conditioning in sex can hardly be overemphasized. Our sexuality—our natural responses, our receptivity, our desires—is shaped by our life experiences, by what we learned about affection and friendship from our contemporaries in adolescence and early adult life, and by cultural attitudes passed on to us by our parents and others.

Most of us have had a good deal of negative training in regard to sensual and sexual attitudes. One of the basic findings of research on human sexuality over the past twenty-five years is that most of us have experienced some sensual and sensory deprivation. As babies at twelve or eighteen months, we were sensual creatures delighted with all the sensory information that came our way. But as we grew older, we became self-conscious about our sensual and sensory nature, and more and more awkward and embarrassed by it. By the time we were adults, many of us were not free with regard to the pleasures of touching and of being touched and responded to.

A great deal of negative training about sex comes from the strong residue of nineteenth-century sexual concepts that still exist in our culture, especially among more traditional and orthodox groups. A double dose of negative conditioning has been received by most women because of the double standard in attitudes toward sex in men and women. Many women have been trained to view their own sexual desire and pleasure as undesirable, unfeminine or even degrading and dirty. Parents need not say a word about their aversive feelings concerning sex for this kind of negative conditioning to occur. If every time Dad makes a sexual or playful gesture toward Mom, she withdraws as if she hates it, very upsetting indoctrination about sex takes place in a child.

These influences in our early experiences get translated into sex problems related to embarrassment, awkwardness and inhibition, and to fear of disapproval or of not being a worthy, exciting or lovable partner. They are responsible for a great amount of anxiety about sensuality and sexuality. This occurs in more than fifty percent of all men and women to the point of creating some sexual dysfunction at some time in adult life.

Thirty-four-year-old Andrea, who called the radio program, was a microcosm of the millions of people who have had powerful negative conditioning about sensuality and sexuality. Raised in a home in which she never saw her parents show emotion, she was unfamiliar with affectionate physical contact and sensuality, and started adult life with intense fears in this area.

"It's very hard for me to show any emotion in front of people, and I have a fear of being seen or heard by my children during sex," she said. "I have to be completely alone. Any physical affection in front of them embarrasses me terribly. And I can go without sex for weeks. Once in a while I'll let myself go in sex, but most of the time I don't. Yet I have a lot of fantasies [about having sex] with different men. I wonder what it would be like with someone else. And I feel guilty."

Like a great many others, in her family experience Andrea had received deep conditioning that sex is a bad thing and that her sexual desire was something to be hidden and avoided.

This had inhibited her freedom to express and experience sensuality. She feared that she was raising her daughter the same way, and this was probably the case.

I believe it was Dr. William H. Masters who once said that the best sexual training a child can have is to observe Daddy patting Mommy on the behind and her being delighted by it. This kind of direct sensuality tells children that their own sensuality is okay. It gives them some degree of freedom from society's anxiety about sex. For years it was thought that exposing children to sexual play between parents would create trauma but we now know this is nonsense. Certainly most psychologists would not advocate that a child actually be present during sexual intercourse between parents, but it doesn't hurt children to know that their parents are physically loving.

The Inability to be Orgasmic

Early life conditioning often causes sexual problems for persons who do not share Andrea's feelings of Victorian restraint. This was the case with twenty-five-year-old Joan, who didn't feel inhibited about sex, but never had been able to have an orgasm with anyone.

"I didn't tell my present husband about it for about a year, because I was guilt-ridden," she said. "I was afraid he would think I wasn't a woman. All of a sudden one day I just blurted it out. He said he wished I had told him long before. He had felt something was wrong and had been reaching to help me but I wouldn't let him. I was shocked. It made me fall apart because I had been carrying this guilt all by myself. I even ran the risk of losing him because he felt something was wrong and I wouldn't let him help me.

"After that, I went for therapy for three months and I found out many things that go back to my first marriage when I was fourteen that cause me to have problems now. My first husband was a very selfish person and in sex thought of no one but himself. I felt like I was being used. When I broke away from that marriage, I felt fine and had an active sex life, but something was missing that I couldn't pin down. When I married again, I was very dumb and happy but still kept feeling that something was wrong. Then I read *The Sensuous Woman*. The writer talked about different methods of trying to discover your body. So I purchased a mechanical vibrator to experiment with. Much to my amazement, I can always have an orgasm with the vibrator. But I still never can any other way."

Joan's inability to be orgasmic with a man when she is able to do so in masturbation has to do with a fear of men. Like eighty to ninety percent of women who are nonorgasmic, she apparently has been conditioned to have angry or distrustful feelings toward males. Even though her present husband is a kind and thoughtful man, she has not been able to let go of these feelings. At some deep emotional level, when a man enters her sexually, she feels invaded. Psychologically she has to throw up barriers and is not able to allow her body, mind and feelings to fully get into the sexual experience.

Many women who have this kind of intense distrust of men have had mothers who didn't really like their husbands. Often their mothers felt used and sometimes brutalized by them. And often women who distrust men did not have a good relationship with their fathers. I strongly suspect that this was the case with Joan. Generally, a young woman does not marry at fourteen if she has a loving relationship with important males in her life. Joan also had a poor relationship with her first husband. She gained some insight into the influence of this first marriage from a therapist who used hypnosis and positive suggestion to help her. Sometimes this can be very useful with sexual problems, but what she really needs is to further engage with a therapist in working through the issue of trusting a man.

It would be best for her to have a male therapist for whom she could learn to have warm, affectionate feelings but on whom she could also act out her anger—one who has the skill to trigger her historical anger and distrust. She needs to break open her internalized pack of angry, distrustful feelings toward men—fears that she will be used, brutalized or treated unkindly by a man—and let it go.

Professionals trained in human sexuality have dealt with thousands of nonorgasmic women in this way with better than an eighty-percent success rate. Joan and her husband apparently have an excellent emotional basis for their relationship. With this kind of emotional retraining she would almost certainly become orgasmic.

A Different Personal History, a Different Problem

A different kind of problem arose in the marriage of thirty-one-year-old Alan and his wife because of something in her historical background.

"When I suggest a different position, she gets shook up and nervous," he complained. "It's the only thing that's ruining our marriage. I try to be patient and a few times she has gone along with me, but she says she doesn't get anything out of it. She says she feels goofy when I try something kind of wild. I wish I could understand why she won't go along with me. She loves me, but she holds back."

"Isn't it good for a marriage to have all these different positions?" he asked.

In some instances it is. It is apparently an important issue to Alan and is causing problems in the marriage.

If both he and his wife were comfortable and satisfied with sex, it is likely they would both feel free. There is some special reason for his wife's anxiety. She may have a fear of loss of control or of being dominated. Or other subsurface attitudes may inhibit a free feeling in sex. Her family conditioning in regard to sex had not been restrictive, according to Alan, who described her parents as "wonderful people, who are very loving with each other." But something in her historical background makes her acutely uncomfortable with sexual contact that is unfamiliar.

It may be that she had pubescent or adolescent sexual fantasies about her father that made her feel wicked. If her parents are very loving, her father was probably very loving with her until puberty. When she suddenly changed from his little girl to a young woman, he may have become embarrassed at close physical contact with her, and backed off from it, as most fathers do. At this point it is very likely that she would have become very competitive as her mother's sexual rival in a fantasy sense. If her guilt about this was powerful enough, it could have influenced her later sexual development so that she would want to restrain herself in sex for fear it would get out of hand as she felt it had in her early fantasies around her father.

An even more likely explanation of her resistance to the unfamiliar in sex is that she was the recipient of a sexual approach by a male before her middle teens. It may have been anything from a sexual overture or sexual play by an older brother or uncle, when she was prepubescent, to fondling by a junior high school teacher. Anything out of the ordinary in sex can bring her disturbingly close to that painful memory.

She needs to get some understanding of what is bothering her. But if she and Alan at least open up the subject of their differences in sexual desires and communicate on a feeling level about what each wants and why, they probably can discover some middle ground where both can be comfortable, confident and happy.

Personal History Interacts With Present Experience

Sexual problems are not caused entirely by our backgrounds, of course. They also have to do with the way a man and a woman relate to one another in the here-and-now.

The experience of Shirley, forty-one, married for eight years, provides a vivid illustration of the interaction between these two forces in a sexual relationship.

"My marriage was perfect for the first three years," she said. "I had no guilt about sex. But I have become so ashamed of sex that I don't even sleep with my husband anymore. It started after we had an argument. We had been going to his mother's every weekend, flying up to San Francisco from Los Angeles. I don't get along with her all that well, and one weekend I didn't want to go. I said, 'Can't we go somewhere alone with the baby and enjoy ourselves this weekend?' He grabbed the baby and said he was going. I said I was not going. And as he walked out the door, I said, 'Ed, why? Why do you have to go?' And he said, 'Because I have more respect for her than I have for you.'

"It hit me like a ton of bricks. I don't know what his problem is. He didn't know me until a year before our marriage. I guess he figures every girl was like the girls he'd known or lived with before he knew me. I had never had sex before we were married. My religion kept me morally straight and I had little time to myself. I went out in groups but I never went on dates.

"Knowing the Bible, I felt that anything done in marriage was perfectly beautiful and should be enjoyed. Then, all of a sudden, after three years of marriage, because I was passionate, because I was doing what I felt, he lost respect for me. I don't understand that. He had been with women before me, but I had respect for him. It reached the point where I turned myself off to him."

Shirley's husband had had negative training about sex from his mother, toward whom he has powerful feelings of love but also, undoubtedly, anger and guilt. As most boys do, he probably found his mother sexually exciting in his early teens and felt terribly guilty about these feelings. One way of handling this is to castigate yourself and ennoble your mother's asexuality. When you do that, you ennoble asexuality (purity) on the part of any woman. He may have been able to suppress this during the first three years of his marriage because he was probably having a marvelous time sexually with his wife. But a powerful sense that he was doing something bad undoubtedly was eating away at him. Visiting his mother more than four hundred miles away every weekend sounds like doing penance for guilt. When his wife protested against these weekly trips, out poured his guilt—his historical inner anguish. It is very easy to project these kinds of feelings onto those whom one is close to.

Since Shirley remained celibate until she was thirty-three, she also undoubtedly had a powerful repository of fear and guilt with regard to sex. She had needed a tremendous amount of approval—the mandate of love, really—to express her sexual feelings.

We all have an image or fantasy of love. If a partner, because of some painful and powerful historical conditioning, rips that image, then the whole structure can come tumbling down. That had happened to Shirley, when her husband's guilt poured out on her. From feeling loved, she had switched to feeling totally unloved, and her inner fears and guilt with regard to sex had broken open and engulfed her. She was in a terribly painful place.

"All I want is out," she told me. "But I don't want to destroy two kids. I've told him I wish he'd go back to running around with girls like he did before we were married. I can't convince him that it would be all right with me. He says, 'Then I'd be living with a jealous wife.' I've said, 'I'll even divorce you, because in the eyes of my church I won't be divorced anyhow. We can still live in the same house and have the kids, but you can be you.'"

But at the same time that she said this, she described her husband as a great person, "the kind of guy that any other woman would give her right arm to have". The message that came through to me was that the two of them still cared about each other. She agreed.

"I tell him so and he tells me so," she said. "But every time he touches me I freeze up. Then I apologize. I've learned over these last few years to turn off. I'm afraid he's going to feel as he did before—that he has something to be ashamed of."

Shirley's learning to "turn off" could be unlearned, but these two badly need the help of a family therapist to resolve the situation. In therapy her husband would get some idea of how badly he brutalized her with that dumping of his guilt feelings on her. And she would realize how heavily loaded he is with guilt and anger toward his mother. Then they both could begin to appreciate the emotional entrapment that each had endured, and the role this played in that devastating episode. They could begin to work through these feelings so they could forgive each other and allow the past to fade. When they forgave each other, their sexuality would turn back on.

Sex and Other Problems

Just as anger, guilt and fear act as powerful depressants on our spontaneous ability to feel pleasure and our physical sexual capacity, other feelings are channeled into the sexual area: low self-esteem, fear of aging, loneliness, general fears about one's ability to cope with life. Sex tends to be the central symbolic area of life, and many people use it badly to deal with a lot of different problems.

Often sex is a hostile act, even between husbands and wives. Many women report extreme aggressiveness by their husbands that denies sex mutual pleasure, tenderness and loving. A lot of husbands report that their wives act out hostility through sexual withdrawal or controlling the quality or timing of sex. Often a couple finds it easier to use sex as a vehicle to carry anger about some nonsexual issue of difference between them than to deal with differences openly. They may have powerful disagreements over child-rearing, or be competing with one another for status and power in the marriage. Unless partners deal with the issues between them, they eventually create a great deal of confusion.

Thirty-one-year-old Ginny, who talks about using sex as a tool for power, was headed for this kind of trouble.

"My husband is a very dynamic personality. He is strong-willed and has to be on top of everything, in business and everywhere else," she explained. "I am just the opposite. I am very quiet. So the only way I can ever calm him down and have control of anything is to say no in sex.

"Generally we have a very good relationship. He is usually very loving and sweet. When I tell him I want him to talk more, he talks more and tells me he needs me and is very loving and demonstrative. And sometimes I look at myself and say, 'It's not him; it's me.' But about the only way I can be anything of real importance is to do what he wants me to do and be how he wants me to be."

Almost every relationship has something of a power struggle in it, but Ginny's way of dealing with hers is a very destructive one. When a power struggle is directly brought into the sexual interaction between two persons, it is very likely to increase and become a negative influence on the relationship. It brings the power struggle into the area where tenderness and a sense of being close to one another and sensually and emotionally important to one another are central.

From Ginny's conversation I got a sense that her husband was actively engaged in self-development—that he was testing his powers and capacities in the world, proving to himself that he is capable of doing many things, and getting a lot of personal reward from doing so. Ginny, on the other hand, seems a somewhat underdeveloped person, who needs to create some separate areas of interest and concern of her own. She needs to take the responsibility for becoming a more energetic, effective, affirmative participant in life, so she can feel better about herself and not use sex as her only source of power and self-esteem.

Apparently, her husband is sufficiently affectionate and easy-going, with enough confidence and good feelings about his life and himself, so that this sexual rejection game of hers has not yet seriously undermined their relationship. But it will if they keep it up. Symbolically, sexual rejection tells a man he's unlovable and inevitably creates an angry, deeply hostile husband. Five to ten years from now the marriage probably will be going very sour and her husband will be finding sexual alternatives.

Sexual Relationships are Changing

Traditionally, a woman has been the passive recipient of a male sexual approach. This came from the traditional view that women lacked sexual desire, which carried over into more recent years as a belief that a woman's sexual desire was less powerful than that of a man. We now know that when the female is unencumbered by negative social and religious conditioning, the only difference from the male in the degree of her sexual interest and activity is that the two reach the peak of their sexual desire at different ages. The typical male arrives at the height of his sexual powers at the age of nineteen or twenty. A woman reaches hers a decade later.

There is nothing inherent in the biology or psychology of a woman that determines that she be less aggressive or free in sex than a man. And most men find having the sole responsibility for rewarding sex an onerous burden. In the new wave of attitudes toward human sexuality the idea of a woman being fully equal as a sexual partner, as free and open in her sexuality as a man, is beginning to gain currency. When we posed the question, "Can you be aggressive in sex?" to women in the radio audience, the number of young women callers who had worked their way through to a good deal of confidence, openness and aggressiveness in sex was impressive.

In a partnership in which both persons feel free and strong and good about themselves and can deal with one another openly and honestly, there is no reason why either one cannot take the initiative in sex whenever either chooses. But it is only in the last generation or two that a substantial portion of the population has had a glimmer of the fact that sex and marriage can be a truly collaborative, cooperative adventure that need not involve dominance or dependence on the part of one or the other. Because of past conditioning to historical sexual roles and attitudes, two people have to walk a tightrope in working out a co-equal sexual relationship. The only way most people can work it through is with very open and intimate conversation. Very risk-taking kinds of communication. They have to trust each other enough to be able to say what they feel without either person being badly offended, rejected or hurt.

Each person has to take the freedom to be a sexually responsive person, and each has to be responsible for his or her own sexual pleasure. At the same time, each must be willing to listen creatively to the other in order to understand what is being communicated, either directly or indirectly. In doing this, if you find that your partner is awkward or uncomfortable, you have to go along with the anxiety, self-protectiveness or avoidance behavior, recognizing that a willingness to experiment and thereby risk more is a process of evolution, of creating trust. It's a tricky, difficult business. Frequently, two people run into problems.

If a woman misses messages from her husband that he feels sexually inadequate when she is sexually aggressive, or that he has negative sexual conditioning that causes him inner pain, there is no way for anything constructive to come out of it. Her sexual freedom becomes his sexual put-down, and the more sexually aggressive and free she becomes, the more he will feel inadequate.

Similarly, if a man gives his wife the message that she's a poor bed partner, perhaps by shoving books about sex at her, the outcome will be negative. He may justify it by telling himself he is only trying to encourage her to loosen up a bit, but she will become more and more angry and humiliated, and withdraw from the sexual arena.

Only if both persons are willing and psychologically capable of communicating openly and "giving to get," can they become sexually free, strong and spontaneous with one another.

A coequal sexual relationship worked out well in the marriage of twenty-eight-year-old Laurie. But her conversation here gives some insight into the mixed feelings we sometimes have when we venture into the scary territory of unfamiliar behavior.

"We've been married for ten years and our sex life has been just perfect. But about four or five years ago my husband said to me, 'Hey, how come you're never the aggressor? I'd like you to be the initiator once in a while.' So I said, 'Fine. I didn't know you wanted that.' So I started being the initiator. And his reaction was, 'Not now. Don't bother me.' Man, he backed off. What would be the reason for that? Why would he ask for one thing, and when I do it, say another? He's not that way anymore, but I was wondering why."

Perhaps Laurie was being aggressive about sexual feelings at a time when her husband wasn't receptive. Or maybe she was taking over some part of the role of sexual initiation that he didn't want her to take over, but he was too embarrassed to make clear to her how and under what circumstances he wanted her to be aggressive. We usually give each other very confused, convoluted messages with regard to sexuality because when we attempt to tell a love partner how we want to be pleasured, we get in touch with our own sexual inhibitions and fears and with deep feelings about our own loveworthiness. Most of us have ambivalent feelings about whether we're going to be given what we basically want. We're afraid we won't and we're afraid we will. The most embarrassing experience for most of us is for someone to genuinely, openly love us. Most of us find it difficult to be loved.

Examine your own feelings when someone you meet, without come-on or hidden implications, says, "I think you're very attractive." Or, "I really admire you. I'm excited and turned on by you." If the person who makes a direct statement of positive reaction to us is someone with whom we have an ongoing relationship, we have a way of partly diminishing it by thinking, "Oh, well, you're supposed to love me." But when we receive an intense, warm response that we're not expecting and not prepared to handle, most of us become embarrassed and find it difficult to cope with.

When I discussed this with Laurie, she agreed readily that it seemed to explain her husband's attitude. "It was exactly as if he was saying, 'That's what I want. But I don't think I'm really ready for it,'" she said.

It's hard to work out those feelings, and all of us have them.

Chapter 4

Extramarital Sex in Modern Marriage

The reality of present life is that "the pill," which separated sex from procreation more effectively than anything in the past, and for some persons separated love and sex, has thrust us into a period in which monogamy is more and more a matter of choice rather than of necessity. Sexual exclusivity, or non-exclusivity, has become an individual matter between two persons that can be negotiated.

A small but increasing minority of marital partners are frankly choosing to have "open" marriages, in which partners agree that both are free to have sex with other persons. While this nontraditional style of partnership works for some people, negotiating such a relationship—bringing the issue of sexual non-exclusivity to the fore and working it through—is very difficult for most couples. Typically, one or the other partner, the male as often as the female, finds sanctioning a marital partner having sexual relations outside the marriage unbearably painful. Even in marriages in which partners do accept the idea of the other having extramarital affairs, most often a spouse doesn't really want to know what the other is doing—the details of who, where, what or when.

Attitudes in this area appear to be one of the most rapidly changing elements in alliances between men and women. But as of now, there are many people who are not likely to be able to make much of a transition on this issue in their own lifetimes without a great deal of inner pain.

Twenty-three-year-old Jackie was recognizing this as the case with her husband when she called.

"We led the same sort of bohemian life before marriage, and I assumed he understood that I wanted an open relationship," she explained. "But it hurts him when he finds out I'm with someone else. I have a good friend and we're really close. My husband thinks I'm playing games. I don't want to hurt him, but I like men. I'm gregarious and he's very introverted. I've always been outgoing. I get bored with one person. It's not the sexual thing. My husband probably thinks it is. But it's not really.

"He leans on me for emotional fulfillment and in a way seems to accept what I'm doing. But I know it hurts him. I expect I have to decide whether to give him up or give up my lifestyle. It's hard because I really love him and we have a lot in common."

If Jackie's husband accepts what she is doing with pain and anger, he will get more angry. It will be just a matter of time until he responds in some intense way. Or he will translate it into a personal put-down. He may develop ulcers or some other form of self-punitive internalized anguish.

If both partners are comfortable with a sexually non-exclusive relationship, the marital situation can be quite different, however. This can be seen in the conversation of twenty-five-year-old Peggy. Her marriage to Tim, twenty-seven, had begun with traditional expectations, but they had decided that a freer pattern better suited them.

"We both had had sexual relations outside the marriage," she said. "Before we got around to talking about it, it was sneaky. It seemed like it was tearing us apart. We're more secure in our marriage now. And now that it's out in the open and we know a closed thing can't work for us, it doesn't seem like it happens as much. It's just something that's occasional. We like each other's company more than anyone else's. We love each other. I wouldn't not let him know where I was. I respect him, I respect his privacy and he respects mine. Before we had this understanding, I resented that if I was interested in someone else, I couldn't see that person. It seemed that Tim was holding me back. Or if I did do something with a friend, I felt like I was taking away from our relationship. Now I feel I can add to it. When I come home, if I want to, I talk about what presented itself that evening. I'm really excited about life. I have doors open for me every day. It's nothing planned. If it's planned, it doesn't work out."

Why Extramarital Sex

While most persons cannot comfortably work out a relationship like that of Peggy and Tim, a great many married persons do engage in extramarital sex. Studies indicate that fifty-five percent or more of married men at some time in their marriages have an extramarital affair.

Women, as often as men, have the curiosity, the need or the desire to test sexual alternatives outside their marriages. In the past they generally felt more inhibited about doing so. In the thirty years since the Kinsey Report estimated that only twelve or thirteen percent of women at some time in their marriage had an extramarital affair, that situation has changed dramatically. Recent studies indicate that nearly forty percent of married women have participated or will participate in extramarital sex.

There is a wide range of reasons why people seek sexual experiences outside their marriages. One of the commonest is that so many people marry very early and have little social, emotional and sexual development before they lock themselves into a presumably exclusive pairing. In later years they often feel that they have been cheated out of broader social or sexual experience. Or they find that the relationship does not give them all they want. Many married people don't have enough friendships or acquaintanceships outside the marriage. When two people are locked into a narrowly based interpersonal situation, often they feel stifled and begin to look outside for something.

This was the case with twenty-six-year-old Donna, mother of two. Married at eighteen to her first boyfriend, she was strongly tempted to have an affair when she called.

"I feel so tied down," she complained. "I have a desire to be free and have no responsibilities. I was satisfied for the first four years of marriage, but during the last four it's been very difficult to refuse offers from other men. I think I still love my husband, but I have this great desire to accept every offer that's given me. I tried talking to him about it, but it was like talking to a wall. He got angry. So I shut up. But it's just breaking me up. He's a very responsible man and he loves his kids very much. And I feel it's either my marriage or this adventure."

With but one friend outside her marriage, and a distant, non-confiding relationship with her husband, Donna feels isolated and lonely. What she is seeking is some recognition of her personal value, some feeling of importance and excitement. At the core, what she wants is to be loved and to be loving, which is what most of us want. Neither she nor her husband knows how to go about giving or getting this with one another. Both have individual growth and personality issues that they haven't dealt with independently. They are frightened of important emotional involvement with each other or with other people, so they emotionally avoid one another and avoid developing friendships. The marriage probably isn't providing a great deal of joy, pleasure or personal recognition for either of them.

Donna fantasizes finding what she wants with a lover who will respond to her physical attractiveness in terms of sexual excitement. Temporarily the excitement of being courted again might conceal her fears and doubts that she will ever get true recognition of her personal value, but it wouldn't give her what she really desires, and she would end up angry and upset.

At this point she badly needs someone to talk to, someone with whom she would feel safe in confiding her feelings. An older woman friend could be helpful—or her clergyman, a favorite doctor, or a marriage counselor.

If she would find such an older confidante (that this person be a woman is preferable), the recognition, mutual understanding and active listening involved in this experience, along with the warmth and affection it would engender, would give her some idea of how she might be able to bring these values into her marriage.

Her husband also needs experience in getting in touch with his emotions and giving these open expression. Participation in a group dealing with interpersonal relations, perhaps a job-related group, would be helpful.

The Don Juan

When the partner seeking an extramarital affair is a man, often it is a matter of acting out early sexual fantasies.

A male usually experiences intense sexual desires in his early teens and generally feels very sexually deprived at that time. Basically, he's afraid to approach a woman sexually. He's afraid of rejection. But he has a fantasy of having an infinite number of girlfriends who are all mad about him and sexually available to him. By the time he's seventeen, he's often angry at women. He feels frustrated, baffled and denied by them. If he never has the opportunity to explore relationships confidently with a number of women, this feeling may be carried into adult life.

For some men, other factors accentuate this emotional immaturity. They never develop a sense that there's great value in establishing a stable, trusting relationship with a woman. The result may be a kind of perpetual Don Juanism.

Michael, twenty-seven, had a serious problem that illustrates this.

"I'm separated now," he said. "I guess my wife couldn't take it anymore. I love her and the kids very much, but I continually look for sex outside our marriage. When my wife takes me back, as she did three months ago, I'm all right for a few weeks, then I change again. I can't stand her or the children, and I have to get out.

"The woman I'm seeing is seven years older than I. She calls my wife and asks what I'm up to, and whether she wants me, and whether I'm living at home. My wife asks me what I want and I don't know what to answer. For the last ten months I have given her lots of gifts, but no love or affection. I've been sort of relieved when she's thrown me out. It makes life easier. When I left the last time, I said to myself, 'Let her bring up the kids by herself.' But now I don't know. I'm confused. What's the matter with me?"

From what Michael told me, he probably has a case of galloping emotional adolescence and is acting out post-puberty fantasies. He didn't go out with girls at fifteen or sixteen, and is doing his experimenting now. But it is also highly likely that, deep in his guts, he doesn't trust women. He may not have had a loving relationship with his mother—one of stability and confidence in which he could be emotionally direct. The notion of romantic fantasy and the chase appears more appealing and rewarding to him than working through tough emotional business with a real partner. It's easier for him to leave home than to take adult responsibility for a marriage. Over a long period of time he may outgrow these attitudes as part of the slow growth process we all experience. But to do it within a reasonably short period of time he needs the help of someone trained to facilitate growth to assist him through the pain and discomfort of changing to another emotional and attitudinal state. I recommended that he and his wife seek marriage counseling.

"I'm afraid they'll tell her to divorce me," he responded. "I guess I really love her. That's the problem."

Michael's fear is unfounded. A marriage counselor doesn't tell people what to do. Some people may think that in counseling or therapy they will be subjected to the objective, external judgment of a counselor, but by and large this is not true. The role of a counselor is to help you clarify all the feelings that are inside you—the conflicting desires and guilt—so that you have a clearer sense of how you are using yourself to try to get what you want out of life.

Sex is not Always the Goal

In many instances, the sexual aspect of an extramarital affair is secondary to other aspects, although it may appear to be primary. More often than not, people are looking principally for significant friendship, a renewal of the feelings of being loved and renewal of excitement and tender feelings. Men in their thirties, forties and fifties who engage in extramarital sex frequently report that what they are really seeking is an affectionate, caring relationship with a woman with whom they can be friends and communicate with honestly, but not feel responsible for. So many marriages carry such a heavy burden of responsibility, obligation, guilt and often anger, that a feeling of warm friendship is hindered.

A desire for uninhibited sex might seem to play an important part in the attractiveness of an extramarital affair in the case of twenty-nine-year-old Yvonne, who was tempted to revive one that had ended six years earlier. But some difficulty in her marriage undoubtedly was behind it.

"I was a faithful little wife for three years while my husband was in the army. Then I met Larry at a wedding reception just a week before my husband came home," she said as she recalled the beginnings of her affair. "One thing led to another and he took me home. It took me by surprise because I'm a nice little Catholic girl, practically raised in a convent. When my husband came home, of course, it wasn't the way I thought it would be. I expected him to spend all his time with me and he wanted to see his friends and family. So, although I had terrible guilt feelings after going with Larry, I wanted to be with him. I thought I was madly in love with him, although I still had an emotional attachment to my husband.

"We had a mad, passionate affair for four months. Then we drifted apart. No fight. And he married another girl. I decided that was it. I loved my husband and still do. Six years went by and I didn't even think about Larry. Then recently we ran into each other at a party. Last week he called me and wanted to see me. I've built these fantasies about him and I want to see him, but I don't want to hurt my husband. My husband is very satisfying to me and we have a good life together with our children, so I can't understand why I want to go back to Larry again. He's very immature. He lives in a dream world. But he is a good lover. I'm thinking, 'Am I going to be stupid enough to ruin my marriage?' But I'm torn. I want to see him."

It is not uncommon for a service wife to have an extramarital episode just before her husband comes home, even though she may have been faithful for several years, because an anxiety usually builds up in her about whether she is really lovable and is going to be accepted. Also, there is latent anger at him for having gone away, although rationally she knows he had to go. In Yvonne's case her affair may indicate that she feared being dominated when her husband came home—that her image of a wife was that she is subservient to the will of her husband. Her comments indicate some degree of power struggle between her and her husband. She described herself as a strong person and him as also strong, but a little resentful of her ability to stand on her own two feet. It could be that their struggle on this issue inhibits her sexual freedom with him. It is very likely that the same fear that led her to an affair before he returned home from the army is what is impelling her to revive the affair. It may be that his way of doing things has largely dominated the marriage and she is at a point where she wants him to accede half the time to her preferences. Or it may be that she has regained most but not all of the autonomy that she had while he was away, and is ready to take the next step toward an equalitarian marriage.

Apparently she associates Larry with sexual passion and freedom from domination. She could get to the same point with her husband, if the two of them were willing to put some effort into it. They would do well to use the "State of Your Union" questionnaire in this book to evaluate their relationship and initiate some expanded intimate communication in areas of poor compatibility. If they reach some resolution of their differences, with caring, affection and respect added to sexual joy and uninhibited pleasure, they will have a much richer experience than just uninhibited sex.

Fears That Spark Infidelity

When a person seeks extramarital sex, part of the motivation may have to do with freedom, choice and openness to involvement with people. But a large part of it often has to do with fear. Fear of aging when we reach those critical years—twenty-nine, thirty-nine, forty-nine—and must face the reality of the sweep of our own lives. Fear of failure when we feel unsuccessful, either economically or occupationally. Fear of being unsuccessful in sex. Many married persons who have sexual problems cannot communicate with one another, so they have no easy way to overcome them. They look down the road of their lives and ask themselves, "Is this all I'm going to have? Am I going to be married for the next thirty or forty years to this person, with no more joy and fulfillment, no more fun or excitement than this?" And their response leads to infidelity.

Fear of aging quite probably had a good deal to do with the occasional infidelities of thirty-nine-year-old Ray over the year and a half before his wife, Eileen, called. Her description of his attitudes suggests he is in the midst of one of the midlife crises that we all experience a couple of times after reaching adult life. His needs to be handsome, charming, successful with women, admired, etc.—needs he has had all his life—have accelerated greatly. His experience of this is exaggerated, but most men go through some form of it in their late thirties. For the majority it is simply a phase that they weather with some degree of discomfort or difficulty. But for a minority, such a crisis is translated into a series of intense or frantic behaviors that are destructive to the quality of life for that person. A man in this condition is in what is actually a temporary psychopathic state. Without psychotherapy he may throw over a business he has spent years building up or break up a marriage that he will feel terrible about losing when the critical period is past. Here Eileen tells about her husband.

"We had eleven beautiful years, but since he changed jobs and became a salesman five years ago, he's changed," she said. "When we're with the family or friends, we get along beautifully. He's a terrific man—considerate and a good provider. But when we're out in a large crowd where there's dancing and drinking, he wants to be the center of attention. The minute my back is turned, he's talking with a woman. He's always liked attention. He's boasted of things that weren't true—that we have this or have done that. But it was never like this.

"The infidelity started when he got into this circle where everyone was doing it. Yet I know he loves me. Sometimes he'll break down and say, 'I don't know what's the matter with me. We've got everything. I don't know what I'd do without you.'

"But I'm beginning to feel insecure. I don't know if I should wait it out. We're both thirty-nine. Six or seven years from now, no one will give me a second look. I've been tempted to have an affair myself, maybe for spite. But I couldn't go through with it. I tried being indifferent and he went out all the more. I don't know how to cope with it."

Ray has been giving Eileen messages for years that he wants life to be more exciting and wants more personal recognition. The two need to communicate on this issue, join forces on it, and negotiate where they want to be with one another, or the gulf between them will become greater. If the marriage is to flourish, they need to take steps to get closer to one another.

If Ray's needs are not so intense that he requires psychotherapy to deal with them, they could do this by making two dates a week with one another, of an hour and a half each, when they would talk to each other about how they feel about their individual lives, about one another and about their marriage—its rewards and stresses and other aspects. They should establish the following ground rules for these discussions: (1) that they will meet in a quiet place where they won't be distracted; (2) that they will be as honest and open with each other as they can be; (3) that neither will indict or put down the other person in any way. If they limit themselves to "I" language and avoid "you" language, they can be sure of being non-indicting.

A great deal of what Ray is looking for with a new woman is the feeling that he is new and different and exciting, a feeling he does not ordinarily get from his wife. But in intimate communication, because his wife is very important to him, she will have an enormous advantage. Since he is important to her, she will be intensely interested in his disclosures of his inner life. When she gives him her undivided attention and is fascinated at his inner life, not only will he receive the satisfying kind of recognition that he can get from other women at cocktail parties, but also the enormously valuable extra dimension of being heard by somebody he loves and who loves him.

If he is given the opportunity to talk about his need for

outside recognition as an attractive man, and is able to articulate some of that, and if his wife is willing to listen to those feelings so that he feels safe in verbalizing them, he is more likely to feel that she is a friend. It is also likely that his need, while it won't disappear, will be kept within manageable boundaries.

Many men, once they become clear in their own minds about their desires, recognize that they want a warm response from a variety of women but don't need or really want extramarital affairs, because such affairs create more stress and upset than reward. Frequently a man, especially one who has been through extramarital involvement, will say, "If I can feel free to be friendly and get some of the fun in that way, I don't need to be involved further. I certainly don't need to be involved genitally, because then somebody else has a claim on my life."

Effects of Infidelity on a Marriage

In most marriages, when extramarital sexual relationships are known to the other partner, they create jealousy and a great deal of pain. Many deep historical feelings, attitudes and emotional commitments to powerful moral, ethical or religious values are often involved. And most people have a sense of possessiveness toward a marriage partner. Women are conditioned to believe their destiny is to be married and to be financially dependent on their husbands. This dependency plays a large part in fostering a woman's feelings of possessiveness. A man's possessive feelings usually have a different source: historical fears of being cuckolded. The idea that when a man acquires a wife, he acquires possession of her physical body and that her vagina is for him alone, has old and deep cultural roots.

Often, when a surreptitious extramarital affair comes to light, it fractures the marriage. This is most often the case when the injured spouse is an insecure person, or has deep convictions that marriage must be monogamous, and feels badly violated. In this situation, the marriage often ends or becomes an embittered, noncommunicative relationship in which one person is identified as the martyr and the other as the bad person. Whatever affection and sexual pleasure once existed between the two disappears, and the spouse who violated the marriage vows has no place to go for affection or sex except outside the marriage.

Nevertheless, there are a variety of situations in which extramarital sex can have a positive effect on marriage, and there are some marriages in which one spouse's outside sexual activity is not objectionable to the other.

Sometimes a partner who has a relatively low sex drive, or a high level of sexual inhibitions, is relieved to be free of the responsibility for providing something he or she isn't emotionally or physically ready to provide. This partner may subtly acquiesce to the desires of the other for outside affairs with the understanding that these will be discreet and concealed. In other marriages, persons for whom intimacy is uncomfortable may give a partner a degree of sexual freedom because of a desire to maintain some emotional distance. For such persons, infidelity is more likely and the infidelity of a partner is more acceptable.

Sometimes, when a marriage is in a state of deadly doldrums, there is such emotional stagnation that both partners have lost a sense of the values in interpersonal relationships and neither has much intimate interaction with anybody. If one or both become involved in an extramarital affair, the sheer stimulation of again actually sharing something with another person is sometimes brought back and contributes to the marriage.

In circumstances in which a man is acting out early fantasies by having an extramarital affair, he often discovers that long, lithe legs or full breasts or long blonde hair—whatever his particular fantasy involves—do not give him what he has imagined. He finds that sex is only a part, and the smaller part, of a relationship, and that one ends up relating to a *person*. Many men learn in such circumstances that their suppressed, inhibited and rejected postadolescent fantasies and anger at rejection in youth no longer have as important a place in their lives. At this point they reapproach their marriages with a new sense of the possibilities in the truly significant pairings in their lives.

In this kind of situation, when infidelity is basically a matter of one person dealing with personal emotional business, if a partner is able to hang in and gain a sense of what the other person is acting out and experiencing, and has some tolerance for it, the situation will soon pass.

However, when an affair relieves deep feelings of emotional loneliness in the straying partner, it may well lead to a breakup of the marriage. Often a man married for years has been so limited in his ability to tell his wife what he feels and experiences emotionally that he feels very lonely. At a certain stage in life he finds that he is able to feel an affectionate familiarity with women that was not available to him as a young man. With a new woman, he finds himself pouring out inner feelings in a way that he has never done with his wife and cannot conceive of doing with her. The ways in which he and his wife deal with one another have become so habitual that he doesn't know how to start a new kind of communication with her. But with someone new, there is an implied question—"What sort of a person are you?"—that leads to self-disclosure. When he reveals his feelings to a new woman, it relieves his loneliness and he develops an enormous sense of gratefulness to her. If that is accompanied by freer and more open sexual experience, he is likely to break up his marriage for the new woman, even though there may be less genuine compatibility with her than with his wife of many years. After six months to two years in a new marriage, he may discover this. A woman can have quite the same experience, of course.

Renegotiating the Marriage

As painful as the revelation of an extramarital affair is likely to be for the other partner, it can have beneficial effects on the partnership, for it opens communication and forces both persons to confront where they are and what they want with one another. In many marriages in which there are caring feelings between spouses, the revelation stimulates a couple to get in touch with these feelings and revitalize the relationship.

This seemed to be a possibility in the marriage of Terry, twenty-six, who had learned just a week before she called that her husband had been having an affair for a couple of months.

"He said it was because he wasn't being fulfilled," she said. "It was kind of an ego thing for him. I can understand his side of it. But I still have a lot of hostile feelings—revenge, anger, a need to be more independent—lots of different feelings. He would like to just erase it now and he's being very nice to me, but I'm having a hard time accepting it."

Terry had expressed her anger to her husband, and the two had talked about the incident as openly as had seemed possible. But they need more extensive discussion of their relationship. They are at a point where a whole new assessment of their marriage—of what they expected of it and one another, and of where and how they are now in terms of inner life—would be useful. The "State of Your Union" Questionnaire might be helpful in this.

By and large, when either a man or a woman commits adultery, marriage partners are not sharing their inner life. Sometimes a partner who engages in an extramarital affair feels guilty, angry and trapped, and desires to avoid the issue. That apparently is the point Terry's husband has reached. But if, in this situation, partners engage in as personal and detailed and honest an assessment of their marriage as possible—of its joys and rewards, frustrations and pains—the bond between them often becomes deeper and richer than before.

However, if two people renegotiate a relationship and the straying partner ends up by saying, "I really do want a monogamous marriage and I won't get involved outside again," and this partner then does have another affair in violation of the new commitment, the marriage generally becomes badly fractured and goes downhill rapidly.

Pairing and Sexual Relationships in the Future

Concepts of sexual fidelity in marriage have varied through history. For centuries in Europe, a man was not expected to love his wife. Love was for another woman. In eighteenth-century France, a man without at least one mistress was suspect. Romantic love in many countries still exists largely outside the marital bonds. This is particularly true in the societies of South America, Southern Europe, Asia and the Middle East.

Twenty-five years ago in this country, most experts concerned with the structure of family life—psychologists, sociologists, cultural anthropologists—felt that the sanctity of marriage required monogamy, and that extramarital sexual activity was undesirable. Today there is a considerable difference of opinion among them as they watch our changing norms. The trend seems to be toward recognizing that, for a substantial number of people, lifelong sexual exclusivity may not be possible and that attempting to maintain it may undermine the inherent stability of marital partnerships. I find myself agreeing with this.

When statistics show that social institutions are failing, thinking people begin to look for alternatives. With the failure rate of traditional marriage approaching fifty percent and the rate of dissolution of teenage marriage much higher, many professionals in the field of family life are looking for means by which long-term relationships can be strengthened and their numbers increased. Pairing is a natural human phenomenon; almost everyone who studies human behavior recognizes that it is socially desirable for it to occur in relatively stable forms. It is important for child-rearing and for the continuity of social institutions.

Although some people will never be happy in marriage, there is a great deal of evidence that the emotional health and physical well-being of most people is substantially improved by long-term matrimony.

Pairing need not involve the attitudes of ownership and possession that are common in many marriages today, however. It can be a partnership—a sharing of life together that does not exclude other important relationships for each partner individually. It may be that for some people a marriage that allows each of the partners the freedom to evolve socially, sensually and sexually through emotional and sexual involvement with other people has a better chance of surviving for a lifetime than a traditional model.

Today, open marriage is for a small minority of married couples. Victorian conditioning and traditional attitudes toward marriage make such a marital model too difficult for a great many people. It creates too much latent guilt or jealousy in one or both partners. In twenty or thirty years, a variety of lifestyles will probably be more widely accepted. By then a sizable *minority* of the population possibly will find open marriage— open sexually, as well as in other dimensions—a preferred lifestyle.

So far as one can reasonably predict a cultural change in attitudes toward an institution as important as marriage, it seems unlikely that sexually open marriage will soon be the pattern for the majority of the population. For most people, monogamy is the most comfortable model for matrimony, sentimentally and emotionally. It has fewer complications and it doesn't create the guilt and the jealousy that are often powerful by-products of the more complex marriage patterns. However, within monogamy we may see variations from tradition. There may be couples who choose to have sexual monogamy without denying each other important friendships with the opposite sex. Some people may have a flexible monogamy, which at particular periods in the lives of the partners accommodates the desires of one or both for sexual experience outside the marriage. Two people can invent whatever kind of partnership they choose.

Chapter 5

Swinging, Swapping and Sexual Freedom

Historically, for most people sex was a minimal experience in which, once or twice a week, Dad lifted Mom's nightie and in three minutes the sex act was completed. There was some physiological tension release for him; for her it was usually simply a matter of "doing her duty." Only a small percentage of women can become orgasmic under those circumstances, and no respectable nineteenth-century woman was thought to enjoy sex or have any sexual desire. Both partners were conditioned to believe that was the way sex was supposed to be. Any sexual playfulness or inventiveness was considered perversion—a transgression of the will of God. Sex was for procreation.

An about-face from these historical attitudes began some fifty or sixty years ago. But the acceleration in attitudinal change during the sixties and since has been so rapid as to seem a short-term revolution.

Today, as a society, we are viewing sex increasingly not only as a function of procreation and marital contact, but as a whole new dimension that we as human beings can explore and be creative about, according to our individual styles and tastes. Basically, we are giving ourselves the freedom to become unembarrassed about sex. We see it as a way to play and to express affection and tenderness, a way to please ourselves and to pleasure one another.

One of the outcomes of this rapid transition in sexual attitudes has been that significantly greater numbers of young people engage in premarital sex. Another is that experimentation in sexual behavior has greatly increased. For considerable numbers of persons, this has led not only to a greater variety of sexual activity between partners, but to experimentation in the kinds of relationships in which sexual activity takes place.

Among the more extreme deviations from traditional views of appropriate sexual behavior to come out of this has been the phenomenon of swinging and mate-swapping. As recently as the late fifties, it was virtually unthinkable for a man to suggest group sex to his wife. But today, several million couples around the country have participated in it.

For most, it is a short-lived experience. Group sex in any form creates pressures and stresses in a marriage that tend to undermine the relationship. Marriage partners who feel alienated and isolated from each other when they enter into it, as is often the case, frequently find that the experience breaks up the marriage, or at least brings it close to divorce and into marriage counseling. Even loving couples seldom are able to work it out successfully for any extended period of time.

For a person like twenty-nine-year-old Sheryl, who talked about her experience on the radio program, at first it's exciting. It is new and scary, yet a freeing experience, highly stimulating and intense. Both partners use it as a vehicle for talking to one another about their sexual fears and fantasies. As with comrades sharing any other intense experience, like climbing a rock face or going down a white river on a raft, they really communicate with one another.

But after a time the excitement wears off and the communication is finished. Then insecurities set in, feelings of possessiveness and jealousy. Partners begin to ask themselves, "Is this a way we're avoiding each other? Does this mean that our relationship is shallow and uncaring?" And then, "What do we really want now that we've experienced this?" After a period of time, most couples find the basic confidence they've achieved with one another seriously threatened. Sheryl had reached that stage when she called.

"We've been married for five years and I've been a swinger for eight months," she said. "It was my husband's idea. I felt maybe he was getting tired of me. He said he wasn't, but he thought variety would improve our relationship. He hated to think that when he was older, he'd think about having passed up all these opportunities. I was very much against it, but finally he talked me into it.

"The funny thing is, it was easier for me to get into it than for him. People we've talked to say that's usual. The husband suggests it and the wife gets into it more easily. I found I didn't have anything against it and I feel it improved our relationship. We were always close, but we began to feel much closer to each other. I never thought that our sex life would be better, but since we started swinging, it is. We're more attentive to each other and try to please each other more.

"But now I've become very jealous and have insecurities that I've never had before. I'm afraid he'll run across someone who is better than I am as a lover. I've never found anyone who's even as good as he is. I've told him that just because I've consented to swing doesn't mean I'll be more liberal about relationships on the side. I feel that swinging is a sharing thing."

When either partner experiences a loss of confidence and feelings of intimacy, it is time for the couple to move away from swinging. If Sheryl's husband has worked through at least part of those sexual fantasies that he hadn't explored as a single person, he, as well as Sheryl, may be ready to resume an exclusive relationship, at least for lengthy periods of time.

To a substantial degree, it is to act out teenage fantasies that most persons become involved in swinging. From postpuberty onward, both men and women have fantasies of completely casual sexual encounters that are totally uninhibited, wildly spontaneous and enthusiastic. For instance, young men sometimes imagine that they are standing on a streetcorner and an unbelievably beautiful woman drives up in a gorgeous convertible sports car and invites them for a ride that is the beginning of an ecstatic sexual encounter totally devoid of complications, responsibilities, guilt or the risk of rejection.

The research data on intimacy and sexual behavior in most primitive societies suggests that if there were no societal or religious proscriptions, the natural impulse of young persons would be to experiment and explore sexually and attempt to fulfill fantasies during teen and early adult years. After going through this learning experience, they would then pair up with long-term partners in largely monogamous relationships.

However, for a long time our society and families quite effectively told young people that they were to remain inactive sexually and that the only good alternative was to make a premature choice of mate.

Today a lot of persons in their thirties, forties and fifties feel cheated by having missed the sexual freedom that is available to youth today, and are engaging in wide-ranging sexual exploration and experimentation, attempting to fulfill early fantasies.

This was the case with thirty-year-old Diane, who talked about a different kind of experience than Sheryl's.

"On two occasions I found myself involved with two men at the same time having sex. Now I can hardly believe I did those things," she told me. "My husband wasn't involved and he doesn't know about it to this day. It happened after the birth of my first child. My husband and I couldn't seem to get readjusted to sex together. I had never reached orgasm before childbirth, and afterwards I just plain didn't like sex. Naturally, I thought there was something wrong with me. I became attracted to another man and began an affair with him, and then I began to enjoy sex. Two different times he said, 'I'd like you to meet a friend of mine.' I was shocked, but we had done so many things I'd never tried before that this just seemed to be one more thing to try. So I did. It seemed to be one of my fantasies as well. It seems like the whole thing was something I had to get out of my system. Now I feel self-conscious in a bathing suit. Yet at that time I was able to parade around nude and have sex while someone else was watching, and think nothing of it.

"Afterwards, I went into therapy because I was having guilt feelings. After a few sessions I quit the affair completely. My husband and I developed a good sex life because of the new things I had done. I only laid one thing on him at a time. But now I'm getting back to that awful bored state. I don't think I'll try swinging again, though. I think I can handle this boredom in other ways. I hope."

A good deal of group sex is the acting out of personal inhibitions. Many people who are undeveloped socially and sexually use swinging as a speeded-up way of trying to live through the social and sexual experiences they didn't have when they were teenagers or young adults, at least on an unself-conscious and spontaneous basis.

When this is your experience, you can go through the kind of wide fluctuation of behavior Diane talked about. On one hand, you can engage in extreme behavior, yet on the other, in what is called a reaction formation, you can be embarrassed and offended in a more conventional situation—on the beach, say. It's understandable in psychological terms as seesawing from one extreme to another with the hope of settling down somewhere in the middle and being comfortable with yourself and your own body within a framework that's socially, sexually and personally acceptable to you.

The Ménage à Trois

The ménage à trois involving two men and one woman—as in Diane's case—or two women and a man in a sexual situation is one very common fantasy, and today more and more people are acting it out. Many live-in arrangements and communal living situations have this element. Much prostitution involves a man seeking out two women. Many single people who are afraid to face possible rejection by attempting a sexual threesome act it out symbolically by having sex with two successive dates in one night.

The presence of a third person during a sexual encounter seems to add to the intensity of sexual excitement for those persons, partly because it tends to confirm one's sexual uninhibitedness even if the third person is merely an observer, as is often the case. It is as if you're bringing in a little piece of the world to see that you can engage intensely in uninhibited sex.

It also heightens sexual excitement because it relates to early adolescent fantasies—in the case of a woman with two men, to daydreams of having unlimited male admiration and desirability; for a man with two women, fantasies of unlimited access to sexual partners.

For many people, acting out sexual fantasies is facilitated in swinging by a sense of unreality in the situation. Diane's comment, "I can hardly believe it was me," reflects this. There's a feeling that these sexual encounters aren't real. It is as if the sexual partner is a faceless person with whom there is no important emotional contact, hence no fear of rejection. Since the relationship isn't important emotionally, you can do things you wouldn't dare do in your primary relationship, and can ask for things that you wouldn't think of asking for from someone important to you, because if that person refused with implied disapproval, it would be very painful.

There is a parallel here to the "stableboy" syndrome in Eastern girls' schools, where some girls from educated, upper-middle-class families have their first sexual experiences with uneducated stable grooms at the riding academies owned by the colleges and finishing schools. With these boys of a lesser socioeconomic class, they are sexually uninhibited and aggressive. Yet with boys of their own class from the Ivy League colleges, with whom they share "important" relationships, sexual inhibitions repress their spontaneous sexuality and they remain circumspect. In their minds, encounters with boys they see as inferior somehow don't count as actual sexual relationships. It is as if the relationships are but a part of fantasy life.

Some Positive Aspects

For some couples, swinging and swapping has positive value in breaking down sexual inhibitions and the rigid positions of role-playing that men and women often get into. The experience enables women to recognize that they are fully sexual persons, and convinces men of this also. Some persons of limited sex skills literally learn to be better sex partners. For those who can swing on a relatively guilt-free basis in a way that doesn't fracture the loyalties and emotional trust of their marriage, it can be a freeing experience and an effective way of living out fantasy. But we are too close to the puritan ethic for it to be used effectively by more than a relatively few people.

As an antidote for boredom in a marriage, social sex sometimes can be effective. Boredom is usually an indication that there is little or no intimate emotional contact between married people—that they haven't recognized and warmed up to each other's inner person, and that sexuality is no longer substituting for true intimacy. With some couples, most often mature couples, group sex acts as a powerful stimulant to intimate conversation about inner feelings connected with the experience, and tends to break down barriers of awkwardness, fear and early inhibitions. When two people start sharing feelings about primary experiences of life, they become extremely interesting to one another, and deep feelings of friendship are often stimulated.

Group sex cannot provide a number of things frequently sought in it, however. It won't revive a dying marriage. It won't create a feeling of contact and communication where none existed previously. When partners who feel alienated and isolated from one another go into social sex seeking some feeling of emotional connection, the experience tends to trigger powerful fears of rejection, amplifying all the things that make people alienated, fearful and angry at the opposite sex.

Social sex generally fails to cure frigidity or impotence, and usually increases these difficulties. Most of the problems one experiences in one-to-one sexuality are also problems in swinging.

When marriage partners are emotionally intimate and caring, but differ markedly in sexual desire or style, social sex sometimes can be a way of allowing a frustrated partner to openly experience and express his or her sexuality without guilt or fear. In this situation, the sentimental attachment between the two may be reinforced. But the marriage is likely to break up if the relationship isn't stable and the confidence and trust between the two are not sturdy enough to withstand the strain.

The basic difficulty that swinging and swapping creates in most marriages relates to the fact that for most people the psychological content of sex is very important. Most of us experience sex as one of the central affirmations of self, and want it to be symbolic of affection, approval and recognition. We want a feeling of being important to a partner and having a partner significant to ourselves. When partners each go off with someone else, each tends to come back feeling undermined in terms of relating loving to physical sex.

Some people are able to disconnect their feelings about themselves and their desires for love and recognition, and experience sex as simply a reduction of tension or a recreational use of one's body with no implications of caring. But they are a relatively small minority, actually much smaller than most people may believe. Eric, whose conversation follows, apparently is one who is able to switch emotional gears and maintain a primary relationship with affection and communication and warmth, and at the same time enjoy sexual variety and exploration with others.

"My wife and I always have had a good relationship," he told me. "Our swinging was suggested sort of mutually about a year and a half ago. We knew a couple who talked about it. It progressed from swinging with them to swinging with many other couples. When we first started, there was a little jealousy. We sat down and talked that out and we both realized that we had each other and that was what we really wanted for life.

"Swinging may have broadened our sex life a little bit. We know what makes each other happy, but we've also run across a few other things that turn each other on. However, the swinging is just a part of what we enjoy. We also enjoy the friendship of it. Seventy percent of the people we swing with, we go out with socially. Of course there are bummers in swinging circles, just like in any circles. We don't care about large parties, although we have been to a few. We like to swing with people we know. We don't swing the first time we meet a couple. We think you have to like a person before you can swing with them."

Although Eric mentioned knowing a couple that had been swinging for thirteen years, the eighteen months he and his wife had been involved is unusually long. The tone of his conversation gives a sense that there is a great deal of intimate communication between himself and his wife, that they talk about their feelings, fantasies and deep sentimental associations. They clearly trust that they are primary to one another and that their relationship will endure. It takes that kind of powerful friendship and immense confidence and trust for marriage partners to reach an emotional state that permits them to give each other this kind of sexual freedom. Most people simply are not there.

Group Sex is Upsetting to Many

For many people, group sex is very upsetting from the start. Partners who want to explore sexually in this way need to be honest with one another about their feelings of guilt and anxiety, as well as the jealousy that will almost always attend this kind of freedom. If a partner who feels deeply about morals or what marriage should be goes into swapping, perhaps because of guilt about not having been a good sex partner, the experience will be humiliating and hurtful and can cause great trouble. If you ignore your own deepest feelings of right and wrong, of what is ethically and morally acceptable, profound feelings of guilt can cause a powerful backlash of self-punitive behavior. A person may develop some sexual dysfunction or a powerful aversive reaction to sex.

Sometimes the morality issue is a "sleeper." All of us have a sense of moral judgment that society or religious and family training cause us to level on ourselves. Occasionally people get into social sex thinking that they have shed all the principles their parents taught them, but later discover that they have not.

More often than not, the experience with social sex tends to be somewhat like that of Cindy, who found her one experience upsetting.

"We were out with some friends one night and ended up in their apartment," she began. "We were playing tapes and it was boring, so the guys suggested that with each song we remove one item of clothing. When my husband got down to his trousers, I got mad that he was going to go through with it. I didn't know what to do. Then I thought, 'If this is what he wants, I'll follow through.' So everyone sat around with nothing on. I was very embarrassed. We didn't swap, but we had sex with our partners. I didn't care what the other couple was doing. But it did make it more exciting with my husband.

"I really feel bad now about doing it, though, and I don't want to ever do it again. It has made me very emotionally upset. I've lost trust in my husband because he wants to keep pursuing it and now he wants to swap. I've turned against the other couple's friendship."

Cindy has traditional moral conditioning that is quite powerful. Her experience undoubtedly triggered guilt and anxiety about whether she was a good person. I suspect that she also has some sexual inhibitions and perhaps feelings of sexual inferiority that make her fear being compared sexually with another woman. Her husband, on the other hand, very likely has not acted out his teenage fantasies of being sexually adventurous and aggressive. He may have had little or no sexual experience before marriage, and is seeking to fill a gap in his sexual and emotional experience.

Two people in this kind of situation can become terribly embattled. Cindy is likely to feel that he doesn't love her and is rejecting her by pressing this painful and unacceptable activity on her. And he, unable to articulate in any clear and comfortable way what he wants and feels, will be baffled by her responses and feel guilty and somewhat angry, but still he will feel what he feels.

A large part of his basic message may well be, "I would like sex to be more exciting." Although Cindy said they get along well in their sex life, that may mean merely that she enjoys being cuddled, and sexual intercourse is acceptable to her. Sex between them may be very limited. Or it may be ritualized and routine. There are millions of American women who think their sexual life is fine as long as it isn't terrifying, painful or upsetting.

These two need to get in touch with their own and each other's feelings and fantasies—the yearnings and desires, as well as the angers. They need to feel, share and respond to them. If Cindy begins to get inside her own feelings and to understand and respond to her husband's, she could learn to become more sexually outgoing, imaginative, experimental and playful.

Very likely, she and her husband will require a therapy

experience to clarify these feelings. And Cindy will probably need the encouragement and support of therapy to overthrow historical fears and inhibitions and begin to feel that it is all right to be playful and inventive in sex.

If she becomes more sexually exciting, her husband is likely to have with her most of what he wants. A good deal of his desire for swapping will disappear because he will be drawn in by the possibilities between the two of them. Studies show that the majority of men prefer a monogamous relationship, because monogamy reduces emotional conflict and diminishes upsetting complications.

A satisfactory monogamous relationship, however, may require a husband seeing his wife (and a wife seeing her husband) as capable of playing out a variety of sexual roles.

Cindy's husband may want to act out his fantasies. He may want to try five or six different positions, or make love in the swimming pool or the bathtub. He may want her to be the aggressor, or to tease him and be titillating in the framework of some of his fantasies.

If she gets in touch with the possibility and excitement of playing out different roles in sexual encounters, they can be playful with one another in any number of different sexual scenarios. One can be passive, the other aggressive. Then the roles can be switched. Or both can be very aggressive. And so on. If he's a man who had the teenage fantasy of being picked up on a corner by a gorgeous woman, she can play out the scene with him. She can make a date to pick him up on a streetcorner after work, wearing a filmy dress with nothing under it and then—as he has fantasized perhaps a hundred times—drive to some secluded spot to spread a blanket and make love.

Conversely, she has fantasies of being swept up and made love to that he can act out.

There is No One Way to be Sexually Free

Many persons feel a kind of peer-group pressure to engage in swapping and other kinds of swinging as a way of expressing uninhibited sexuality and ending forever their sexual hangups. But uninhibited sexuality is not the same for all of us, and for many, many persons, swinging and swapping are not appropriate for their normal styles. They aren't a natural outcome of their attitudes and feelings and experience of life, and offend their sensitivities.

There is no one way to be sexually free, because the variety of natural tendencies is very broad. We vary in our sexual urges and desires, our fantasies and sexual images. We vary in terms of what excites and pleasures us. And we vary in our sentimentality. In some ways, the differences among us are far greater than the similarities.

A New Set of Sexual Problems for This Generation

It was a common belief in the younger generation, which largely led the way in the sexual revolution of the last two decades, that sexual freedom and joy were a matter of relating to many different people and being able to have sex with whomever one wanted, whenever one wanted. But that has turned out not to be true. Many who have successfully shed the influence of our Victorian heritage and been among the more daring in sexual experimentation have not found sex the joyful and rewarding experience they expected. They have found that a new set of fears and problems has been substituted for the old set. This has happened because human sexuality is not a one-dimensional aspect of human feeling, but a very complicated one.

Most of the sexual research over the past forty-five years tells us that at least four elements are involved. The first is the biological impulse that comes out of our genetic heritage. It arises strongly in males right after puberty and has a powerful influence on male adolescent attitudes, behavior and feelings. It occurs in females at a much lower level after puberty, then builds up to peak around the age of thirty.

A second important element, critical to adults being free and loving with one another, has to do with infantile sensuality. As infants, it is tremendously important to us to be held, hugged, snuggled and loved. Out of our early experience of this evolves a desire as adults to feel the warmth of someone's arms around us, to hold and be held, to fondle and touch and feel this kind of expression of tenderness.

The third element in truly spontaneous loving is play. Adults play in sexual and sensual ways. Adolescent and postadolescent horseplay—wrestling and chasing one another—is an example. If human physical love is to be truly free and rewarding, playfulness in the full range of adult imagination has to be a major part of it.

The final factor is emotional recognition—when each partner recognizes the other as being very special, as beloved. Curiously enough, this rarely occurs in most societies.

Sex that lacks one of these elements is limited in nature. Within the emotional framework of the very young, and particularly the young male who has fantasies of having sex with every physically attractive woman in sight, sheer variety in sexual experience without emotional recognition tends to be satisfying. But over a period of time this is not the case. When you have sexually explored and experimented widely, you become more and more aware of the shallow nature of superficial sexual relationships, and they begin to be boring. You are then confronted with the problem of emotional contact, with the reality and meaning of affection and the problem of gaining the experience of being loved. A loving relationship in which there is genuine recognition becomes the more exciting arena. This is a wholly different emotional and sexual experience.

So the new difficulties relating to sex are problems in loving. The problem becomes one of gaining the kind of warmly affectionate, deeply caring partnership in which, unless two persons have some painful negative conditioning concerning sex, feelings of loving and being loved generally carry over into physical affection.

Young people who, on the whole, are much freer and more exploratory about sex and their own sexual responses and feelings than their parents or grandparents, have found that their greater sexual freedom has given them but one dimension of the possibilities. They now have to develop ways of communicating, of being honest and of sharing growth experiences with one another.

It is true that a great many people of older generations have gone through their whole lives without ever creating this kind of deeply caring, affectionate communication and emotional closeness. Marital expectations of the twenties, thirties and forties did not include a great deal of communication between husband and wife. Revealing inner feelings to one another on a subject of such mutual concern as pregnancy, for example, was not considered appropriate. But the new sexual freedom has brought with it a revolution of expectations in the whole interpersonal sphere. Sexual freedom has loosed upon this younger generation the expectation of being genuinely happy in a genuinely loving sexual partnership. This can be very difficult to achieve.

Chapter 6

Great Expectations and Other Problems

We expect a great deal of marriage today. We expect love and personal security and pleasurable sex. We expect close emotional contact, involvement and communication to a degree simply not sought in marriage in the past, when communities were more stable, and extended families, old friends and acquaintances filled more of our emotional needs. At the same time that we seek greater emotional closeness, many of us also seek to go separate ways to some degree. Not wanting to be locked into the limited routine of our parents' lives, we expect to have separate interests and friends who share those interests, including friends of the opposite sex.

Some of us have expectations of marriage that come out of a misunderstanding of the nature of the relationship and its possibilities. Often marriage is seen as a cure for loneliness, although it cannot resolve the problems of the chronically lonely. Sometimes one feels that in marriage one can acquire the qualities of one's mate. A shy person marrying a gregarious one, for instance, may expect to gain somehow the social abilities of the mate.

Frequently we have the notion that a spouse will assuage all of our painful feelings from an unhappy childhood, providing the affection, emotional support, encouragement and other indications of our personal value that we wanted and were never able to get from our parents. Often we futilely try to obtain these from a partner in the same way that we tried to get them from parents—by being angry or hurt, rather than by making clear what is wanted.

The Confusion About Love

Disappointment in marriage may be related to a misunderstanding about the nature of love, on which we rest so many hopes. Above all, we expect love in marriage. However, our images of love are confused. The words "I love you" do not always convey warm, tender feelings. They may be used as a cover-up for almost anything: for domination and control of another; for neurotic confusion; for destructive behavior to oneself or to a partner. Nevertheless, according to a popular concept of romantic love, those magic words take precedence over the capacity for judgment of any practical considerations about an individual's intelligence, social and personal capacities or economic potential. A young couple often plans marriage when it seems apparent that the relationship will be painfully unrewarding or one or both are deeply in doubt.

I think that love, in ideal form, was best defined by a great psychologist, Harry Stack Sullivan, who said that when the satisfaction or security of another person becomes as significant to you as your own satisfaction and security, a state of love exists. It is fairly rare that one fully gets to this state of feeling, but solidly based adult-to-adult love represents some approximation of this.

What we usually describe as love is really romantic fantasy—the romantic idealization of another person whom you perceive as having qualities that are a projection of what you want to see, a kind of marvelous extension of yourself. It is being in love with love and endowing the other with all of your longings to love and be loved and to be recognized as superspecial. It's overwhelming sexual attraction stoked by Cinderella, love songs and soap commercials, with their common theme that someday your own true love will appear and sweep you off your feet.

Romantic fantasy is useful and important in triggering relationships. It's the rocket that propels them into orbit. But it inevitably fades. After marriage you learn the real nature and quality of what you have with another person. It may be very different from what your fantasy projected. We all tend to con one another somewhat in courtship, making a presentation of ourselves that we hope will fulfill the expectations of the other.

There may be things about your partner and yourself that you couldn't possibly have known because in many ways most of us don't know ourselves well enough to articulate who we are.

Often, two people go into marriage with vast differences in early training and expectations. As individual preferences, predilections and avoidances become a part of their everyday life, each begins to see the other as having behaviors, attitudes and feelings not perceived earlier. Disillusionment, or at least some feeling of letdown, sets in. This sometimes happens, painfully, on the honeymoon. But usually it reaches a peak sometime within the first three years. When this occurs, partners need to accelerate communication about their differences, as was discussed in the chapter "Recipe for a Loving Relationship," in order to translate their romance into a genuine loving partnership—a caring friendship containing affection, respect and mutual valuation. Otherwise there will be anger and a feeling of being cheated. The marriage will begin cycling in a negative way with each partner punishing the other for not being what each had idealized.

This was happening in the marriage of Barbara. Her conversation gives a sense of how troubling the fading of romantic fantasy, of being in love with love, sometimes can be.

"When I first met Burt, I was so impressed with his thoughtfulness," she said. "He was always doing little things for me. He doesn't do things from the heart anymore. I don't expect flowers like I got every Friday before we were married, but it would be nice if he called me once in a while and said he loved me. I'm basically an insecure person and I need reassurance.

"I didn't go into this marriage with the idea that everything would be roses, but he did. He says he loves me but he feels marriage is a disappointment. Now I am forced to play the masculine role. Sexually, I am forced to be the aggressor. I feel as if I've lost all my femininity, and he has told me I'm not feminine at all. If it weren't for me, we wouldn't be together. We separated once. He won't give me an explanation. Right now we're in marriage counseling and it's helping me learn how to argue properly. I'm very emotional. I get angry fast and get over it fast. My husband can't do that. He pouts for days and it drives me up the walls."

I suspect that Burt comes from an emotionally cold family in which there was little open demonstration of affection and physical contact. He may have been demonstrative in the process of wooing, but with the fading of romantic fantasy, the affectionate warmth that was translated into physical contact and sexual desire in that period has diminished. Now he probably wants and expects the kind of low-key relationship with which he is familiar and comfortable. If that is the case, a wife accustomed to more openly expressed affection who makes demands for more physical contact and continuing reassurance will make him feel inadequate or as though he doesn't satisfy her. By being aggressive, Barbara may be amplifying feelings of dependency and fears of being aggressive that he may have. And if, from childhood, he has some sense of not being loved and perhaps of not being lovable, these feelings are triggered by the feeling that his wife is not happy with him.

Generally speaking, this kind of relationship will end in divorce, or result in the more warmly responsive person, in this case the wife, becoming so bitter that life becomes very grim for both. Since they are in marriage counseling, there is hope they may have a better future together, but they should have a marriage counselor who is also a trained sex therapist. They need to be led through the early stages of sexual reawakening so that Burt can become more familiar with his own sensuality and sexuality and more comfortable with his physical capacity for touching. Then he is likely to begin to enjoy and get excited about it, and will substantially expand his repertoire of affectionate sensual and sexual behaviors. Most people not accustomed to associating loving with being physically demonstrative are quite capable of learning to do so, for it is a natural impulse. But many of us unlearn it in early to middle childhood because of family style or circumstances.

How Your Experience With Parents Shapes Your Marriage

Frequently, problems in marriage are related to the kind of roles played by the parents of the two partners. A child's association with parents is an early-life primary relationship in an emotional sense, much as marriage is in adult life. What we learn about important relationships in this early experience shapes our expectations in marriage.

When the basic message we get from our parents in childhood is that loving and sharing feelings and closeness are the central elements in an important relationship, when communication is open and mutually respectful and parents understand and tolerate our testing our power as growing children, we go into marriage with an expectation of an equalitarian adult-to-adult partnership. We expect to share inner life feelings, to actively listen to a partner and be listened to. We expect to treat the other person in a respectful manner, to clarify and negotiate differences. And we expect a partner to so respond to us.

But when parents are authoritarian and our basic message from them is that what they want most is to control and direct us, we learn to expect control and domination as central elements in any important relationship. This expectation may be modified by important friendships in the teenage years and early adult life, especially through important friendships with older people (teachers or employers, for instance) with whom we have a quasi-parental relationship which may be transformed into a mutually respectful equalitarian one. Participation in sports and social groups in high school or college also may provide opportunities for relearning. But this learning often does not penetrate the deeper levels of feeling. The expectation of control and dominance in a primary relationship remains.

When two people marry who have very different kinds of experiences with parents, and consequently different expectations of a marital relationship, the two have a difficult time. They carry such dissimilar emotional expectations into the marriage that each is painfully confused by the attitudes and behaviors of the other. It is as if one spoke Greek and one Russian, with no translator around.

However, mutual expectations of a dominant-dependent framework in marriage also are often a basis for problems.

If your relationship with your parents was painful and your struggle to free yourself from their domination involved a great deal of anger and guilt on your part, unless you have identified your feelings and renegotiated the relationship so that you can forgive your parents for their shortcomings and share an adult-to-adult friendship, you carry into marriage or other pairings an expectation of being controlled and devalued, of having anger, guilt and humiliation. In the period of intense romantic idealization this expectation tends to be obscured, but as romantic love declines and differences begin to offend one person or the other, your old anger and guilt, your sense of embattlement, reassert themselves. Then you tend to act out with your marriage partner your struggle against your parents.

Angry Emotional Dependency

Another extremely common problem in dominant-dependent relationships, one in which one partner usually needs considerable individual counseling, is angry emotional dependency. A high percentage of young women (and some men) who have not become independent adult persons before marriage, go into the relationship wanting from a spouse the feeling of being taken care of, and the approval, direction and control that their parents provided. We all seek from a spouse some degree of this feeling of being taken care of and the validation of our worthiness and attractiveness that we had from our parents. But when you have fought through teenage rebellion, redefined your relationship with your parents and become an independent, competent adult before marriage, your major role in marriage tends to be that of one adult person seeking a loving relationship with another. When a still needful, dependent person locks into marriage, the message given to a partner is, "Make me happy, make me feel comfortable. I need this. I need that." Eventually, an angry, dependent person says essentially, "I'm not happy and it's your fault." This was the position of thirty-four-year-old Janis, mother of four, who was married when she was very young.

"I like being a mother and a housewife, but my husband makes me unhappy," she told me. "He doesn't mean to. I think he's depressed, too. We have four kids, a house, no money, and one car that somebody ran into the other day. It's just one thing after another, but he is so opposite from me. I open up everything. He gets depressed and goes for days without talking to me and I can't stand that. It drives me up a wall, because I have nobody.

"When you get married, don't you expect a partner to be your companion? Someone to talk to and be with? I was raised by my grandmother, who is now eighty-four, so when I was growing up I had no one to talk to, and I still don't. When I talk to my husband, most of the time he tells me to stick it in my ear. He doesn't want to talk to me or look at me or touch me. I just sit in the corner and feel like a little puppy who's going to be thrown a bone any minute."

Janis is a classic instance of a young woman who married very young and has never developed a sense of herself as a separate, independent individual, not just a mother, wife and needful person. Even at thirty-four, after fifteen years of marriage, she is still underdeveloped, lacking the basic confidence necessary for her to get what she wants out of life.

Raised by her grandmother, she had nobody to talk to in her childhood, and is accustomed to feeling that she is not important or is a nuisance. She keeps acting out this script with her husband, seeking from him, needing from him, but feeling helpless and unloved.

Her husband is a person who withdraws inside himself when under stress. That kind of personality has to try to cope alone. When I explained this to Janis, pointing out that her demands exaggerate his withdrawal, she didn't really hear me. She didn't want to tune in on his problem or to see him as a man lacking in emotional development. She has a self-fulfilling prophecy that she is unimportant and unloved. She expects rejection and that is what she gets.

In all likelihood, her husband will become interested in her only if she becomes an interesting person. She would shake him up if she greeted him one night with, "Hey, Rudy, Thursday night you and the kids have to fend for yourselves because I've joined an amateur theatrical group." Or, "Rudy, I've met some exciting new people where I'm doing volunteer work, and I've invited them over for dinner Saturday night." But instead of going out and creating excitement and vitality in their lives, she acts out hopelessness and helplessness. Tragically, at thirty-four she has largely given up on herself.

I recommended to Janis that she become involved in community activities or part-time work, and that she set as her number-one priority the development of a number of important friendships with both men and women. I wasn't suggesting romantic relationships with men, but friendships. I also recommended marriage counseling with a clinical psychologist who, in individual counseling, would take steps to diminish her sense of powerlessness and fear of life and try to give her a sense of its possibilities and fun. She might be given vocational-guidance tests to help her find personal vocational direction, and she might be advised to take part in a women's consciousness-raising group to gain some sense of her own personhood. An effort might be made to focus on avocational pursuits that she has played with but never really used. She would also be encouraged to expand some area of her social life outside the home.

Basically, she needs to develop her own adult person, to identify her own unique way of viewing the world, her feelings and desires, and gain a sense of her inherent human dignity, pride and power. Then she will be able to free herself from a dependent role in which she seeks a parent in her husband.

Changing the Dominant-Dependent Relationship

Sometimes a young, dependent marriage partner develops into a more independent person during the early years of the marriage and a more satisfactory relationship evolves, with redistribution or reshuffling of responsibilities toward an optimum of equal responsibility and load-sharing. But partners often become stuck in the forms of relating with which they began the marriage, and in fixed allocation of tasks even though these no longer fit the changing personality or changing self-regard of one or the other partner. An implicit emotional contract that may have been satisfactory early in a marriage may later cause ferocious strains because it no longer meets the emotional needs of the two people.

If this is your experience, you can negotiate with each other to share authority in areas that have been monopolized by one partner or the other. Then, when you have negotiated for a modified role in one area and accepted a modified role in another, you may take responsibility for doing what you said you would do. It is important that anyone attempting to acquire a greater share of authority be willing to see responsibility not as something to be avoided, but as something that adults accept as a part of adult life.

Without communication and this kind of negotiation, a marriage can become badly fractured as a dominant partner, finding responsibility for the other person a burden, or a dependent partner, feeling limited and demeaned, rebels against the constraints of the habitual role. This had happened in the twenty-three-year marriage of Virginia, 45, as she and her husband went about painfully breaking out of dominant and dependent positions in which they had been stuck unhappily for most of their marriage.

"Things were fine until about three years ago, but now I'm married to a man who doesn't want any part of the responsibility for the home," she began. "I do everything: paint the living room, pay all the bills. I don't know whether it's because of his work or something happened. He's just lost interest in doing anything or even going anywhere. We moved to California ten years ago, not knowing a soul, and we haven't done anything to get acquainted with people. We don't have any friends at all.

"I've had terrible fights with him about taking over some of the responsibilities. I finally thought, 'What's the use?' I can't get through to him. I've tried and tried. He won't talk much and he won't admit anything is wrong.

"Recently I went back to school and I'm looking for a job. I'm also seeing another man. I don't think it will solve my problem. But I feel like I'm getting a taste of freedom."

Twelve years before Virginia called, she had had a breakdown, which she described as "an anxiety phase when for eight months I wouldn't go out of the house." That can be seen as a kind of temper tantrum, an expression of: "I'm just going to sit here and let the world go by and I won't do anything for anybody." At that point her husband probably became angry at her for letting down. There are sometimes seemingly incredible time delays before these kinds of things are dealt with in a relationship. Now he is having his temper tantrum. For a good many years, he was the responsible one in the family while Virginia was a very dependent person, I gathered. Now he is saying, "To hell with responsibility. I've had all the responsibility and obligation and pressure I want."

At the same time, Virginia is now becoming more independent.

My guess is that these two people are so out of touch with one another that they hardly have any idea of the feelings of the other person. They have a chance to renew this marriage, but they probably need a professional third person to draw out each of them in the presence of the other so that they develop an empathetic understanding of each other. Then they can begin to communicate.

Chapter 7

Dealing With Anger

Often, couples believe that expressing anger is bad for marriage. Many try to avoid confrontation and make a relationship seem pleasant even when there is an unspoken agenda of mixed feelings between partners. This suppression of anger diminishes the capacity of partners for open, honest communication. When you avoid disclosing your feelings about differences, you avoid the intense, intimate dialogue that can cause people to feel close to one another. A person who is angry needs to be able to express the anger with some intensity and focus, to ventilate it and let it go, in order to become willing to negotiate a common position that both people can feel good about. When anger is not openly expressed, communication typically gives way to sullenness and distance.

How costly avoiding confrontation can be in a partnership can be seen in the seven-year marriage of Linda, twenty-six. She had not allowed herself to express the anger she felt when her husband had an affair, for fear he would leave her. Her marriage at that time had been "too shaky to rock any boats," she said. So the angry feelings, which had had no outlet, were still gnawing away at her several years later, making a close, warm, supportive relationship with her husband impossible. Here she describes her experience.

"I can't seem to forget the affair my husband had a few years ago. I smell for perfume or look for scratches and inspect his clothes for hair. It makes him mad and keeps us apart. At the time, he was upset with me. He said I was ten pounds overweight and wasn't keeping the house, that I was a crybaby and too dependent. He said I had been this way ever since we got married, but it had built up to where he didn't think he loved me anymore. It really panicked me and I started trying hard. I didn't cry anymore and I acted cheerful.

"Around that time he was gone a lot at night. Sometimes he would come home at three or four in the morning. I was so stupid it never dawned on me that he had another girl. Finally my parents figured it out and he admitted it. I was crushed and was going to leave him, but then I thought, 'That's stupid. The only reason I'm going to leave is because I want him to come running after me. If I jump out of the scene, that will give her a clear field.' So I decided to stay and try to win him back. Two months later he said he thought he was in love with me again and he wasn't going to see her anymore.

"But at the present time I'm driving him crazy with this inspection every time he comes home. I don't know how to stop it. He has smelled like perfume a few times. I find long blonde hairs on him. He says I'm crazy; he's not seeing anyone else, and my acting this way makes it hard for him to feel close to me. I hate to be so suspicious, but on the other hand I don't want to be stupid like I was before."

The fact that Linda cannot forget her husband's affair is a product of her anger. It's her way of reminding him that he was the disloyal, miserable blankety-blank that deep inside she feels him to be.

If her husband had encouraged her to fight through the issue at the time, and had participated so that she had vented her anger, the distress his infidelity caused in the marriage might have been finished then. But having no proper outlet, the anger is still very much a part of her emotional life, driving her to keep on acting out her suspicions, even though she recognizes this to be hurtful to their relationship.

The Confusing Ways of Suppressed Anger

There are many other kinds of circumstances in which the suppressing of anger has negative effects on a marriage.

Parental disapproval of a child's expression of anger was formerly considered desirable in socializing children, so that in childhood most of us were not permitted to express it beyond a certain point. A great many adults, who learned when young to associate anger with being bad or with deep feelings of guilt, are unable to experience it freely. Yet anger is an important human emotion, a natural product of the stresses, malcommunications and frustrations of life. When you are afraid to let angry feelings come up, the entire spectrum of your capacity for feeling is reduced to some degree, because all of our emotions are interrelated. Your capacity for joy and optimism, your capacity to be emotionally responsive to a partner, your capacity to respond to other challenges and opportunities are all diminished.

Often, anger that isn't expressed openly emerges in other ways that distort and confuse a relationship. Many of us direct suppressed anger inward. This is a habit learned in childhood, which causes a great many physical as well as psychological illnesses. It is a root cause of depression and much compulsive behavior—overeating, overdrinking, and so on. Some people act out internalization of anger by injuring or demeaning themselves.

Many other individuals turn much of their anger, whatever its cause, on their love partner. This happens when a child who has been taught that it is naughty to be angry views the parent of the opposite sex as unloving, controlling and disapproving. The child expresses anger at this parent while suppressing anger otherwise, and uses this one outlet for all anger. Any important person of the opposite sex is cast in the parent role in later life.

If you're a person with this history, when you are angry for any of the reasons that people get angry—because of a bout of bad health, because the economy has slowed down and plans you had for economic advancement have been halted, or because you can't work out a good relationship with your children—you will tend to direct this anger toward the person of the opposite sex who is most important to you.

This may well be the experience of eighteen-year-old Jennifer, who avoids openly expressing her anger and lets it out in ways designed to irritate her husband. Generally speaking, what she describes here is a way of gaining attention and creating low-level irritation, that permits one to focus anger at a partner without having to admit it and deal with it. Many persons similarly irritate a spouse rather than express their anger openly. The kinds of behavior that people use to do this are as various as human inventiveness can devise. Moving the furniture around constantly ("three times a week, the whole house") was Jennifer's way.

"My mother changed the furniture for years, too, and I did

it when I was living at home," she said. "My father would come home from work and trip over the furniture. He wouldn't know where to step. My husband is getting really upset. I move the TV and he has to hook it up again.

"I look at it like I need a change. I get extremely tired of looking at the same thing. I come into the house, and if it's been like that for a week or so, I want to change it around and brighten it up. I move from room to room.

"I also have a compulsion not to be on time for anything," she added. "My mother was that way, too."

In moving the furniture around, Jennifer acts out anger without having to take responsibility for it. She also does this in being habitually late, a habit that frequently conceals angry feelings. It's a way of saying to the world, "I've been controlled and dominated in my childhood and I don't want to be bugged anymore." By telling the world to wait for me, I exercise a form of angry counter-control. It also may be an attention-getting device, a way of creating negative emotional response in other people when you don't think that they are responding to you in a positive way. Some response may seem better than no response. Probe down through two layers of feelings and again you find anger, the most inhibited and denied of the primary human emotions.

Part of what I heard from Jennifer was that she is bored. She doesn't feel that life is an exciting, rewarding event for her. She feels weak and inconsequential, and she's angry about it. But instead of attacking the problem directly and taking action to find challenging involvements in her life, she's caught up in moving the sofa around.

I also sensed that an important factor in her anger is that she is very angry with her father. Although she told me that her parents were very close, I suspect that her mother also was very angry at Jennifer's father. He is dead now, and Jennifer probably feels guilty enough about her anger that she can't confront it. Instead, she puts her husband in the role of a father against whom she can act feelings out indirectly.

Situational Anger is Limited

People act out anger indirectly, or suppress it, because they have been taught to fear the consequences of expressing it. But bringing anger openly into an important relationship doesn't mean that you destroy the partnership or that the other person is torn apart by it. Anger experienced by people who allow themselves to be angry and so have not built up a backlog of unexpressed rage is situational and lasts only a few minutes. It is limited by the context of the anger-producing situation. It is also limited by the hypothalamus, the part of the brain that acts as a control mechanism to keep our actions within the constraints of appropriate social behavior. For some people, appropriate behavior is shouting and yelling. For others, caustic remarks. One's perception of what is suitable varies with cultural background.

If a person experiences anger freely—as simple, raw emotion such as a child who is disappointed might feel—the emotion takes a wave form, rising, peaking and coming down rather quickly. People differ in the duration and intensity of this wave, just as people differ in metabolic rates and other qualities, but most anger is experienced and expressed in from one to five minutes, with the typical wave period being about three minutes. Angry episodes between partners often last much longer, however, because the two do not know how to handle anger.

Dealing With Anger

When one partner is angry, the best response the other can make is to acknowledge the anger ("I see that you're angry. I'm listening. I'm concerned.") and hear it out without counterattacking. Being able to express negative emotions—to get mad when you're mad—is an enormous relief to a person. If you listen all the way through to a partner's feelings, the anger will be followed by a second and different wave of feeling in which he or she often will be willing to explore the feelings, desires and issues behind the anger. After the anger has subsided, if you say, "I see this is troubling you. Can you help me understand it a little more?" the message comes through as, "I care about you. I want you to be as happy and comfortable with life as you can be." This kind of good feeling and giving response begets good feeling and giving response. The second wave of feelings of the angry person who has been listened to in this way will include some new degree of willingness to compromise or cooperate in negotiating a resolution of differences. Two people who are important to each other have a powerful impulse to give what the other wants—or at least as much as can be given without shortchanging or demeaning themselves.

However, there is a natural timing to this process. If you press a person to explore the basis for the anger before the full wave of anger has been experienced, the anger will go into a self-justifying cycle that can go on and on with self-pity and indictment of a partner and of a cruel world that feeds the anger again and again.

This is a very common experience in married life, for, typically, when one partner becomes angry, the other either dissolves in tears, devastated by feelings of being at fault, or aggressively fights back.

The art of listening to anger without either of these reactions is to recognize the anger as an experience someone else is having without putting yourself in the role of victim—of being responsible for the other's feelings, disappointments and other emotional business. My anger is a representation of me, of my disappointments or frustrations. Even if your behavior has provoked my anger, my anger is simply my experience of frustration—my way of responding to the fact that this human being's perception of the world, purposes, desires or timing are not the same as another's. However, much of my anger may not have to do with you at all, but may be a consequence of my own personality issues and personal history. In expressing anger I may be acting out emotional business with my father, mother, or siblings, or acting out issues that have to do mostly with my view of the world or some particular construction of reality.

The art of expressing and experiencing anger without cutting off the possibility of a good outcome in a relationship is to stick with the experience of anger ("I'm furious! I'd like to kick the walls in.") without translating it into indictment of the other person.

After your anger is expended, you can ask the other person, "What are you feeling?" The answer may well be, "I'm angry at your anger." But if it is also, "But I'm hearing it and I'm willing to listen," then after a couple of minutes you can say, "What just happened between us? What went on?" You can then share the experience in another dimension—in terms of how each of you was offended and affected. In a partnership this inevitably leads to, "What can we do that will diminish the likelihood of another such angry encounter?"

If two people move only one percent closer on an issue in an encounter in which both feel they have been really listened to and responded to without being indicted as bad people, the outcome will be good. Both will feel relieved and pleased;

each will have gained new perceptions of what the other is experiencing. The next time around, with good will and a desire to reinforce a loving relationship, they will get another two or three percent closer on their differences. In this way they learn to react to one another in a positive way, with trust and confidence.

When two people become somewhat experienced in having positive outcomes from experiencing and expressing their anger, they can risk expanding the process so that each person takes a turn in the role of angry partner, while the other listens before negotiating issues.

If partners deal with one another with honest emotions in here-and-now situations and really listen to one another, they begin to have some idea of the frustrations that may have been building up in each other over a long period of time. Each gets a sense of the cumulative experiences of life, the combinations of feelings and historical reactions that have put the other person in a particular emotional state. The process can be a major tool in reinventing a relationship.

Historical Anger

Anger that comes out of a partner's personal history is frequently an important and disturbing factor in a marriage. A great many persons have locked inside them intense anger caused by parental disapproval or by a lack of the love, security and encouragement they wanted from parents in childhood. A part of it is internalized as a feeling of undesirability, unlovability, unworthiness, etc. Often it is a passive, self-destructive anger that leads to drug addiction, alcoholism, "workaholism" or suboptimal academic achievement. Or it is expressed in coldness and aloofness, an unwillingness to engage in an affectionate and caring manner with any other person.

To a degree, most of us have stored up some internalized hostility. This happens not only because of our personal histories, but because of conditions in society with which we have to cope. In the present era, a major contributing factor is rapid social cultural change, which causes people to feel insecure and to have feelings of self-doubt that get translated into anger, either passive or overt.

For the twenty million people who move out of their neighborhoods each year, the moving itself is highly stressful and anger-producing. The loss of what has been known and comfortable and the need to develop a new set of acceptable circumstances make people very angry.

Internalized anger that is carried into marriage and work situations and into relationships with children can increase considerably the anger felt in frustrating situations that develop in the here-and-now.

Locked-in anger may be so intense as to be actual rage. If you have built up a huge backlog of historical anger, the most valuable thing you can do for yourself and your relationships is to reduce your anger level by ventilating, identifying and clarifying the anger so that you can forgive your parents for what you didn't get from them and allow yourself to forget. This may require therapy, for it cannot be done intellectually. The best studies of human emotions tell us that only fifteen to twenty percent of latent historical anger can be dissipated by recognizing rationally that your parents turned their own anger into spousal and parental behavior and by understanding how this affected you.

Over a period of time, this anger may diminish somewhat with positive life experiences, but intense historical anger often leads to choices that deny positive experiences.

With noncognitive, nonintellectual techniques of therapy, which may involve intense psychological role-playing, you are often able to act out with another person the historical rage, frustration, fear and guilt. You can break through this pocket of historical emotions toward your parents, vent the anger and let it go. You may then move on to create new affirmative experiences that give you a new way of seeing yourself.

If You Are Unable to Express Anger

If, as a child, you were denied the ability to feel what you felt, you may not only be unable to express anger openly, but even to identify angry feelings as anger. Many people have denied their anger for so long that they experience it as something else, such as sadness or fear. If this is your situation, you owe it to yourself to break through the inhibitions and repressions and learn to identify and express angry feelings. You can help yourself to do this by seeking opportunities to play-act anger, and so gain some experience with it without having to take responsibility for it. Join a play-reading or amateur theater group. Find a character whose feelings you can identify with and throw yourself into the role. Or take a course in assertiveness training, which often involves a good deal of role-playing. Take the role of the angry, overbearing or aggressive person, not the shy one. Or buy an inexpensive tape recorder and after reading your daily paper, tell it how mad you are about what is going on in the world.

In ventilating your anger in these ways, you discover that anger is not as frightening as you had thought. It seems less wicked and guilt-causing and is something you now have some familiarity with. With this kind of experience, you can learn to identify your own anger and become able to say, "Hey, I'm really angry," when you feel that way. When you can shout that in a loud voice, you will have given yourself a great amount of emotional freedom, a great reduction of stress and tension, and new possibilities of dealing with a partner openly and honestly.

Getting Angry for the Wrong Reasons

If you become angry inappropriately at your partner because a person of the opposite sex is your habitual outlet for anger, you will probably need some feedback from a third party to get a clear understanding of what you are doing so that you can learn to redirect your anger. Partners so often respond to attack with counterattack that it is not likely that a couple will be able to examine what is happening in periods of anger without this outside aid. A friend whom both you and your partner value and respect might be able to provide the necessary feedback if you suspect you have this problem. You might make a practice of turning on a tape recorder whenever an angry exchange begins with your partner. Such a tape could be submitted to a respected friend for a written critique of the dialogue. This is a tool frequently used by marriage counselors.

If You Are Chronically Angry

If you are chronically angry because of intense dissatisfaction with an unrewarding life situation that can't be expressed, self-help efforts are not likely to work well. You may be a parent with a low nurturance capacity, for example, and find parenthood an unrewarding, frustrating experience, but feel guilty about confronting and expressing your angry feelings. In this situation you are likely to be engaged in considerable self-beratement, as well as anger at the world, and need professional counseling or psychotherapy.

However, if you have some understanding of what is causing your anger, you can begin to deal with it yourself. To begin, you need to identify where you are and what you want out of living. In doing this, the writing techniques of keeping an "intensive journal" or creating an autobiographical "life script" (both self-exploratory systems taught in adult education courses in high schools and colleges) can be useful. Psychodrama also would be helpful.

Group Psychotherapy

Both individual and group therapy can be valuable in dealing with suppressed anger. However, group experience should be begun with some caution. It is always desirable to have a few individual sessions with the therapist who is leading the group so that he or she knows you well enough to assure that you will have a positive learning experience in group. This is especially true with suppressed anger. Certain kinds of pent-up historical rage can be upsetting or even dangerous to other persons in a group.

Group therapy is the best approach that has been invented for dealing with some kinds of internalized anger, however. I don't recommend confrontational groups, but groups that become emotional families in which there are positive, caring feelings.

Thirty-six-year-old Harry is an example of a person for whom such a group could be very helpful.

"It took me a long time to realize that I've been an angry person most of my life," he said. "I'm high-strung and I had a miserable childhood. I have a duodenal ulcer. I'm afraid to say the things I feel, and my stomach pays the price. I'm afraid to say things because I don't want to hurt the other person, or I think it will cause more problems."

In a psychotherapeutic group, Harry would be able to risk saying what he feels to someone not so important in his life. Once he learned to use this freedom to express his feelings in a group situation, he would learn that in doing so, he could end up with a warmer relationship—that he could experience and express anger and end the encounter with both himself and the other person feeling good about themselves and about one another. Ultimately he would gain the capacity to risk saying what he feels and needs to say to his wife. He would have learned in therapy that when you are free to experience frustration and anger with people who are important to you and they are free with you, too, a basic trust evolves that you will stay together, that you will experience what you need to experience and that you will be how you need to be with one another.

Violence

With some persons harboring internalized anger, violence is a problem. Violence as an outlet for intense anger is learned behavior, however. Even intense, internalized, historical anger has relatively little potential for violence unless the person has had violent parents or has been part of a culture in which violence was condoned and encouraged, either implicitly or explicitly. But some people have learned to view violence as an appropriate response to anger.

This was the case with Carolyn's ex-husband, who had lost a leg.

"His father used to beat his mother when he was drunk," she said. "He'd feel sorry afterward. My husband used to brag, 'I hit you and I'm sober.' He has a false image of what a man should be. He used to keep saying, 'I am the man and you are the slave,' and shouting about how he was the head of the house. I said to myself that someone who has to keep shouting isn't so sure of himself. Also he would beat the children with a belt and want me to beat them with a belt. It was very bad for the children. He wouldn't work, so we were on welfare, which I couldn't stand. I left him because I could go no further."

The anger of Carolyn's ex-husband was probably related to feelings of powerlessness or of being less than a man. I suspect he felt a need to gain within the family a sense of power that he didn't have outside the home. Having been conditioned by the violence of his own home to see violence as appropriate masculine behavior, he used it to express his accumulated anger.

In this way and through child-beating, violence in a family is likely to be self-perpetuating through generations. The beaten and brutalized child has no normal outlets for the anger that builds up. The child locks into his or her inner feelings a sense of powerlessness along with profound rage, producing a distorted personality. This overwhelming subliminal rage, a perversion of honest anger, may burst forth in an uncontrollable way or in a malicious desire to brutalize or injure. Consequently, battered children typically grow up to become adults who batter their own children.

Twenty-five-year-old Betty, who had such a background, was trying desperately hard to avoid becoming a battering mother when she called the radio program.

"My stepfather beat me and my three sisters continually as far back as I can remember," she said. "For example, every Sunday we had to go to church, prayer meetings and the whole bit, and we had to be perfectly dressed with our shoes polished or we would get a beating. One time I couldn't find the shoe polish. I was really scared and called my mother. We weren't supposed to do that either. When my stepfather found out I had called, he picked me up and threw me against the wall and beat me so badly I couldn't see to go to school for a week. I would tell my mom and she would mention it to him and I would be in more trouble. So I learned to keep my mouth shut and take whatever came. If I came home late from school because a bus was late, he was waiting at the front door. He counted from the time I was at the end of the driveway until I reached the front door. If he counted up to 102, that's how many times I'd get hit with the end of a belt buckle. Finally, it didn't matter anymore and I stopped crying when he hit me.

"Now I have a two-year-old boy. Sometimes I work myself into such a frenzy that I want to hit him, but I'm afraid that I would keep on hitting. So I find myself breaking glasses, hitting walls and throwing telephone books rather than hitting my child. It's my way of self-control."

It is ironic and tragic that Betty, who suffered so much in childhood, has to work so terribly hard to avoid over-controlling and beating her own child. The suppressed rage that her early experience created is easily provoked by the behavior of her little child. When it is provoked, she wants to do the same thing that was done to her. In this kind of situation there is an almost overwhelming compulsive urge to beat just as you were beaten.

So far, she has managed to restrain herself, but that kind of intensity of emotion under such ferocious inhibition and suppression is dangerous. She will either end up with some physical illness from so tremendously inhibiting herself psychophysically, or she will go through the guilt of being a violent person. Anyone who has been brutalized in childhood and must fiercely control and inhibit himself in order to keep from being a brutalizer should go into therapy, where this tremendous backlog of helpless, hopeless rage of childhood can be broken out of, experienced and let go. This rage is not anger in the usual sense. It is pathological.

Not all infantile rage, which piles up in childhood and comes out in adult violence, has been caused by child-beating. The wife-beating husband of thirty-one-year-old Jean had had a different kind of childhood experience, which was responsible for the anger he took out on his wife in violent ways. He was a mother-dependent man, whose over-controlling mother probably nurtured feelings of guilt and unworthiness in him. He had largely cut himself off from his mother when he married Jean. He probably had hated his dependency on her. But it is deeply buried in his guts. So he had transferred his emotional dependency to his wife, putting her in the role of a mother substitute to whom he deferred for approval on any decisions, major or minor. As he felt himself transferring this dependency to his wife, he apparently stored up resentment. Then, when he got drunk, out came the resentment. Here she tells about her experience.

"He first hit me after we had been out drinking with another couple and the other guy started hitting his wife in the back seat of the car," she recounted. "Evidently my husband thought it was a great idea, because when we got home he gave me a broken jaw. The next day he went out drinking with his friends and when he came home, he hit me in the stomach, even though I was pregnant at the time and he was happy about the pregnancy. I've been thinking how demented he is, but I must have been just as demented to have taken it for four years. One time when we went home from a party because I wasn't feeling good, he was mad because we left and started kicking me. I still don't know what triggered these attacks, but when we went to a psychologist much later, I said it was probably all my fault.

"A lot of times when my husband would get mad at me, he'd punish me by sleeping on the couch. Once he came home drunk when I was five months pregnant and I said, 'Will you please sleep on the couch tonight? The smell is making me sick.' He threw me outside over a bush in the snow. I lost the baby and I found out later that he didn't think I was going to live. We've been apart for two years, but I still see him. I've had three proposals from other men. They have always treated me nicely, but I look for the smallest thing I can find wrong in a man. I don't know if it's that I can't let go of him or that I'm afraid of marriage."

Jean seemed to have a strong image of women as maternal figures to this type of man. She also has latent guilt feelings that come out of her background, which make her a natural victim. So she and her husband made a particularly bad combination. Each fulfilled the other's expectations of the opposite sex. Part of Jean's unwillingness to let go of the relationship completely, despite the divorce, is probably related to her not knowing how to relate to a man who treats her kindly and lovingly.

Trusting Your Anger

Approving the expression of anger in ourselves and in anybody important to us is a part of our strength in dealing with life. It is necessary to our self-confidence and to a clear sense of our own purposes and motivations, to our sense of identity. Without anger, we lack the assertiveness to insist upon respect for our rights and dignity.

The issue we face as adults is being able to trust our anger, to trust ourselves to experience what we experience in the way that we experience it, confident that we will not do anything that will demean or dehumanize someone else. The person prone to violence needs treatment. A comprehensive physical examination may reveal serious neurological, endocrinological or metabolic disturbances that sometimes create violent behavior. Sometimes a diabetic or prediabetic person will be violence-prone. When violence is the product of psychological conditioning in early life, therapy is needed.

But when anger is within tolerable limits, when there is not a hidden backlog of rage and you can identify the sources of your frustration, you can best deal with your anger by letting it out, knowing that it will be ventilated within a few minutes and that your way of doing this will be appropriate within the framework of your life and your important relationships.

Chapter 8

No-Win Marital Games

Constructive fighting is sometimes necessary in marriage. But much marital fighting, rather than contributing constructively to the relationship, is inconclusive and destructive, neither resolving problems nor effectively communicating feelings. One person may express some anger and frustration, and the other may respond with self-protective denial or counter-frustration. But no negotiation occurs on the differences between them. Later, again and again, the couple repeats this basic scene, going around in a painful kind of marital game. There are a dozen or more scenarios typical of these no-win marital struggles, which psychologists refer to as "games" or "tapes" because of the repetitive cycling of frustrations without any real effect in resolving differences.

We fall into these ways of relating for a variety of reasons: feelings of low self-worth and fears of rejection; fears of the opposite sex; high levels of anxiety about getting into close interaction with anybody; or mere unfamiliarity with saying to one another what we feel and asking for what we want. Often we have lacked good marriage models. There are many, many experiences in life that make it easier to relate to someone important to you in a negative way than in a positive one.

A game can be a way of sending a message without openly

communicating what one wants. It can be a way of not hearing a message from the other person when the message is an emotionally disturbing one, perhaps an indication of differences that one isn't prepared to deal with.

Whatever the underlying reason for it, this destructive kind of fighting frustrates both partners, denying them the rewards and joys of a fulfilling relationship. One of the many ways of doing this can be seen in the conversation of Denise, thirty-four, who had been married for thirteen years to the kind of man I call the Disaster Seeker.

"It's a one-sided fight," she said in describing his way of interacting with her. "Walter is a perfectionist and always looks on the negative side of things. I'm not perfect, but he picks on me for everything. I'll try to do something earnestly and honestly, but if it doesn't come out to his standards, he will say I'm stupid or an idiot. It cramps my style and depresses me.

"He also likes to ridicule. When he's in a light-hearted mood, he'll make little jokes to play a person down. He doesn't do it to everyone. If he believes that a person knows his subject well, he has great admiration for this person. But if he has the feeling that someone isn't so perfect, he plays the person down."

Through early experiences, Walter developed an aggressive style with which he seeks to be in control of those around him. He also attempts to find a cloud over every rainbow, undermining everyone with whom he has an important relationship. A person acting this way may have had an aggressive or unfeeling mother, or may have had a great deal of early-childhood anxiety from other causes. According to Denise, Walter is extremely fond of his mother, but his father died when he was less than a year old. That kind of experience, in which a boy is deprived of a strong male model, creates much anxiety in a child, who, on becoming an adult, tends to be either very dependent and anxious, or an aggressive, dominating, controlling person. It probably has been very important for Walter to feel he has control of his life.

An intimate relationship in which one partner chronically heckles and attempts to minimize the other's worth is very painful for the one being put down. I advised Denise to talk through with him his style and the ways in which it was creating frustration and anger in her and diminishing her power as a person.

Unrealistic Expectations That Lead to Games

A common thread running through many games is an attempt to identify the partner as a bad person, or at least an insensitive or unfeeling one, in order to justify deep disappointment in the marriage.

When two people have romantically idealized each other to a great degree in the early stages of their relationship, a good deal of anger can develop between them as the full dimensions of their differences emerge, if they have not begun to underpin the relationship with the beginnings of a trusting friendship.

The anger is based on the feeling that someone you love ought to share your views and respond to life in the same way that you do. The expectation that anyone will find somebody on earth who matches himself or herself in attitudes, emotional predispositions, style of life, physiological cycles, energy level, etc., is unrealistic. But marriage counselors spend a good deal of their time listening to spouses ventilate their frustrations that their partners' responses to life differ from their own.

In a way, the view that one's partner ought to be an extension of oneself is a carry-over from childhood. You start out in life seeking your parent's approval. What is important to them is important to you, because you want them to like and approve of you. As you grow older and begin to develop as an individual, at some time you must also begin to give up on getting their full approval in order to have views somewhat different from theirs.

If you have a good relationship with your parents, they tolerate differences between you and themselves as you develop. Unfortunately, many parents feel that a child who is not a straightforward projection of parental views, attitudes and style of life is disloyal, and they are personally offended by any such deviation. This attitude was much more prevalent two generations ago than it is today, but it still plays a powerful role in the lives of many people and conditions them to feel that a marriage partner should respond to life as they do.

Often this feeling is the basis for a power struggle in marriage. Each partner may attempt to dominate or control the other in order to be the one *giving* approval rather than the one *seeking* approval. When partners are not able to play out the parent role and control the other, they become angry. At that point the destructive games often begin.

Frequently, these games are very complex and subtle. At least a dozen psychologists and psychiatrists, beginning with William James before the turn of the century, have attempted to identify the destructive scenarios. Descriptions have varied with the psychotherapeutic theories behind each psychologist's interpretation. But most of the major games are pretty clearly described by all, although these have many variations. People are infinitely inventive in finding destructive ways to relate to one another. A truly embattled couple will have several games going simultaneously.

In one of the most common scenarios, partners mutually engage in putting down the other instead of dealing with their differences. Karen, twenty-six years old and pregnant, and her husband were playing one version of this "I don't like you, I'm mad at you" game when she called.

"He doesn't approve of many things I do," she said. "If I'm reading a book, I'll try to show him something interesting in it, but when I look at him, he's looking out of the window. I guess I force myself and my ideas on him. I try to enlighten him about everything I'm interested in. Instead of just taking an objective look at it and saying, 'I don't agree with it and this is why,' he just says, 'I think it's a lot of bunk and I don't want to hear about it.' When we're arguing, sometimes he says things he doesn't really mean. Like the other day he said, 'For all I know, it's not even my baby.'

"There's a racial thing, too. I have a half-Mexican daughter and he seems to get along with her. But at times he says things about other Mexicans and blacks. I really hate racial prejudice. I can silence a whole party by spouting off if someone starts in with racial jokes that put people down. When I try to discuss why he feels this way, he doesn't want to discuss it. He'll say, 'It's just the way I am.' And I'll say, 'That's a pretty poor excuse. My parents are racially prejudiced and that's the way I was brought up, but I've changed myself.' You get out in life and look at the opinions your parents have given you, and as you view your experiences maybe you see things a little differently."

In that last paragraph, Karen is saying that she is changing and growing and developing new attitudes, whereas her husband is not—a viewpoint that is strongly disapproving of him. And he bluntly disapproves of her whenever she mentions something exciting and interesting to her, even to the point of insulting her in a very painful way about their expected baby.

I suspect that both are people with deep feelings of self-doubt who try to build themselves up by putting the other down. Many people are caught up in this attitude that the only way they can feel good about themselves is to have somebody to whom they can feel superior. When this game is highly developed, it is very difficult to stop, for to do so, the persons involved are required to give up crutches for their self-esteem that they have used for a long time, in all probability since long before the relationship in question was established. As a first step, they must recognize what they are doing and identify it as a corrosive and destructive influence in their relationship.

They also need to face up to their differences in attitudes, feelings and styles of life, communicate about them and negotiate some resolution where possible, rather than lacerating each other from a distance.

If Only My Spouse Were Different

Such avoidance of dealing with differences in a way that will effect some workable compromise is common to all the marital games. However, the particular scenarios a couple chooses vary with the personalities involved. Often a game reveals behavior patterns habitual since childhood.

I suspect that Roberta, fifty, married to her third husband for less than a year when she called, had played "If Only My Spouse Were Different" over and over again with the men in her life. In this game she takes the role of surrogate mother, which allows her to avoid dealing with her husband as an adult responsible for his own behavior. The habits she complains about here give her an excuse to disapprove of him, to identify him as "not okay" and, by implication, identify herself as the superior person in the relationship.

"He has a few traits I wish he didn't have," she said, explaining her position in this game. "It's nothing for him to pick his nose twenty-three times in one day. He chews gum with his mouth open. And his table manners are awful. Before we were married, he did everything perfectly, but once we got married, he relaxed. I guess he felt he could be himself.

"These things upset me. When I criticize him for them, he goes into a temper tantrum. He says whatever he feels like saying—horrible things—and I'm very uncomfortable. Half an hour later he's agreeable again, but I don't want to be around him."

When differences in style between two people create some dissatisfaction in a marriage, and they find it painful to fight through these differences and find mutually acceptable ways of relating, frequently one will focus on troublesome behavior, as Roberta does, making it more important than it really is. And the other will release tension by getting really mad.

Apparently, Roberta's husband is one of those people who has a style of exaggerated expression carried over from childhood petulance. Such individuals say things like, "I hate you. I wish you were dead. I'd like to kill you." But it has almost no meaning for them. It is merely a statement of, "You're making me angry. Get off my back." Once they experience and express the anger, they're perfectly happy. But the pain for the other person, in this case Roberta, who deals with it as a real evaluation of her or of the relationship, is just beginning.

That Roberta plays this game suggests that she may not have had a warm, affectionate experience with her father and is fearful of attempting to relate to a man on a coequal basis.

There may be some elements in her husband's personality that lead him to seek some mothering from a woman. I suspect that if he were a strong, confident man, Roberta would not have married him. But a wife attempting to give maternal guidance and control to a man in his fifties is incompatible with his pride, dignity and sense of worth. So he rejects it with a temper tantrum and seeks to restore the balance of power.

Other factors also may be playing a part in their behavior, of course. He may be doing things deliberately to goad her into maternal controlling behavior if, as a child, that was the only way he got the feeling that someone cared about him. And if the only way Roberta, as a child, could get attention from her father was to make him angry, in picking on her husband she may be acting out her childhood experience with men. Picking a fight can be a way of transforming a feeling of deadness or apathy into a feeling of aliveness, of saying, "I'm here, I'm alive." Sometimes very hurtful games are played in adult life on just that kind of a basis.

Emotional Avoidance

The game that probably brings more people into marriage counselors than any other is emotional avoidance. Women describe this in terms of the husband coming home and refusing to talk to the wife, who has been with little children all day and is starved for attention and affection, or responding to a request for conversation with an annoyed, "What will we talk about?" A man who fears intimacy may give generously to his wife of money and gifts—everything but himself.

It works the other way around, too, of course. The husband may come home wanting affection while the wife may busy herself with housework or fiddle around with the kids. She will do almost anything but pay attention to him.

Basically, the avoider is saying, "You can have my body or my money, but you can't have my attention or my involvement."

Emotional avoidance also plays a part in other marital games—being ill or exhausted when a partner wants to deal with a problem or is angry, for instance. The tragic thing is that this often leads to real and chronic illness. This is more frequently a game of females, although it may be played by the "impotent" male.

However, avoidance should not be confused with a partner's needing some time alone. Fifteen or twenty years ago, at the height of the movement for family togetherness, marriage counselors sometimes suggested to couples that they ought to spend all their free time together and share all possible experiences with the children. Studies clearly undermining this view tell us that most people need time alone to experience themselves.

The avoidance-game player chronically avoids the emotional involvement of sharing feelings and communicating about differences sufficiently to work them through. Typically, this game is played by people who find close relationships and the open expression and experiencing of emotions difficult.

This apparently was the case with Matt, who had been married to thirty-two-year-old Alice for fourteen years.

"When Matt and I have an argument, he clams up and doesn't talk to me," she said. "He's a great person if it weren't for this, but I'm at the point where I'm ready to tear my hair out. When he's around other people, he's outgoing and a regular guy. When I try to talk to him, he calls it nagging. Of course, we have our problems like any other married couple. But Matt won't talk about them. He's told me I must learn to open up and not hold back my feelings if anything is bothering me, and I keep reminding him to practice what he preaches, but it doesn't help. He's a good father and a good provider.

Our sex life is quite good, but sometimes I think I'm just being used and that turns me off."

The inability to talk about inner emotions is often trained into young children by parents who react unfavorably to emotional states other than that of being pleasant. Sometimes a person carries that inability from early childhood into adult relationships, and simply cannot verbalize feelings. More men than women are caught in this situation because expression of emotions generally has been thought more acceptable in women than in men.

Matt could overcome his tendency to avoid emotional interaction in group psychotherapy. An alternative to group therapy that might be helpful would be for Alice to write a series of brief notes to him, telling him feelings she would like to share with him and inviting him to share his feelings with her. These need not always be on heavy topics. She could be playful and from time to time express her pleasure in his positive aspects. Her messages should clearly be invitations to enjoy life together more.

She also might try involving Matt in activities with a group of people who are very open in expressing feelings. She might arrange to go to the theater on a regular basis or take a university extension course with a group of the liveliest, most interesting and emotionally responsive people she can find. He might catch on and become more open himself.

The Failure Seekers

The "Failure Seekers" game is often played by people who have felt unloved or unappreciated in childhood. Typically, their parents' experience of married life has been more negative than positive.

They start marriage expecting an unhappy, unrewarding relationship in which they will not be well treated by a spouse. They behave in a way that inevitably brings this about, then they indict the other person.

This happens because a man (or a woman) whose parents had a bad marriage has powerful learned attitudes that predispose him (or her) to respond to a spouse as if his (or her) marriage were an extrapolation of that same relationship between his parents. He may recognize intellectually, and even emotionally at a surface level, that he is different from his father and that the woman he chose to marry is different from his mother—maybe very different. Nevertheless, he carries into the marriage some of the attitudes, defensiveness and destructive games of his parents. These involuntary mental sets and preconditioned responses exist because his parents' marriage was the primary model of a marriage that he saw during his childhood and teenage years.

If he starts to experience his marriage in negative terms, some of the deep anger that he felt toward his parents for not being happy and not giving him a loving, supportive environment as a child will be turned not only upon his mate, but upon the marriage itself. With any disillusionment, almost inevitably he views his marriage in more negative terms than are justified. Easily discouraged and inclined to give up on it, he is likely to begin to identify unconsciously with his parents and play more and more of the hostile, hurtful games they played.

Often, almost deliberately, he will make the relationship worse than it is, in part because of anger over not having the wonderful marriage that he had fantasized, and at not being the "special" or "different" man that he dreamed of being.

Charlene, thirty-eight, and Pete, forty, divorced twice from each other and again dating, were old hands at the "Failure Seekers" game.

"It was bicker, bicker, bicker when we were married," Pete said in describing their married life. "Sometimes it was loud and ugly. Sometimes it was just a surface tension that never quite went away. To live day after day under that kind of strain was impossible for both of us. We were both miserable. But we can't quite seem to turn loose from each other. There's a tremendous physical attraction, and we still care about each other. We've talked about remarrying and we both say no. I know we can't live together. But why is it that when a divorce or separation is finalized, we immediately seek each other out, and when we don't live together we get along great?"

Separated but friendly, enjoying each other when they choose, may be the only way Pete and Charlene can have an enjoyable life. There is strong evidence that a significant portion of the population cannot be successfully married. For persons in that segment, and Pete and Charlene may well be, marriage is inevitable disaster. Their conditioning, their deepest emotional feelings are such that as soon as they get married, they feel oppressed by demands. Marital obligations seem a heavy burden of responsibility. They feel guilt and anger and start to injure and undercut each other.

When I suggested to Pete that he and Charlene maintain their single, friendly state, he worried about the impact on the children. Obviously, the kind of relationship the two of them have will have an impact on the children. But I suspect that seeing parents as friends, enjoying each other, would have a more positive impact than having as their model of adult married life the kind of marriage Pete described, which sounds dreadful.

More Games

Another game, a particularly painful one that teenagers are especially likely to play, is "I'm As Good As You Are." In this scenario, partners seek the feeling of strength and worth that all human beings need, by competing with each other for power. In the process they indirectly undermine or belittle each other. For instance, in a social situation a young husband may cut off his wife's views on an issue by implying that she is not knowledgeable, or may make the same implication when they are alone by giving her a detailed lecture on a subject on which she has expressed an opinion. She may respond by complaining, either directly or indirectly, about financial problems, implying that he is a poor provider. When a young couple gets married, the change in roles between man and woman makes this power struggle particularly confusing. It frequently degenerates into savage competition in which the only outlet is in putting down the other.

Another aspect of these marital scenarios is the "Counter-Complaint Game." When one spouse attempts to deal with a frustrating situation in the marriage, the other complains about something else and the two go around and around, with neither issue being effectively fought through.

One of the least rewarding games of all is "Dominance-Dependence," in which one partner is strong, dominant and controlling and the other is needful, dependent, frightened, etc. Eventually, the powerful one feels like he or she is carrying an enormous burden and feels put upon. The dependent one usually ends up angry because the position of powerlessness is such a putdown.

In another game, one partner, who feels that life is grim and frightening, is extremely fearful of taking any action involving even remote risk. This almost paranoid attitude comes, in part, out of that person's childhood and adolescent experience. But it frequently becomes a marital game in that whenever the other partner wants to take a risk to better the lives of both—buy a house, make an investment, start a new business—even though it may be a very reasonable risk, the fearful partner will frustrate the other's desire.

Still another common scenario is the "You're Going to Abandon Me" accusation, which dependent persons often throw at their spouses whenever they are not getting what they want. It is a way of controlling through guilt feelings. Although this is occasionally done by a man, it is more commonly a ploy of women who have been taught to feel that women aren't worth much. This game, of course, tends to be self-fulfilling.

Testing the Limits

In many of these painful games that adults play, marriage partners are testing limits with one another. They are attempting, either by subterfuge or direct demand, to see how much they can control the other person. Again, this way of behaving comes out of childhood. As children, we get into games with our parents, siblings, other children, and adults. We see how far we can go in getting what we want. We test parents to see if we can dominate them—if we can persuade them to give us a diet of candy and ice cream or let us stay up all night, even though these things are not in our own best interests.

Children test the limits in other ways, of course. They attempt to determine the boundaries in all dimensions of living. ("How fast can I run? How high can I jump? How many cookies can I eat? How long can I keep myself awake?")

A loving parent who recognizes that it is natural for a child to test the limits of parental control, but also recognizes parental responsibility, gives the child all the affection and recognition that the child is essentially demanding, but firmly and clearly sets guidelines for behavior. This is the primary role of a good parent—loving the person of the child, but defining acceptable versus unacceptable behavior.

When parents overrespond to children's misbehavior with disapproval that does not differentiate between the behavior and the child, children may perceive the parents' response as disapproval of themselves. They may grow up with deep feelings of being unlovable or unworthy people.

Throughout life, we continue to test limits in one way or another. Whether we do it in affirmative or negative ways depends in part on our self-image created in childhood. A person with a strong sense of self-value may test limits largely in terms of opportunities for achievement. One who has a desperately low feeling of self-worth may test limits by becoming suicidal. For most adults, one of the most significant areas in which we test limits is that of intimate relationships. Most human beings are not comfortable in asking directly for loving affection, and are painfully awkward in accepting affection from people from whom they most want it. So a good deal of this testing tends to be done indirectly.

If two people do not receive from one another the love, respect, appreciation and genuine attention they seek, they are likely to become involved in behavior typical of the marital games. In seeking to prevail in the marriage relationship, they are testing the limits of their importance to their partners.

One person may do this by playing "I'll Gladly Give You What You Don't Want and Look How Generous I Am." Another plays "If You Love Me, You'd Know What I Want Without My Having to Tell You." Still another chooses "You're Hurting Me and It's Making Me Sick."

Whatever the negative marriage game, the result is the same. Each partner denies the other the closeness and loving affection that they were seeking in the marriage.

Chapter 9

When Sex Turns Sour

When we asked the radio audience, "Has your husband lost interest in sex?" calls jammed the station switchboard in unprecedented numbers.

This widespread problem is usually a symptom of deep marital distress, which carries with it painful feelings of guilt and responsibility for a man. It can be triggered by a considerable number of factors, from the arrival of a first baby to anxiety about the effects of aging. High-tension stress on the job, obesity and lack of exercise, too much alcohol or drugs, or simple misinformation about sex and a man's sexuality can play a part. But most commonly, it relates to inner fears of inadequacy or rejection related to onerous feelings of responsibility for the sexual pleasure and satisfaction of his wife.

The male in our society has been conditioned to feel that he is responsible for the success of sex. This attitude is a terrible ego threat for most men. Sexual prowess is the subject of a lot of joking and teasing among young men, and often becomes very important to masculine pride. For many men, the idea of not being a sexual hero is untenable. Yet men have as many fears and inhibitions relative to their sexuality and as much anxiety about rejection as women do. The responsibility for being a successful lover can be very painful.

When men find that they are not eleven feet tall in the bedroom, they tend to withdraw from sex. A man's retreat is viewed by his wife as an indication of her lack of lovability.

She then seeks sex as reassurance that she is loved and appreciated.

This puts a man in a painful spot. He feels that performance is demanded, and this can arouse more anxiety about his ability to meet his wife's expectations, along with embarrassed guilt or anger. These stressful feelings affect the autonomic nervous system in such a way that secretions are sent into the bloodstream that tend to suppress or diminish an erection. With both psychological and physiological factors suppressing his sexual capacity, an unrewarding sexual encounter is almost guaranteed.

Often a man finds this too embarrassing to talk about with his wife because, in a sense, he will have to admit that his masculine drives aren't up to her expectations. Without communication, each partner repeats and reinforces this negative pattern, and the couple's sex life goes downhill drastically.

The Arrival of a Child

Frequently, this kind of distortion of the sexual relationship occurs after the birth of a child, which brings a new element into the partnership. Pregnancy is a mystery that some men find quite upsetting and difficult to cope with, and with the arrival of a child, partners are no longer carefree playmates in the old sense. A child's arrival puts a man in competition with the baby for his wife's attention and brings him into direct contact with his feelings about fatherhood and his attitude toward women, which often includes a basic distrust. This sometimes happens because when a woman becomes a mother, her behavior changes in many subtle ways. Usually, she has feelings of increased dependency on a man, which can arouse fear of rejection and abandonment when she is most needful. And inevitably she is somewhat angry in a special kind of a way because dependency creates anger. Whenever you feel dependent on anybody, you harbor some degree of resentment. At that point, a woman may seek love partly through demands for reassurance. The husband may back off because of new, awesome and frightening feelings of responsibility, which make him uneasy. Then a man who has felt powerful, aggressive and masculine in sex may feel subject to demands for sexual performance that he can't meet, at least not with comfort, confidence, pleasure and joy. This is bound to make him feel unmanly and get him in touch, at a fairly deep level, with feelings of anger and frustration toward women, which have their roots in childhood. Then a sexual relationship, which may have been quite rewarding earlier, starts to cycle negatively.

This had happened in the marriage of twenty-six-year-old Dolores, married five years.

"As soon as I became pregnant with our first child, he completely ignored me," she said. "He does not like fat women and I did become quite large, but I have lost the weight. Still, he has never resumed the vitality he had before we were married. He can go for two weeks or a month without touching me. If I bring up the subject, then I guess he feels obligated and we'll have relations, but it's as if he has to be reminded of it. I can't understand it, because of the way he was before, and I can't cope with it. I have suggested marriage counseling to him, but he doesn't seem to think he has a problem. He's kind of a closed person and won't talk much about anything, but I try to bring him out."

The sexual problem between Dolores and her husband is a symptom of disaffection between them. Each is very angry with the other, but for quite different reasons.

A baby symbolically creates a tremendous feeling of family, which brings all of one's historical associations and sentiments about "family" welling up. Those of Dolores's husband are painful. His parents were divorced when he was very young, and he had no continuing contact with his father. Lacking a loving and supportive father substitute as a child, he almost inevitably became very angry at his mother, feeling that she cheated him out of a father. This anger at his mother, translated into anger at women, is carried into any relationship he has with a woman. As his wife became rotund in pregnancy, it began to gather direction and force as the baby's impending arrival triggered old feelings of "Where's my daddy? Why didn't my mommy do what she had to do in order for me to have a daddy?"

His wife inevitably felt his anger and responded to it, either overtly or covertly. Her response was based on angry feelings of her own—feelings that you can't trust a man to love you if you put on a few pounds, or to be loyal and supportive in a crisis, when you're pregnant and anxious about childbirth.

After the birth, she undoubtedly focused her attention on the baby, her anger probably leading her to pay less attention to her husband. Even if he had wanted to compete with the child for her attention, his own anger would have kept him from doing so. So this period after childbirth, which is always a difficult time, could easily have escalated their angers and was probably extremely difficult for them.

Only if they examine together their reasons for anger, and go through intimate disclosure of feelings, with each one actively listening to the other, is this troubled relationship likely to improve.

When a Wife's Sexual Initiatives Cause Upset

In some marriages, negative cycling in sex gets started when a woman approaches her peak of sexual desire at about the age of thirty, and she begins to evolve a sense of sexual freedom and openness. A man who is saddled with the idea that men are sexually aggressive and women sexually passive, often sees this as an assuult on his prerogatives and finds it upsetting.

A part of his anxiety frequently comes from partially repressed feelings that sex is evil. Another part may be associated with a historical reservoir of negative feelings about being emotionally intimate with any other person, particularly a woman. His anxieties may also be related to fears of aggressiveness by his wife in other areas of life. Many men feel that if they are supportive of a woman's sexual freedom, she may demand equality in other ways, and their dominance in other dimensions of the relationship will slip away.

The husband of thirty-two-year-old Maria was typical. Although other factors undoubtedly played a part in his loss of sexual desire, he was a strongly macho male with traditional conditioning.

"About three years ago I was sick off and on, and then I had surgery," she began her account of their problem. "Afterwards I felt pretty well and wanted my husband. I tried to be the initiator of sex with him. It seemed to turn him off and he hasn't really wanted me since. At the time, he seemed to feel I was a scarlet woman. And he became very jealous, even though he didn't want me anymore. He felt that since he wasn't taking care of me, I must be going out with other men.

"I think some of his attitude had to do with our being Mexican. He has old-fashioned Latin ways of being the man and the aggressor and all that. We were brought up in parochial schools, and I had hangups from that, but in my late twenties I got over them, I think. Some of it may have had to do with the fact that he had drinking problems.

"It was pretty hard for quite a while, and our marriage did break up. But after working and all the problems, I felt it would be just as well to go back with him, and I did. We have three children. He's an excellent father. I do care for him and I know he cares very much for me. I didn't think I could ever find another right man who would be willing to accept my children. I tried dating when we were separated, but most men just want a sexual relationship, and that's not all I want. It would have to go along with the whole package.

"But in many ways I'm not satisfied now. There isn't much sex. He's stopped his drinking and is getting back some of his sexual desire, but I don't think it will ever be the same or better."

What happened between Maria and her husband didn't happen without some basis. I suspect that her husband has guilt feelings associated with sex and his own sexuality, and that he experienced anxiety and a certain amount of sexual turn-off when she became ill. A husband often doesn't know how to deal with his sexual desire if his wife is ill, especially if her illness is serious. The confusion of tenderness and sexual desire or passion are frequently upsetting, especially to men like Maria's husband, who are not emotionally communicative— who can't say what they want or can't talk about what they feel. When Maria became desirous of sex, he was probably experiencing a complicated set of upsetting feelings toward her and toward his own sexual nature.

Anxiety About the Effects of Aging

In later years, a marriage often runs into trouble sexually when a man becomes distressed by what he perceives to be the effects of aging on his sexual capacity. Men go through biological transitions, just as women do. Whether or not you put a name to it, there are "changes of life" for both sexes. A man's sexual drive peaks in his early twenties and declines slightly from decade to decade. However, with good health and an understanding of the facts about his sexuality, he can remain sexually vigorous and sexually interested into his seventies, sometimes into his eighties and nineties. But when a man in middle age notes that his sex drive is not what it once was, he becomes anxious about it. For many men, sexuality has been so attached to their sense of masculinity, power, worth and dignity that it is terrifying to experience a slackening of sexual desire. Their fright and embarrassment can create psychophysical stress that depresses their sexual capacity further. Continued negative cycling of these psychological and physical factors may drastically reduce sexual ability. This had happened to fifty-five-year-old Todd, married for thirty years, who felt that his sex life was over when he called.

"For the last two years, maybe three, sex has seemed like a chore," he said. "My wife can't understand the change she sees in me. I put her off. I try to be kind, but I can't get enthusiastic. Then, if I just give her a little kiss, she takes it for an invitation to the kind of thing I'm not interested in. She asked me to see a doctor about it, but I've compared notes with a few of my friends, and I'm not the only one who feels finished with the whole thing. I don't think a doctor could help."

I suggested to Todd that a few sessions with a counselor could be very helpful in restoring his sexual vigor. The reassurance, information, and understanding of his situation that he would gain in counseling would very likely alleviate the pressure to perform that he feels in sex. Dissipating his anxiety could thus remove the downward pressure these feelings place on his sexual responses.

A part of a man's anxiety about his sexual capacity as he approaches middle age often has to do with the variations in the strength of his erection during lovemaking, which become more noticeable as he ages. A man may start a sexual encounter with a firm, hard erection, but in the course of lovemaking, cuddling, talking and snuggling, it will start to fade. There is no problem in this unless he thinks it is a problem. A penis normally softens from time to time over an extended period of lovemaking. A normal erection hardens and softens, hardens and softens. At the age of twenty-five and earlier, this waning and waxing is almost imperceptible. As a man ages, the amplitude of the cycle increases and many men become anxious about losing their erections. A man with this anxiety needs to learn that it is normal for the penis to soften during lovemaking, and that when he wants to have active intercourse, his erection will be there. It really will be there.

Todd would also learn in counseling that as one grows older, a greater amount of sensual behavior—holding, fondling, stroking, touching—becomes more and more necessary for successful sex, for it increases hormonal secretions and neurological responses. In addition, along with reassurance about his sexual capacity, Todd and his wife would be given exercises in touching and sharing feelings to create new excitement in the relationship. They would be told to take showers together and start a program of daily nude cuddling. They would have an exercise in body examination in which each in turn would stand, one behind the other, in front of a mirror. The one in front would describe inner feelings about each part of his or her body, from the top of the head to the tip of the toes, while the other listened silently. In another exercise, they would experiment with touching each other's bodies in different kinds of ways—roughly, gently, and in variations somewhere in between—with the person being touched describing how it feels. In these ways they would stimulate an opening-up of feelings between them. The self-disclosure and hearing the inner feelings of the other would revive the sense of excitement between them.

You're Not Stuck With Unrewarding Sex

Often, partners can break out of negative cycles that have very different causes than do Todd's problems, if they are able to open communication and be really honest with one another.

There are two main steps to be taken. First, you need to determine whether or not there is enough caring and attraction between you and your partner so that you both are willing to make a considerable effort to achieve a good outcome. This can be a scary and painful step, because forty percent of persons in a deeply troubled marriage, who engage in open communication on the subject, will find that there is not. However, if you are not prepared to test that, going to step two is useless.

In the second step, you must disengage yourselves from old expectations based on romantic myths that a loving partner should know what the other wants or is pleased by, and face the fact that you and your partner are separate individuals; that each of you has individual feelings, attitudes, personal history, fantasies, desires, timing and wishes; and that, at times, each will intrude on and offend the other's sensibilities. You can then begin to communicate about these things, going through a whole process in which each of you defines your own conditioning, training and attitudes toward sex and toward self, confiding anxieties, hopes, desires and dreams.

In a marriage of considerable length—ten years or more—partners who decide they care very much for each other frequently get stuck in trying to work through this second step, because so much anger, disappointment and upset has built up over those years. If you have strong feelings of having been denied, humiliated or rejected by the other, you may lapse into a painful, uptight state with one another in trying to say, "I feel... This is how I am." Then you need to bring in a professional third person as a facilitator.

Professional Help With Sexual Problems

A third of a century ago, there was little effective help for people with sexual problems. A large amount of knowledge about human sexuality has been acquired since then, and additional information is emerging each year from a number of research centers around the world.

A considerable number of skilled persons are now working with people in the sexual area, and a great many sexual problems are being solved—some of them in surprisingly short periods of time. Sometimes, just two or three visits with a counselor can be exceedingly useful. Inner fears, pain, anger and guilt come pouring out, and all kinds of misinformation and misperceptions of self and other people are cleared up and put in perspective. Some persons have considerable misperceptions about themselves, which play a primary part in sexual dysfunction. Sometimes they have been disturbed for years by their sexual fantasies. Persons who have had powerful conditioning that associates affectionate feeling for a person of the same sex with homosexuality, often are plagued and terrified by homosexual fantasies, in the process of inhibiting and disguising these, they put a lid on all their sensual and sexual feelings. When a therapist clarifies the historical conditioning and helps clear up misperceptions, they recognize themselves as normal and start to give themselves permission to feel, react and fantasize.

Many persons have misperceptions about the opposite sex and/or false notions about sexuality; these are a major cause of sexual problems.

Some young women are astonished to discover in family therapy that men have feelings of vulnerability, sensitivity to rejection, and fears of being inadequate as a lover or provider. Men, of course, hide these feelings because they have been considered unmasculine in our culture. And many men have hidden their emotions and sensitivities so successfully that their grown daughters believe that men do not have them.

Another frequent misperception on the part of women is the

idea that men are naturally more sexually aggressive than women. The strong sexual impulse that develops in the male in the early teens leads women to the expectation that men will be the pursuers and aggressors in sex all their lives. Nothing could be further from reality. Since a man believes that a woman is expecting him to be the sexual initiator or the more aggressive person sexually, usually he acts it out. But after the age of thirty-five, much of what passes for masculine sexual aggressiveness is male role-playing. Increasingly, the male is seeking companionship, affection and approval more than he is seeking sex.

It is a rare woman who recognizes that after thirty her sexual desire exceeds that of her husband, however. So when a male's sexual initiative diminishes in his mid- to late thirties, a woman tends to think that he no longer loves her, or that he is bored with her. There may also be some loss of interest because of lack of variety in sex. But at least a part of his loss of interest is usually due to a natural physiological decline in his sexual enthusiasm.

Often, a woman does not recognize that this is a time when she can seize the initiative and rekindle intense sexual pleasure and erotic desire. She can surprise and excite her husband by words or by aggressively horsing around with him, taking hold of his genitals, caressing him with head massage, back massage, foot massage. There are many ways in which a woman can be sexually provocative if that is what she chooses—if it is pleasurable to her, and if it is acceptable to her man.

A man with a considerably more sexually active partner often becomes anxious and uncomfortable in this situation, because he has not learned ways of dealing with it. This is often the case when a man has a much younger wife. Frequently, men do not know that a mature male with a somewhat diminished sex drive can have pleasurable and comfortable sexual intercourse much more frequently than his own sexual drive would initiate if he learns that he can bring his partner to orgasm in intercourse without climaxing himself. A nineteen-year-old who tried this would have an uncomfortable or painful after-reaction as the seminal vesticles filled up with seminal fluid. But a man in his forties generally has no painful reaction. There is no pressure on his testicles, which fill up to a point that is usually very pleasurable. He can have sexual intercourse without orgasm once or twice, say, for every time he climaxes. In this way he also avoids the feeling of exhaustion that some men in their forties with very sexually active wives report.

This information was needed by the forty-three-year-old partner of twenty-five-year-old Sonia. Her sexual emergence in the year they had lived together had apparently frightened him. His consequent reaction threatened their relationship. Here she tells what has happened between them.

"When we started going together, I was a little shy about sex, about expressing my desires and showing my response to whatever he was doing or we were doing. David was unhappy about this and kept trying to get me over it. Then I reached the point where I really could let myself go. I was even sexually attacking him. But now he's constantly avoiding the whole thing. He says he doesn't want to hug and stuff like that because he's afraid I'll want to continue it for two hours.

"I thought that this was going to be a really long-lasting relationship and that if things continued going all right, we'd get married. We get along on so many levels. But I'm not interested in getting married if it's obvious there are going to be problems. His turning me off on sex seems a big problem. I even look at him and I can't control myself anymore. I'm going out of my mind and it's hard for me to get him to talk. If he's not willing to work this out, I can't see spending a whole lifetime climbing walls."

What Sonia describes occurs frequently. As long as David was clearly the aggressor in sex, and was in a superior position as the teacher, showing her new things and being excited about being able to show her new things, I suspect he felt good about himself. But when she became freer sexually and began to initiate sex, this probably threw him into self-doubt about his role and about how much sex he really desires. A female's emergence as a full sexual partner often causes a man to feel that performance is being demanded of him and that a whole new set of emotional responses is required. This can be a big problem for a couple. Partners need to develop an understanding of what is happening between them.

I suggested to Sonia that if David were important to her, she should write him a series of letters, each one explaining exactly how she feels. Such letters should have no element of condemnation or putdown. She should make only positive statements of what she would like to have with him and what she thinks the two of them could have, if they work things through.

Often, there is confusion between wanting sex and wanting to be loved. This apparently plays a part in the conflict between these two.

Many men don't understand that when a woman is pressing for sexual intercourse, a good deal of what she may really want is to feel loved. A partner can give her this without intercourse by playing with her in sensual and physical ways—by hugging and fondling or reaching out to touch her as they pass each other in the house, or by wrestling or dancing around the living room with her. Part of what I hear from Sonia is that essentially she wants affection and a good deal of this kind of emotional physical responsiveness. If David gets a sense of her need, the two of them might find their way to a new and more comfortable accommodation.

Other Differences in Sexual Drive

Some differences in sexual drive between partners are not primarily a matter of age or differences in male and female physiology. Part of our sexual response is shaped by what we learned from our childhood environment. (There are some males who have a penis so anaesthetized by anxious attitudes about sexuality that they report having almost no feeling in it at all.) Another part of sexual desire is determined by our genes. As with every other human trait, biological sexual drive varies according to a normal distribution curve. There are people at the low end of this curve and people at the high end. Those at the low end biologically don't have much sexual desire and don't want to have much to do with sex. For those at the other end of the scale, sex is a central part of life. They may engage in a great deal of sexual play with many different partners, regard sex as a sport and keep score. The major portion of the population, perhaps eighty or eighty-five percent, is somewhere in the middle.

Sometimes, compatibility in sexual drive is not tested out in a relationship before marriage, and a man with a very high physical sexual desire as part of his biological personality marries a woman who is very low on that scale. Sometimes the reverse happens. It seems fairly likely that this is the case in the marriage of twenty-three-year-old Stacy.

"I don't know what is considered the average amount of sex you're supposed to have a week, but I seem to have a problem with my husband," she began. "He's twenty-seven and it seems as if he should have a good healthy appetite. But maybe once a week or so we have sex, and I have to ask him or approach him. This is deflating to my ego. I am an attractive woman. I never had to be sexually aggressive when I was single.

"I think part of our problem is that he's a handsome man and has always had women chasing him. They call even now that we're married. I'm not worried about him being unfaithful. But he's used to sexually aggressive women and I think it's hard for him to take on the aggressive role. I don't know what to do about it. I've told him I don't mind being the aggressor sometimes. It can be exciting. But I don't like to have to ask for it all the time. You know how you're always reading articles where women avoid sex with their husbands by saying they're too tired, or have a headache. I get that line from my husband. It seems that he only gets sexually aggressive when he notices other men admiring me. Then he lets me know that he likes and desires me. But I'm not the type of person who has an affair on the side. I'm not mentally able to handle anything like that."

As a handsome man, Stacy's husband may well have a good deal of his need for sensual, sexual and social approval fulfilled in the form of social flattery. And he may have feelings about sex, about himself, and about being approved of and being lovable that have become distorted. If he and Stacy are to become playmates in a loving sense, they need to discuss this issue of his feelings and the issue of her being put in the position of having to create jealousy on his part in order to have a fully participating love-play partner. Nevertheless, it is likely that he would be a good deal more sexually active if he did not have a low sex drive biologically.

A biological difference of this kind cannot be changed. It is one of the most important issues that some partners face in attempting to find a happy life together. It can cause terrible problems between two people unless there is enough basic goodwill and caring between them to make it worth reaching across the difference to find an accommodation. We can reach and stretch for someone we care for because it is worth it to us to create pleasure and delight in them. But if it's physically unrewarding to us, we may not persist.

People learn to accommodate each other with techniques such as those suggested earlier for Sonia and David. A man who is naturally comfortable having sex three times a month can have it six or seven times a month if he learns that he needs to climax only three times a month. A woman who would like sex twelve or fourteen times a month can settle for six or seven times if the sensual, playful part of the relationship is expanded with hugging, caressing and holding.

The ability of two people to make this kind of an adjustment depends upon the presence of deep caring feelings and an intimate knowledge of what the other person needs, wants and fears. Working out a satisfactory sexual relationship requires communication in which there is an awareness of a partner's points of sensitivity and ways of self-protectiveness, and recognition of how the other is asking and not asking for what is wanted.

If there is a lot of unreconciled anger, disappointment and disillusionment between two people, they will not be willing to accommodate each other in this way.

Males Stuck in Teenage Sexuality

For some men, giving a partner physical affection that is not genital is difficult. Because of circumstances in their early lives, the parts of their sexuality that have to do with sensual playfulness or sentimentality have not been developed.

Frequently, a male child—and sometimes a female child—has very little physical affection shown him after the age of five or six. To an adult with this background, hugging and touching outside of intercourse not only does not occur, but is psychologically uncomfortable. A man who has not had unabashed physical contact with his mother in prepuberty and postpuberty tends to separate sexuality from loving and feeling close to another person.

Not having developed the sensual, playful part of one's sexuality also may have to do with the messages about sex that one receives from one's parents. If the messages were negative or upsetting, a young man may have felt extremely awkward and inhibited about his sexual feelings when he was sixteen, seventeen or eighteen. The embarrassment, guilt and anxiety may prevent him from becoming a fully sexually responsive person. He may be able to permit himself to have sex, but feel that he must get it over with as quickly as possible. He may not be able to permit himself to be sentimental, affectionate and playful.

A man stuck with sex that is almost entirely genital is essentially stuck in teenage sexuality.

Most very young men connect sex almost exclusively with

their genitalia. From thirteen to seventeen, the male sees girls, at least in part, as walking vaginas. To a considerable degree, young women are sexual objects to him, and there is a lot of ribald teasing and joking about girls within this attitudinal framework.

At a later point in his development, he begins to develop sentimental feelings of affection and friendship toward women, and begins to see them as persons. Then, more and more, he sees his sexual desire as but a part of his feelings toward women. This change in attitude usually begins when he falls in love with a young woman, but it may occur through direct and open communication about his feelings with his mother. If he has been conditioned in his family to associate physical contact and play with feelings of affection and friendship, this carries over into sex. But if not, sex may remain primarily genital for him. However, many men in their later teens who have some affectionate contact with women spontaneously go through a learning experience that associates affectionate touching and cuddling with sexuality, rediscovering the pleasure of it.

To some extent, there was more likelihood of this learning in earlier eras, when sexual intercourse outside of marriage was largely prohibited by social rules and by young women, at least early in a relationship. Today, since many young women are willing to engage in sexual intercourse almost from the beginning of a relationship, the relationship often does not develop a tender, cuddling, touching phase.

If a man experiences the entire developmental process of becoming a potentially loving man within an important heterosexual relationship, his early attitudes of responding to a woman as a sex object atrophy. He responds to a woman in the various ways in which human beings can relate to one another—as a friend, a confidante, an intellectual companion—with sex as a part of the relationship. Since we never leave attitudes completely behind, something may occasionally trigger ribald humor of a kind that relates to teenage attitudes, but this is generally a momentary response that the man recognizes as coming out of adolescent feelings and images.

However, a significant number of men get stuck in the teenage attitude that women are sex objects to be used or acquired. They may have some growth and added sophistication, but at twenty-seven, thirty-seven or forty-seven, their most powerful visceral reaction to females is unchanged.

Underlying the persistence of this attitude is anger at

women. A very young male generally does not have a sexual partner and often feels terribly frustrated. One of the consequences of this is low-level anger at women, and sometimes a substantial degree of distrust of them. A male may carry these teenage feelings of sexual denial and deprivation by women into later life, even though he may have reached a point where sexual partners are readily available to him.

Much of the sexism that feminists have identified as depersonalizing and dehumanizing to women has to do with this feeling of sexual deprivation on the part of males.

The man who remains stuck in this attitude typically had feelings in early childhood of being controlled and manipulated by women, which created considerable anger. This anger became powerfully reinforced by teenage feelings of sexual deprivation. A man like this never really communicates or shares with a woman. He never reaches the point of deep sentimental ties or of assuaging loneliness. And he often spends a good part of his life and energy trying to fulfill the teenage fantasy of having sex with every attractive woman in sight.

Common Sexual Problems

Often, minor sexual dysfunctions which can be resolved quite easily seem enormous problems to the persons involved, and create great personal pain for years. Premature ejaculation is a common problem of this type.

In his first sexual experience, almost every young male has premature ejaculation. Sex is an unfamiliar and scary experience, and anxiety triggers the involuntary ejaculatory mechanism. Since it is rare for a very young woman to be so intensely sexually responsive that she can be orgasmic in the fifteen to ninety seconds that is the normal span of control of a seventeen- or eighteen-year-old male, he has to learn how to control his ejaculation. Typically, as he becomes more familiar with sexual intercourse, he will last longer and longer before having his climax. But for some men, feelings of fear, doubt, guilt or embarrassment about sex continue to trigger a premature ejaculatory response. Sometimes a part of the problem is simply a lack of sufficient information about sex. A large number of men in their thirties still have the notion that the nature of sexual intercourse is for them to thrust and remove, thrust and remove as rapidly as they can. And that, of course, brings about very early ejaculation.

Until the last decade or two, it was thought that premature ejaculation was incurable or at least very difficult to deal with. We now know that the cure is quite simple. A husband and wife can substantially relieve the problem in two or three days, and over a period of six months can completely solve it. So there is no reason for any male past the age of nineteen or twenty to endure this kind of distress.

To overcome this problem, a man needs adequate knowledge of the alternatives and possibilities of sexual intercourse. He needs to learn that he can enter the vagina and be quiescent for a bit, then thrust actively, then be quiescent again, that he can invite movement of the female and can tell her, "Slow down, I'm getting too close." And he needs to learn enough about female anatomy to trigger her excitement without triggering his own.

There is a chapter on premature ejaculation in the summary of the Masters and Johnson research, *Understanding Human Sexual Inadequacy*,[1] which anyone having this problem should read. If partners follow the instructions there, it is likely they will eliminate the difficulty.

If adequate knowledge about the alternatives possible in sex doesn't solve it, then certain psychological issues are involved. For some couples, hidden anger, irritation and frustration have built up over the situation. Then partners need to open communication about their sexual feelings and experiences with one another. Taking a course in sexuality together or participating in a marriage encounter weekend or a seminar workshop on intimate communication can facilitate this. But sometimes, the help of a third party is required. If you work with a marriage counselor or therapist, these issues usually can be solved rather straightforwardly.

When a man has had a pattern of premature ejaculation for years, he has habit formation and has often built up a great deal of anxiety. So he is particularly likely to need help from a counselor in reducing his anxiety and slowly switching over to new behavior.

He also probably will need the "Upsy-Downsy" trick that Masters and Johnson and others have developed for dealing with this problem.

In this technique, when he feels he is about to ejaculate, he removes himself from the vagina. His partner takes hold

---

[1] *Understanding Human Sexual Inadequacy*, Fred Belliveau and Lin Richter, Bantam Books, 1970.

of his penis, pressing it for four seconds just below the head. The penis becomes semi-limp for a few seconds, then erect again, but has lost some of its intense sensitivity. He then can reenter and last a good deal longer. Each time they do this, his capacity to maintain intercourse without ejaculation extends. Over a period of several months, a process of reconditioning takes place.

Use of one of the ointments that desensitize the skin of the penis, Nupercainal for instance, can be helpful during this process. About two hours before intercourse, a man squeezes out two inches of ointment and spreads that over the top of his penis. He then folds several layers of Kleenex around the area so that it doesn't rub off on his underclothing. In two hours the ointment reaches full effectiveness and can be wiped off with a damp washcloth. For about four hours after that, the tip of the penis is desensitized from fifty to seventy percent. A woman is totally unaware of the ointment and there is no possibility of any negative effect on her sensitivity, for it takes two hours to become effective.

When Sex Gets Off to a Bad Start

For thousands and thousands of couples who started marriage as two embarrassed, awkward youngsters and have never been able to get into a more comfortable frame of mind, sex is discouraging and destructive, creating a great deal of stress. Often they give it up. Thirty-four-year-old Elaine and her husband, married fifteen years, had had this kind of experience.

"He's complimentary and affectionate, but there is just no sex," she told me. "It's been about five months since we've had relations, but there's really never been any to speak of. It started on our wedding night. Both of us were amateurs. I think he feels a failure and has given up, and I have, too. I'd just as soon not be bothered.

"I always felt I had more of a drive than he did. He was the one who said 'Let's wait until we're married.' So that gives you a little insight. At one time early in our marriage, I was attracted to another man. My husband didn't want to know, but he surmised. But he's forgiven me and has never brought it up. He's a beautiful person, really.

"I have suggested therapy, but of course there's the male ego and he would rather not. Actually, I'm not even frustrated anymore. I just don't care. I get a lot of compliments on my physical appearance. I don't know whether that takes care of it or not."

Very often the male thinks that if you go to a counselor or therapist, there is something seriously wrong with you. But in many instances, the only thing "wrong" is that early influences have created attitudes not conducive to a comfortable, confident sexual relationship. Many men are afraid to reveal a sexual problem because any form of sexual inadequacy threatens their egos. Unfortunately, our culture causes us to feel that sexual pleasure is a man's responsibility, although it really is not. It's the responsibility of both partners, and should be a collaboration. But if a man isn't willing to risk some initial embarrassment in order to gain or enhance sexual joy, pleasure and reward for both his partner and himself, he is self-defeating.

A substantial number of couples who have the kind of experience Elaine describes can quickly develop a new and rewarding sexual life between them with the help of a qualified therapist. Many couples who have not had sex for five to fifteen years are able to have normal sex within a few months.

In therapy, marital partners like Elaine and her husband are taken through a reconditioning and reeducation process. For a period of several weeks in which sexual behavior is not permitted, they go through training in sensual discovery and exploration. The man is taught to reexperience his own physical sensuality and the woman to rediscover, or perhaps initially discover, hers. They learn to masturbate, to discover the other's body and then to experiment in sex in ways quite different from what they have done previously. (It is likely that their past sexual repertoire has been so narrow as to be almost nonexistent.) As embarrassment drops away, they gain sexual freedom to play this way and that, and eventually begin to associate sex with new feelings of openness, freedom, joking, laughing, etc., rather than with failure and awkwardness. With less embarrassment and a new awareness of the possibilities in sex, they become free to touch, hold, cuddle, massage, taste and examine each other's bodies. The excitement of this new freedom creates a momentum of its own in continuing sexual excitement.

Poor Sex Can Destroy a Marriage

There are a number of important reasons why a couple in a nonsexual situation should seek help in achieving rewarding sex in a relationship. Not only will a revitalized sexual relationship add a powerful dimension of emotional and physical delight to the lives of both partners, but a satisfactory sexual life triggers the release of hormones that keep a person vigorous and active. Without it, we tend to age prematurely. In many instances, poor or nonexistent sex will destroy a marriage. One like Elaine's might last a long time without changing the sexual relationship, but a marriage involving a sexually aversive female and a male who feels actively rejected, as in the case of twenty-eight-year-old Colin, who discusses his marriage here, is likely to be in crisis in a fairly short period of time if sexual relations are not improved.

"Carol doesn't like sex. She was a virgin when we got married, so she didn't know she didn't like it," he said. "But she hates it, so we don't have much. Most married couples have sex several times a week. Maybe it's only once a week for us. I work at night and she works in the daytime, so she's usually asleep when I get home. I feel deprived and I wonder why she doesn't enjoy it. We don't fight about it. I don't say anything. I just ignore it. I don't know what to do about it. I was inexperienced when we married, too."

Unless Colin and his wife develop a more rewarding relationship sexually, his sense of worth and power may decline dramatically over the next ten years, and he will probably experience and express anger in indirect ways. If Carol is basically a warm and affectionate person, she too is likely to feel a sense of deprivation. It may not sock her for five or ten years, but at some point, she will feel as if she has missed something extremely important in life.

Fifty years ago, these two people might have remained in this kind of relationship for forty or more years, both locking inside themselves a sense of hurt, rejection and loneliness, and becoming embittered. But they won't do that now. Perhaps by the time Colin is thirty-five, a somewhat sexually aggressive young woman will lead him into an affair. Either one of them is ripe for an affair, as a man sure of his own sexuality might awaken Carol sexually. Otherwise, by the time Colin is forty, he will have reached a period in life in which, to put it bluntly, you use it or you lose it. He will very likely have experienced secondary impotence.* At this point, out of sheer desperation,

---

*Primary impotence describes the male who has not been able to have confident penile erection. Secondary impotence describes the male who has had erectile confidence, but who, later in adult life, partly or wholly loses it.

he will find another sex partner to reassure himself that he hasn't lost his sexual capacity. He will probably be filled with guilt in doing this, and if Carol finds out about it, she too will feel guilt. By that time, their relationship will be in bad shape, and very likely will be destroyed.

The marriage need not follow this dismal course. Their problem is a matter of their learning not to be embarrassed and painfully awkward about sex. Learned behavior can be unlearned.

Because of negative sexual conditioning and uncomfortable, unrewarding early experience with sex, Carol probably has suppressed her sexual responsiveness so that few of the physical changes that normally occur in the vagina during sexual arousal take place. So sex is uncomfortable, perhaps even painful to her. She may have *vaginismus,* a contraction of the lower third of the vagina caused by anxiety, which results in painful intercourse. In extreme cases, it is impossible for the penis to enter.

If she and Colin were to go to the Masters and Johnson clinic, or similar clinics for sex therapy, they would be given a large amount of sexual information. Both would learn a great deal about each other's bodies. The woman therapist on the team would encourage Carol to explore her own body and her genitalia. As she learned to manipulate herself for pleasure, and began to create some physical excitement in herself, she would begin to feel what it is like for the vagina to fully lubricate and the pelvic area to become engorged with blood. She and her husband would then participate in *sensate focus,* engaging the other's body to pleasure themselves without intercourse.

By the time they were permitted and encouraged to touch each other genitally (but not to have sexual intercourse), Carol would begin to allow herself to experience sexual excitement. Once you permit yourself this, or mentally approve it, sexual excitement arises, for it is a natural function of the body of every human being.

Only Halfway Free

A great number of people who are in a much less painful place than the last two couples could make good use of some sexual reconditioning. Thirty-three-year-old Helen seemed to be in this category.

"It's my dear sweet husband, whom I love very much," she began. "He has never said anything, but I have the feeling sometimes that he would like to get out and sow his oats, because he didn't do it before we married. I've got a card for him. It says, 'Don't try telling me anything about sex. Show me.' But he would just die of guilt if he did. Is it something I'm not doing? He loves me dearly, but he's just dying."

It is likely that both Helen and her husband have a very active sexual fantasy life, and have developed sexually beyond the point that they have put into practice. However, I suspect that they have not acquired enough sexual freedom and playfulness to allow themselves to tie their fantasies in with their real sex lives.

"Why this hangup with me?" Helen asked, when I suggested this to her. "Why is this wall there? Does it go back to your upbringing? To being hurt? You're afraid to love and afraid to care? I just cannot let myself go with him. I've tried and I just can't. How do you do it?"

Part of the problem may be related to various factors Helen mentioned. But an important part can be attributed to basic early training in sexuality. Because of this, often you can get to the point of viewing yourself intellectually as relatively uninhibited and spontaneous, without being able in your guts to give yourself that same amount of room. Becoming emancipated in our heads doesn't transfer directly to our loins.

It is very difficult for long-term partners to change with each other. Sometimes it is easier to effect a change with someone new. But that can be very costly in terms of the relationship or in guilt.

The Sexual Weekend Workshop

For many people like Helen and her husband, sexual assertiveness weekend workshops, which provide short-term sexual reconditioning, are proving to be a help in breaking out of old patterns. Basically, it is an experience in which sexual fears and anxieties are desensitized and communication is opened up between partners. These goals are achieved by a variety of methods.

The workshop usually starts out by providing a great deal of information about human sexuality, much of which people generally do not know. When new information implies that you've been denying pleasure to yourself or a marital partner for a number of years, it can be very upsetting and difficult to accept. So information is provided in a way that evokes emotions in a group environment where strong personal convictions and feelings can be ventilated.

Then sexual fantasies, fears and other sexual feelings are discussed. Discussion may start with group leaders making sexual statements that are shocking to many of the participants. By degrees, the leaders become more explicit about typical sexual fantasies and desires. Participants join in talking about their own sexual imagery, desires, etc., and as the weekend goes on, people who started out very timidly in this respect become more and more open.

This desensitization process also includes seeing erotic movies and having other experiences new to most of the participants—perhaps dance therapy or sitting nude with others in a Jacuzzi.

Another aspect of the weekend involves a series of instructions for marital partners to explore various ways of physical contact with one another in a private room. They are expected to talk with one another about their feelings concerning this. Here, the primary value is in opening communication. Sometimes this is encouraged by suggesting the use of pen and paper. Each partner may be asked to write a list of secret fantasies, or to keep a diary that may be read by the other partner.

At the end of the weekend, every couple is given a program to follow at home, specifically designed for the particular situation of those two people.

Success in Dealing With Sexual Dysfunction

Starting roughly in puberty, the vast majority of us human beings have a sexual experience every seventy to ninety minutes during sleep every night of our lives, whatever our sexual experience, or lack of it, during our waking hours. A male gets an erection, apparently automatically triggered by the hypothalamus in this seventy- to ninety-minute cycle. A female has the female sexual responses—clitoral enlargement, vaginal lubrication, pelvic engorgement—that usually precede intercourse.

Man alone among the animals has this ongoing readiness for sex. This indicates to biologists and social scientists that sex is a natural human function, serving the human being not just for reproduction or biological equilibrium, but for psychological pleasuring. It relates to a psychophysical need of the human being for gregarious connectedness—for touching, cuddling and affectionate human contact, as well as sexual intercourse and orgasmic responses.

For all but a relatively few people, sexual dysfunction is a psychological problem. More than ninety percent of the people who go to sex clinics for help have no organic basis for their sexual dysfunction. According to Masters and Johnson, this percentage becomes a phenomenal ninety-nine percent when people with two major health problems—advanced alcoholism and diabetes—are not considered.

With reeducation and reconditioning, a great deal of success in assisting sexually dysfunctional individuals has been achieved. With some problems, the Masters and Johnson facility (The Institute for Reproductive Biology, St. Louis, Missouri) has had over ninety percent success, even though success is recognized only when it has been maintained over a five-year period.

However, many people go to sex clinics to deal with sexual dysfunction when that is not their real problem, but is a symptom of other problems that may relate to feelings of alienation, anger, guilt, etc. The most frequent basis for impotence, for instance, is anxiety. Anxiety about sexual performance may be mostly responsible for impotence, but it is also caused by a generalized sense of fear or apprehension about life. Somehow, sex tends to be the central symbolic area in which we act out negative feelings—expectations of failure or rejection—as well as good feelings and joy.

If two people have not resolved nonsexual issues between them—basically, the issue of having a positive life together and having access to each other's feelings—or if a person is troubled by anxiety or depression, an unsatisfactory sex life is likely to be an important symptom of the situation. Unless the basic problems are resolved, treatment of the sexual dysfunction is likely to be ineffective. Some people become sexually functional at a sex clinic with the help of the warm, positive feelings generated there, but later slip part of the way back to where they originally were sexually. For them, psychotherapy for a longer term, perhaps six or eight months or longer, is the probable answer.

Chapter 10

Jealousy is an Awful Pain

In my travels through life, I have yet to meet an individual who did not, to some degree, have feelings of insecurity or inadequacy. The amount of self-doubt varies enormously, of course, ranging all the way from extremes of anxiety that practically incapacitate a person to a minimal amount in those who feel quite self-confident and complete in themselves.

It is in this basic feeling of insecurity that jealousy, one of the most painful, destructive and pervasive of human emotions, has its roots.

Those who have deep anxiety about whether they will ever experience themselves as worthy and gain the esteem of others may be jealous constantly. Feeling shortchanged in personal endowment—physical, intellectual or emotional—they may be continually resentful over what other people have or are or can do, and over the response that others receive from the world in comparison to themselves. Even among less anxious persons, some degree of jealousy is so common as to appear to be endemic to human experience. Studies show that more than ninety percent of the population will admit to having had painful jealousy within any six-month period.

This experience, which is basically the feeling that someone has usurped a position you thought was yours or wanted to be yours, is associated with many relationships. It affects parents in regard to sons- or daughters-in-law. It affects children in regard to parents and step-parents. In work relationships, it may be aroused by a boss who seems to favor another employee. It plays a particularly distressing part in the lives of many people in connection with sexual pairing. Some of the most hellish jealousy is experienced during dating in the mid- and upper teens when young people are testing their desirability as social and sexual partners in the love/infatuation market. Later, jealousy is a painful and upsetting element in many marriages.

In marriage or any other significant pairing, the tendency to be jealous that comes out of a person's inner feelings of insecurity is considerably augmented by traditional conditioning to feelings of possessiveness toward a primary partner. In mild form (when jealousy is essentially a way of communicating that another person is really important to oneself and that one has a need to be reassured that a primary or sexually exclusive relationship exists between the two) it may be a normal framework for possessive feelings in our society, though upsetting and painful.

However, in any relationship in which jealousy is a chronic problem when there is no factual basis for it, it is a tool to control a partner. "I love you and therefore I don't want you to..." says a jealous spouse. Often, jealousy is a weapon in a destructive game of "putting down" as well as controlling a partner. Ernie, thirty-five, was troubled by that kind of jealousy in his wife, Evelyn, when he called.

"I've never had any kind of relationship outside of our marriage," he said. "But my wife often accuses me of doing things. She has always been much too jealous. She had a husband before me who ran around quite a bit, but we've been married seventeen years. She has a lot of good qualities, and this is the only thing wrong with our marriage. But it causes a lot of problems. I don't think she realizes what her jealousy does to me. It really makes you feel like a crumby person when somebody thinks you do all those things all the time."

Actually, Evelyn is quite aware that her jealous accusations make Ernie feel, as he puts it, crumby. She wants to make him feel badly to compensate for fears and doubts she experiences about her own self-worth.

"I think not having much education has made her feel insecure at times," Ernie said, when I raised this point with him. "But she's done well on her own. She's had several good jobs. She's done a lot of things. She's very pretty and a very nice person—one that people find very attractive. They don't find me so interesting, but I've always trusted people."

Evelyn may have considerable success in the outside world and still be plagued by intense feelings of inferiority or inadequacy that come out of her childhood. Her insecurity may date back to when she was three, four or five years old. Perhaps she wasn't given enough loving attention and positive encouragement by her mother. The fact that her first husband had relations with other women is an element in her jealousy, but she wouldn't maintain and reinforce her jealous attitude so long in a second marriage if she didn't have a deep sense of insecurity from earlier years.

The message to Ernie in her jealousy is "I can't believe you really love me." But there is no way that a partner can reassure a jealous spouse. These feelings would be projected in the same way on any important person of the opposite sex.

Other Jealousy Games

Jealousy is often used as a weapon against a partner when a person harbors some deep anger toward the parent of the opposite sex. It gives men a way of being constantly angry at women and gives women a way of being constantly angry at men, because, no matter how much a partner denies being unfaithful, you can always create a basis for justifying your jealous anger.

"I saw you being charming to that woman at the party," a woman may say. Or, "I saw the way you looked at that woman on the street." No matter how shallow or fragile the basis for the expression of jealousy, the accuser doesn't have to confront the fact that he (or she) feels that he never has been treated kindly by anyone of the other gender.

In some relationships, jealousy is used as a weapon in fighting out a power struggle between partners when there is no hint of extramarital sex. In others, partners who don't feel comfortable with their sexuality use jealousy to create upset in the marriage in order to diminish the sensual and sexual aspect of the marriage.

Sometimes, jealousy in the form of fear that a spouse will engage in an extramarital sexual encounter is a simple projection of the jealous person's own desire to do so—a desire the person cannot admit even to himself or herself. It's not at all uncommon for a woman to come into my office, as one did recently, and say, "I've been jealous of my husband for years, but in the past two years I've been terribly jealous of him. Five months ago I got involved with another man myself. I don't quite know how it happened. I met him at a party, and when he asked if he could call me for lunch, on pure impulse I said yes. It's unthinkable, but for the past five months we've been having an affair."

Sometimes a person who is psychologically uncomfortable in being the recipient of warm loving feelings uses jealousy as a way of upsetting and confusing a partner so that love is turned away or defused. In some relationships, two people who each have a good deal of self-doubt and find a close, loving relationship uncomfortable vacillate between encouragement and rejection of each other, taking turns as the jealous spouse over a period of years. As one withdraws from involvement, the other pursues with intense feelings of possession and jealousy. Then, when the loving feelings so eagerly sought begin to be returned, the pursuer withdraws and the other takes on the pursuit.

Psychological discomfort with emotional closeness, to a degree amounting to a fear of intimacy, is usual among extremely jealous persons. Typically, they are lonely people who have a desperate need for love but feel undeserving of it or unlikely to be loved. An extremely jealous person usually forms very few close relationships and feels an ambivalent need to cling desperately to an important one.

Jealousy, a Sign of Lack of Intimacy

Generally, a lack of intimacy is a factor in any jealousy-troubled marriage, even when possessiveness is not extreme. Often, partners lack familiarity with intimacy. This apparently was the case with Kathleen and Tony, married eleven years.

"My husband's mother is a super-martyr type," Kathleen began her story. "She doesn't have much. She takes care of his sister's children and lets his sister kick her around. My husband has a hard time communicating with her and I guess he feels guilty. But in all these eleven years, I still can't get over being jealous of the weekly letter my husband writes her. If he'd just tell me what he writes in the letters, I don't think I'd be so jealous."

Tony's mother, with whom he has a relationship apparently based more on guilt than warmth and closeness is certainly no threat to Kathleen. Her jealousy is understandable only in terms of her own relationship with Tony, which she described as "up and down."

"We can have some fantastic times, then all of a sudden it will just blow up," she said. "I can't anticipate when that will happen. I guess part of it is that Tony likes to do things a certain way and I don't always go along with him. Like when he's watching television, he doesn't want any interruptions. And if some special event we have planned doesn't go off just so, he gets very upset. We have two boys, and the oldest, who is five, is always saying, 'Daddy, I love you.' It's almost as if he knows he's got to give him some positive feedback because he tries very hard to please him.

"Usually, Tony won't talk about differences between us, and I'm afraid to force the issue for fear of making him angry. But when I do talk about something, he listens somewhat, though he doesn't comment. Then he usually makes an improvement within the next few days."

This whole family seems to be substituting emotional possessiveness for emotional communication. The fact that Kathleen cannot anticipate her husband's anger underscores this, for anger that can't be understood by a partner is not situational anger. It is anger that has built up over a period of time in a family in which people are not free to be annoyed, frustrated or angry—not free to feel and communicate whatever they feel.

Kathleen's jealousy is related to this noncommunication with her husband and some of the feelings operating between the two of them. Tony apparently is not confident and comfortable in intimacy with a woman, whether it is his mother or his wife. But Kathleen could safely risk pushing for closer communication with him. If he is loyal enough to hang onto such a marginal relationship with his mother, he is loyal enough to stay with his wife through some rough spots.

Understanding Jealousy

To understand jealousy, you have to look to childhood experience. We learn feelings of possessiveness from our parents, when they assume they own each other and own their children, rather than valuing and respecting each as separate individuals whose style may be different from their own. If parents demonstrate that they care about you by being authoritarian and controlling, you carry a strong bias that the way to show that you care is to monitor and control a partner's life, rather than to accept and enjoy the other person as he or she is.

From childhood experience, we also learn feelings of trust or distrust toward those who are important in our lives. If your parents are trusting people who feel good about themselves and life, and have loyalty and deep affection for one another, their message to you is that the world is a nice place, that there are many nice people in the world. Then you enter childhood and early pre-adult years with feelings of optimism and anticipation that good things will happen to you.

But if you have seen your parents experience a lot of pain with jealousy, whether or not it was connected with extramarital affairs, you are likely to be jealous and possessive in adult relationships.

If you viewed one parent as the responsible one who was home and met family obligations while the other parent played around and was irresponsible, this can powerfully condition you to feel that this is the way love is. You may have learned that one partner is loving and giving, and the other irresponsible and taking, that one is victim, the other victimizer. You may have a deep feeling that love will entail suffering, and that part of that suffering will involve the other person's playing around sexually.

If you have this expectation, even though you marry a person who does not have a natural proclivity for sexual infidelity, you are likely to act out intensely jealous feelings, suspecting a sexual overture in the most innocent contact. You may keep this up until a spouse is provoked into behaving as expected. Twenty-one-year-old Michelle, who has a deep suspicion of men, was in the first stage of acting out such a self-fulfilling prophecy when she called.

"I have a hard time trusting guys," she explained. "I've had quite a few boyfriends who played around behind my back, and I feel I have to keep close tabs on my present boyfriend, because I feel he will do it if he has a chance. I'm extremely jealous. I don't want him to talk to other girls or anything.

"It bothers him that I can't trust him. He says he almost feels like going out and proving that I can't trust him."

If Michelle marries with this attitude, she will quickly create in her husband a sense that he is in a jail cell, making it highly probable that he will have an affair. In expecting it, she is likely to bring it on.

The message in her extreme jealousy is that she doesn't expect to be loved by a man, or to be treated as an equally valuable and worthy person. She fears that unless she locks him in by cutting off his contact with all possible competitors, she will lose him. Her jealousy is a tremendous self-putdown.

During our conversation, Michelle recognized that she lacked confidence in her attractiveness and related this to her childhood, when, daily, she had come home from school crying "because I felt I was ugly."

"As I grew up, guys started noticing me and I turned out to be really pretty," she said. "But I still felt ugly. I feel I have to compete so tremendously with myself. If I gain two pounds, I feel everybody sees it."

Like Michelle, many of us carry into adult life our self-image and feelings from childhood, long after the basis for the feelings has passed: And frequently, we use ourselves in self-defeating ways that come out of this early self-image.

Michelle badly needs to rid herself of this feeling that she is unattractive and unworthy. I suggested that to increase her sense of her own worth, she join one of the self-awareness or consciousness-raising groups of the National Organization of Women. I also suggested a few sessions at the counseling center of her college, preferably with a woman counselor. Everything she can do to build up her sense of her own value will decrease the frightened, powerless possessiveness she acts out.

A major factor in her lack of self-confidence, as in the case of many young women, unfortunately, is that she is convinced that the primary attraction she holds for a man is sexual. She is powerfully conditioned to believe that her only value as a person lies in her physical attractiveness and her sexuality.

Sadly, pretty girls, more often than others, are frequently caught up in this way of valuing themselves and of relating to men. They experience painful times because they tend to attract certain kinds of males who are not very bright and do negotiate on this basis. Brighter, more educated males tend to be afraid of the pretty girl, for whom being pretty is a primary concern, preferring to relate to someone who has more depth and breadth of character. It is difficult for a young woman so strongly influenced to be convinced that she can build a solid foundation of identity by developing other aspects of her self—her charm, vivacity, intelligence, education, etc. But the quality of her whole life depends upon her doing so.

Sibling Jealousy

While the various childhood experiences already mentioned play a part in jealousy, most often one is powerfully conditioned to be jealous by the sibling relationships of childhood in which one competed with brothers and sisters for parental attention, approval and acceptance.

One may also have competed for parental attention with things one can't define, such as parents' involvement with the outside world. Many fathers are "workaholics," building their lives around their work and giving little attention to children. Sometimes a mother is so involved in community affairs that she becomes unavailable to her children, who are fiercely jealous of her involvement with other adults.

Sibling jealousy fades out with time if parents respond to each child as a person and cause their children to feel loved for who they are as individuals. This usually happens if parents are reasonably fair and don't have favorites among children in a strong emotional sense. But when parents emphasize performance, putting the children into fierce competition for parental approval of their achievements, or if parents get some emotional reward from sibling rivalry between their children and reinforce it, sibling hostility can last a lifetime.

If this is your experience, when a spouse has any involvement with another person, that person may symbolically fill the role of a competing sibling, one who is winning. Jealous feelings also can be aroused without the involvement of a third person. You may cast your spouse in the role of "competitive sibling" if he or she is rewarded with attention or success that you want. For instance, if you were a plain girl with an older brother who was thought to be very handsome and you marry a man who attracts attention for his good looks, you may resent it, feeling as if the attention he receives takes something away from you. Many husbands and wives are jealous of their spouse's occupational or social success. Frequently, a woman confesses in the candor of a therapist's consulting room that she does not dare exploit her talents to the fullest because her husband is so jealous, and she fears that further success or recognition would end the marriage.

Jealousy of a mate's previous spouse and competitive feelings toward stepchildren are also common problems growing out of unreconciled sibling rivalry. Thirty-two-year-old Diana talks about such jealousies here.

"When I married my husband, he had three children—two teenage boys and a girl, now nine," she began. "His first wife died of cancer after nineteen years of marriage. We now have a fifteen-month-old son of our own, and my husband loves our son, but he also loves the other three children, as any father would. He wants us to be one family unit. It's a very hard situation for me. I dearly adore my husband, but I feel I'm probably not doing as good a job as his first wife would have done. I'm not used to these big boys, who were very fond of their mother, and I think I've caused some discipline problems. The little girl calls me 'Mom,' but I don't feel I'm a good enough mother to her. I resent her. I associate her with her mother, and I'm very jealous of her mother. I'm jealous of my husband's relationship with his first wife. A couple that spent nineteen years together must have had something.

"My husband says, 'I'm no longer a child. I have reached maturity. Why can't we start from now?' We talk about it for hours. Then he gets mad and we don't talk. Then we do again. We sit in the bathtub and talk. He says, 'I cannot neglect my other children,' and I can understand his paternal feelings. And he says, 'Maybe you will grow to love the children.' And I think, 'Yes, but it's not that easy.' When we go for a ride and take the other kids with us, I resent them. Yet I know that I'm a very important person to this little girl. She does love me. The boys probably realize that I resent them. Yet they're nice boys and they do try.

Sometimes I know that I'm not fair to them, and I feel really bad because whatever I do affects my husband and his whole family. The boys are nearly grown, so I'm not worried about their personalities. I am concerned about the girl's, because her mother was sick for years so she was never close to her. She would love to be close to me now."

Diana's image of being her husband's only focus of love and attention is in conflict with the realities of her life. Her situation cannot be dealt with on a rational intellectual basis, however. She undoubtedly has painful and complicated unfinished emotional business that she needs to deal with. Possibly she was jealous of her mother for her father's attention, or jealous of her father for her mother's attention. Perhaps she was jealous of both in different ways and degrees. Her conversation suggests that she is a cauldron of pain regarding her early relationships with her parents. Very likely she also had a sibling rivalry which never has been reconciled.

In addition to this complicated set of painful feelings, she has a relationship with a man who has a lot of mixed feelings of his own. He has loving feelings for three children from his previous marriage and memories of warmth and affection and good times with his first wife. Probably, he also feels guilty because she died and he lived. And he may have confused feelings about the anger as well as the love that one feels when a spouse becomes seriously ill and then dies.

So the two of them are in a complicated situation that could work out very badly. If they would go into family therapy where a third person would listen and reflect back to them what they are feeling, Diana would have the opportunity to experience and let go of her childhood pain. If they stay in their present situation for ten or fifteen years, her stepchildren will be grown and gone from the home, but the emotional scars and anger are likely to be considerable. She is well on her way to alienating the two boys, to whom a sentimental connection with a mother substitute is probably still important. And she may become rigid in her guilt-ridden but hostile posture toward the little girl.

Adult Jealousy of Children

Stepchildren are by no means the only youngsters who cause jealous feelings in adults. Jealousy of one's own children is a common phenomenon in which one parent, most often the father, is jealous of the affection and attention that the other parent gives the children. Most frequently, it starts with the birth of the first child, a time when the father often feels left out and unimportant. Often, the child hasn't actually made that much difference in the relationship, but it is not possible to convince the jealous spouse of that.

What generally happens in such marriages is that young partners have married without knowing how to be warm and tender or actively affectionate with one another. Feeling awkward and embarrassed about seeking this kind of caring from each other, instead of communicating their desires for it, they start to blame each other for the lack they feel.

"You don't spend any time with me. You're always out playing basketball with your friends," she may say. "You don't try to look good for me," he may respond.

About the time they have begun this kind of criticism, she becomes pregnant without either of them having actively chosen to have a baby. The arrival of the child makes her very important—to the extended family as well as to the child—and gives her an excellent basis for punishing him for real and imagined offenses before and during the pregnancy by paying very little attention to him. He suddenly feels very pushed out and jealous of the child.

This kind of jealousy can continue for years in a marriage when partners who haven't developed a sentimental, affectionate relationship never build intimate communication. This had happened in the marriage of Camilla, thirty-seven, and Andy, thirty-eight. The first child had arrived when they were both still in their teens, and had been quickly followed by two more. Both had tried to fulfill their family responsibilities, but after twenty-two years together, they were very alienated from one another. Andy was jealous of the children and probably identified them, at least in part, as the source of the alienation. But it is unlikely that they were the cause to any significant degree. His jealousy can be understood as a possessive reaction to his feelings of disappointment and futility in the marriage, which has evolved so unsatisfactorily. When two people have a sense of hopelessness, anger and disappointment, and no longer expect positive things from each other, they often view each other as personal property in a negative way. There is the feeling: "I should have joy, pleasure and reward with you, but if there's any pleasure, you have it with someone else. You find pleasure with our kids, with a lady friend, or at a bridge club." Or, when the roles are reversed: "You have fun out playing poker with other men, or at a football game with others." The jealous reaction might be expressed: "How dare you! You're my property and you're not giving me any fun."

Here Camilla gives her view of the situation.

"Andy works long hours. He is gone from seven in the morning until ten at night and works Saturdays, so my life has always been very involved with the children. We have four daughters, nineteen, eighteen, sixteen and five. The eighteen-year-old is married and the other three live at home. Andy is very jealous of the attention I give them. When he comes home at night, no matter what has happened, it's always my fault. But if I try to reprimand one of the girls by taking a privilege away, he says I am doing it to try to hurt him. So no matter which direction I go, I'm wrong. I don't have any outside life other than with the children, so I stay in the house and he says, 'You never put on makeup or dress up for me.' When I put makeup on and dress up to go someplace with the girls, perhaps to a school function, he jumps all over me with, 'Who are you trying to impress?'

"We seldom go anywhere together. I can't remember the last time we went to a movie. Of course, there's always the problem of finding someone to watch the five-year-old. The older girls have their own lives and you can't depend on them. We did more things together until about ten years ago, when his father died. He seemed to change a great deal after that. His father was a very domineering man, but Andy seemed to respect him very much. It's hard to know just how he felt about his death. He won't go to the cemetery and he doesn't like to talk about it. He seems to hold his feelings inside."

Not really involved in the family life, Andy sees himself as outside the family circle and unrewarded by it. He probably feels that all he does is work and deal with irritations and frustrations at home, and that life is going by without much fun and joy. Camilla is in the same boat when it comes to having fun or reward. I suspect that each is blaming the other, either consciously or unconsciously. Each makes the other the enemy instead of collaborating to change their lifestyle in a way that will give each of them some pleasure. They are stuck in hurtful ways of relating, and need to make a major overhaul of the marriage. They need to look at their relationship, identify what each wants out of it and fight their way through to positive goals.

Dealing with Extreme Jealousy

That kind of mutual effort will not resolve jealousy when one person in a partnership is caught up in the extreme possessive feelings talked about earlier in this chapter, however. There is no easy way out of the jealous games that couples often play in that situation. Basically, the jealous person keeps sending the other person the message: "I don't trust you, and my image of marriage (or whatever the relationship) is that I ought to own you." Since there is no way anyone can prove that he or she can be trusted, the relationship can be improved significantly only by changing the attitudes and self-perception of the jealous person.

This can be seen in the remarks of thirty-seven-year-old Vince, who had learned to recognize that his jealousy was unfounded but, nevertheless, had not been able to overcome it.

"I seem to be of a very suspicious nature," he said. "I'm constantly looking for things that aren't there. I've been this way from the day we got married. That was seventeen years ago. And I still keep looking for things, even though I haven't found any in all that time. I know it's my fault and I don't know how to correct it. My wife tries her darnedest."

Vince told me that he is generally regarded as a confident person, and that he feels himself to be confident in much of his dealings with the world, and this may well be the case. But quite plainly he is very insecure when it comes to feeling lovable. He undoubtedly had some painful experiences in seeking and receiving love when he was a child, and is carrying feelings from those experiences into his marriage. Although he recognizes that his attitudes are preventing him from comfortably enjoying an affectionate relationship with his wife, he continues to project his childhood anger and anxiety onto her. Only by confronting and experiencing his painful historical inner feelings can he make the changes in his basic attitudes and perceptions that will modify the relationship for him. To do this, therapy is likely to be necessary.

When a jealous spouse in therapy talks about feelings concerning a partner, strong feelings of ownership and the right to control the other person are revealed. A woman will describe how her husband is doing things she doesn't want him to do and causing her to feel terrible pain and jealousy. Essentially, she sees him as disobeying her. When a therapist feeds back to her how completely she has circumscribed her husband's freedom by her demands that he do this and be that, and how little freedom of action he actually has if he is to remain in her good graces, she begins to sense the reality of her ownership and possession. She also begins to sense the pain that it will cause her to loosen her control.

If control isn't loosened, the partner may flee. Yet, frequently, an extremely jealous person would rather lose the object of jealousy than make the self-change necessary to attenuate the jealousy and loosen control. The loss can be less painful. The partner can then be identified as the bad person who went away. If, in childhood, you could never get the affection that you wanted from the parent of the opposite sex, your feeling that members of the opposite sex are unloving is reinforced.

When Jealousy is Within Reasonable Bounds

When self-doubt and childhood pain are not so excessive that jealousy is extreme, two people who agree that their relationship is a positive one and important to them can take steps on their own to relieve the upset it causes.

They can start by beginning to explore and share inner feelings and attitudes. They might begin by sharing images and fantasies of what they wanted when they were eight years old, how they felt about these dreams, desires and feelings at twelve, fifteen, eighteen, etc., and go on to how they are feeling in the present.

Typically, two people in a primary relationship with strong feelings of possessiveness are not tuned in or responsive to the individuality of the other person. They see each other as a wrapped-up package filling a role. ("You're my wife. Your name is Betty and this is where you live." Or, "You're my husband, John, and you work at such and such a place and we have kids together.") They know little of the other's feelings, fears or dreams. They hear expressions of frustration, dissatisfaction, uneasiness and even hopes and dreams as a ritual of complaints. They do not actually listen to or deal with one another.

When two people begin to listen carefully to each other, trying to identify their separate attitudes on the whole range of important issues with which they are dealing in life—the uses of money and property, child-rearing, relationships with extended family, love and hate—they begin to see each other in a new way. They come to recognize, often with astonishment, that the other is a unique and complicated and largely unknown individual, a very interesting individual with a whole special set of characteristics and attitudes. Then they begin to respond to the uniqueness and the specialness of the other, and become genuinely interested in each other as people. They begin to ask the other, "What do you want out of life?"

In this process of experiencing and expressing self to one another, feelings of possessiveness and the related feelings of jealousy diminish substantially. Couples begin to make room for each other to have separate interests, dreams, enthusiasms and involvements, as well as those which both share.

Sometimes the resulting increased knowledge also operates

rather directly to decrease jealousy. This can be seen in the case of a woman who is offended, as many women are, when her husband looks admiringly at attractive, nubile, very young women. Typically, she feels she is being compared unfavorably with a teenager whom she can't possibly match in physical attractiveness, and she feels resentful. If she is willing to risk asking, "What feelings do you have when you look at that eighteen-year-old?" and her husband is willing to share those feelings with her, she will probably find that she has little reason to feel that she is in competition with the young woman. She may find that looking at the teenager triggers some historical feelings and sexual fantasies in her husband. But as he talks about his feelings, if she asks, "Can you conceive of yourself actually having a sexual relationship with that girl?" his reaction, especially if he is past the age of thirty-five, may well be, "My God, no! I just want to look. I just want the sensual and sexual reactions of looking."

As he tests the fantasy, he may say, "When I was eighteen, if only a girl like that had been sexually free and available to me! Wow! What that would have done for my self-confidence. I might not have been so frustrated." In this way, the woman will probably learn that she is not being compared with the girl, that his fantasy does not have to do with himself as he is now, but with his eighteen- or nineteen-year-old self.

Similarly, a man who feels he is showing some signs of aging may be jealous when he notices his wife being stimulated by an attractive younger man. He needs to understand what is happening. The two of them need to talk about where they are with one another in the here-and-now in regard to fantasies. If they do, he too will probably find that the situation is not as threatening as he thought.

Often, when partners share feelings about jealous attitudes, they recognize that their propensity to jealousy is strongly culturally conditioned. Among persons of Mediterranean family heritage, for instance, men are expected to be deeply concerned about the possibility of being cuckolded. In other cultures, the wife traditionally views the female as the preserver of marriage, and is more likely to be concerned about the likelihood of a spouse straying.

Frequently, partners have not perceived previously the degree to which they have been acting out their particular subcultural heritage. When they gain this understanding, often they can modify their attitudes. People can give up old ways of seeing things when there is a clear, strong reward for making such a change. In this case the objective is that each will feel a good deal more comfortable in the relationship. Heather and Tom, married eleven years, are an example of a couple who would find sharing inner feelings very useful in diminishing the pain of jealousy.

"We're both jealous," Heather told me. "He doesn't show it, but then neither do I. When I confess to him that I'm bothered by jealousy, he says that he is too.

"Before we were married, I used to flirt, but I never have since. And I've never had any reason to suspect him, but when we were first married, I was terribly eaten up by jealousy. I did come to grips with it and I have reached the point where I can go for a couple of years without feeling jealous. Then all of a sudden, something will happen and it will hit me. Yet I really don't know when he would have time to do anything with anybody else. I always know where he is. Once, when we were talking about my being jealous, he said that I have all day to do whatever I want, so I guess that shows he does have jealous feelings.

I think my problem goes back to when I was eighteen and went with a guy who was my first real love. It only lasted a few months, but I was really in love and we were talking about marriage. Then, during the courtship, I found out that he was unfaithful with anyone he could find. He was stringing me along. I had trusted him completely, so it was a real blow. After that, I never trusted any man until I got married."

Heather still doesn't trust any man. But before she called, she had come to realize that communication with her husband about feelings was "the most important thing" they could do to ease their situation.

"But it's kind of hard, you know," she said.

It is. It's difficult for a couple to trust one another deeply enough to share their inner lives. It's risky and scary. But that is what these two must do to overcome their jealousy and create a more rewarding partnership. They need to keep pushing away at expanding the space in which they mutually share feelings without judging each other.

The second thing that Heather and Tom and others troubled by this kind of jealousy could do to diminish upset is to make a contract recognizing that they are separate individuals and each has individual rights. They might go through a "bill of rights" exercise, in which both write out what they think are the inherent rights they take into marriage. Such an exercise often opens up specific issues of concern, as well as general feelings about one's rights as an individual, and gives partners a great deal to discuss.

If two people acknowledge to one another that they have separate realities and separate ways of experiencing and dealing with the world, they can fracture the "fusion delusion" so common in marriage. Jealous feelings are then likely to diminish, because jealousy is a powerful attempt to pretend that we and our spouses are not separate or alone as individuals.

In making a contract recognizing their separateness and individual rights, partners agree to give each other more space and time alone to be separate persons. In a sense, they agree to trust one another.

What most of us want from other people outside of our primary relationship is recognition. We want to be friendly and to have people pay attention to us. If each partner can say to the other, "You can have all the room you want to be a friendly person, to relate to other people, both men and women, on a warm, friendly, even affectionate basis," they will both have taken an important step toward ridding themselves of the terrible bugaboo of fear of sexual straying and lack of loyalty.

When two people are in the posture of being jealous, this is difficult to do, but if they explore and share inner feelings and attitudes, they will become more comfortable with it.

Chapter 11

Reinventing a Failing Marriage

"You don't have a husband," I said to twenty-eight-year-old Connie, as she ended a woeful description of her marriage. Although her husband continued to spend a few hours a night in the same house with her and their two children, essentially he had abandoned her.

"What are you going to do about it?" I asked.

In generations past, when a person was expected to stay married no matter how unrewarding or painful the relationship, no one would have put that question to Connie. The expectation would have been that she was locked into her situation by social, religious and family bonds. Those bonds no longer hold.

Divorce will probably be Connie's answer to her problem sooner or later, although for many unhappily married persons it is not necessarily the best solution, even in this era. One-half to two-thirds of all marriages that are in difficulty or in the process of divorce could become anywhere from reasonably fulfilling to very fulfilling for both partners with the help of adequate marriage counseling or family therapy. But for a marriage to have this potential, both partners must be willing in their deep inner feelings to make the effort necessary to renew contact with one another and recreate the relationship. If one person refuses, it is not a viable partnership. Refusal seemed to be likely in the case of Connie's husband. Here she tells about her marriage.

"I had thought my husband was happy. Then, some time

after the birth of my second baby, he told me he had been very discontented for the last five years," she began. "He had stored things up. I was shocked. I had felt a little discontented too; our marriage had seemed a little boring. But I had thought that it would work out.

"I decided to do all I could to make him happy. I signed up for a course in 'Fascinating Womanhood' to learn more about how to make a husband happy. For six months I really bent over backward and I thought it was working. We got along well. No arguments or fights. I really enjoyed it. Then he told me he wanted a separation. He wanted me to work and make it easy for both of us. Well, I had an eight-month-old baby and a five-year-old. So I said a separation was impossible. He said okay, and nothing more was said. But he is rarely home now. He stays out most of the night and then gets up to go to work at five-thirty. When he is home, he spends time with our five-year-old, but he does not love our baby. And I'm tired of not having any kind of relationship with a man. Sometimes I feel like having his bag packed and saying, 'Get out.' But I have two little girls. I need to at least get my littlest one up on her feet. I am able to be a secretary and can earn a living. But I do not want my child to be raised by someone else all day long.

"I tell him I want to make the marriage work, but he won't talk about our situation. He is so full of hostility toward me. One day we were sitting at the table and I said, 'I am so frustrated by our situation.' He said, 'Frustrated!' and walked out. I have mentioned counseling to him, but he won't go for it at all. He says he is resigned to this type of life for the sake of the children."

By accepting a life that demeans and humiliates her and denies any meaning or reality to the marriage, Connie, in a way, has encouraged her husband to think that he can have a relationship with her on less than a minimum basis for marriage, which is an emotional and physical partnership. In doing this, she is collaborating in the death of her marriage as well as in undermining her own sense of self-worth. Her cooperation in her own rejection is apparent from the time her husband first mentioned some dissatisfaction in the marriage. Then, rather than the two of them taking joint responsibility for improving their relationship, she assumed it was her responsibility to please her husband.

She needs to develop a sense of her own value (a few sessions with a counselor would help her do this), and from that position make some new choices. She should try to negotiate with her husband a minimum set of behavior standards. If she can't get a minimum set of commitments from him, the relationship isn't worth hanging onto.

Accepting misery in marriage as a way of life, as unhappily married people usually did fifty or seventy-five years ago, isn't in the interest of either her children or herself. There are too many unhealthy side effects. Loveless, angry spousal relationships lead to psychosomatic illnesses, depression and other negative effects on mental health. Children who have models of parental relationships that are hostile and sexless carry these models into their own marriages.

As costly and upsetting as divorce is, most sociologists and social psychologists today see it as preferable to having people locked into angry, punitive relationships. However, the fact that a partnership is angry and unhappy does not mean that divorce is the only remedy. Sometimes, making one change in a marriage, resolving one nagging problem or renegotiating one area in which one person feels shortchanged, will affect the entire relationship beneficially much as a break in a log jam releases all the impacted logs into the flow of the river.

Sometimes strong pressure by a counselor or therapist on marital partners to spend a considerable amount of their time doing things that both consider fun revives a marriage. Many couples so identify marriage with responsibilities and obligations that they can hardly imagine having fun in it. They haven't developed ways of playing together to sufficiently offset the problems and demands of day-to-day life.

Sometimes, renewing a marriage is a matter of partners taking a hard look at their style of living and how they feel about it. Couples often have lifestyles that both partners have been conditioned to think is the right way to live, when it is not what either one truly prefers. When the two communicate their desires to one another, they may choose a new lifestyle that is more rewarding to both, perhaps giving up city life for small-town living at a lower economic level.

The Roots of Marital Trouble

Whatever the particular situation in a troubled partnership, degeneration of the marriage commonly begins with lack of communication of inner feelings and negotiation of differences.

The substantial differences that any two people carry into marriage out of their personal backgrounds and experiences are sufficient to set the stage for conflict. Usually, young married people have great doubts about whether they have the right to tell the other person that something about the relationship or the other's behavior offends or disappoints. As unresolved grievances pile up, both partners become unhappy, frustrated people who are very angry with one another and perhaps feel they have chosen the wrong person.

Frequently, one or both spouses have attitudes that make achieving a happy partnership especially difficult.

Many people enter marriage angry at the opposite sex. If a man has not had a warm and affectionate relationship with his mother, particularly if there was more control and criticism than approval from her, he will very likely view his wife as attempting to control or manipulate him, either directly or indirectly. Even a male who has had a relatively good relationship with his mother may have picked up this view from his experience with teachers when very young. Then, in teen years, the male typically has a difficult problem working through his relationship with his mother. The hostility, guilt and fear that may result from his struggle to free himself from his mother's influence may considerably dampen his enthusiasm for his bride. Once the marriage takes place, he may react almost immediately with the thought, "God, I'm trapped."

A young woman who has experienced rejection or a lack of affectionate closeness with her father goes into adult life with the expectation that she will not be treated well by a man, and frequently she is not open to emotional closeness with a man. Often, a woman who has felt jealous of male freedom and prerogatives from early childhood feels shortchanged in relation to men.

Sometimes people who saw their parents being hostile and hurtful to one another have dreadful preconceptions of their roles. Some men have the view that a man is supposed to be brutal, to subject his wife to his will. Some women have an image that women are supposed to be secretively manipulative and control a spouse by indirect, subversive techniques.

Sometimes one spouse has the notion that sex is a club that one uses to subdue the other, or that children are tools with which to brutalize and dominate the other.

Even when you actively reject a good deal of the hostile behavior of your parents in marriage, you have a tendency to repeat the style and behavior patterns of the parent of the same sex and expect the person of the opposite sex to respond in the mode of your other parent.

Feelings and attitudes brought into a marriage also often affect relationships with a partner's parents or friends, or affect reactions to the other's style of life. Often a woman transfers some of her past hostility toward her mother or her grandmother to her mother-in-law. The slightest hint of criticism or disapproval from the new older woman in her life will serve as a peg on which the young wife will hang an enormous sack of historical resentment.

The Uses of Professional Counseling

When two partners are angry and frustrated, they need to become aware of these inner attitudes and expectations that have been brought into the marriage, in order to get a clear sense of what actually is happening between them. They need to get in touch with their own feelings about themselves as individuals, and how they have grown and changed during the marriage. They also need to become aware of all the games, ploys, machinations and emotional business involved in the relationship.

It is often very difficult for two people to attain this kind of awareness without feedback from a third party. On their own, people tend to see their marital behavior in terms of episodes. They tend to self-justify and, in a way, to rewrite history. Sadly, one or the other partner in an impacted situation will often view seeking counseling as indication of weakness or sickness. In fact, two persons who are quite healthy in terms of stability and capacity to deal with the world can have a marriage that is in rapid decline.

The task of the therapist is to listen for what is said and what is not said, to pick up all the nuances of emotional communication—body language and many other clues—in order to get and feed back to a couple a clear sense of the nature and quality of the relationship, of the way two people relate to one another and what they individually want out of life.

The therapist holds up a mirror to the marriage and elicits the kind of communication and emotional contact necessary to clarify whether or not the marriage has a basis for survival. If it does, the therapist helps the couple develop more positive ways of relating.

Usually, a perceptive professional can recognize within a couple of hours with both partners whether or not the relationship has the potential to become a satisfying marriage. This determination rests on whether or not both are within the symbolic circle of a connubial relationship—whether, under all the anger and pain, the two people still have positive feelings of attraction or caring, and identify their partners as being special or central to their lives and expectations. Some degree of latent attraction or affection between two people is needed to motivate them sufficiently to go through the self-clarification, growth and change, and the attendant frustration, pain and anger that are necessary to recreate a rewarding relationship.

Twenty-year-old Betsy and her husband, Hank, were typical of many young, unhappy couples who have the potential for a good relationship, although they were separated when Betsy called.

"I wasn't happy in the marriage, but..." she began, then started to cry.

"We just started going in different directions," she said when she had pulled herself together. "It was so many little things, not any big things. We've been growing apart little by little. When we first got married, I was content to be a housewife, which is all he has ever wanted me to be. He's a real powerful guy and he was running the whole show. Then he went into a new religion and his personality changed. I started resenting staying at home with the baby all the time. I felt I had brains and could to something. I didn't feel important anymore. I wasn't important to him. I'd try to tell him something, and he'd be watching reruns on television.

"Then I got a job and things got worse. So I told him I was going to leave him. I planned to save up money and do it. But we had a big fight and I moved out. Now I'm living with a girlfriend. I quit my job and she's single and it's hard living here with a child. I feel like I'm imposing. I wanted so badly to be independent, but now I'm so afraid.

"Before we separated, we went to a marriage counselor a few times. We went once a week, and for three or four days things would go well. Then our next appointment would approach and we'd start battling again. Every time we went, we were able to get along a little better for an extra day. But then the counselor said he wanted me to go into a group by myself. He said I wasn't happy with myself, so I wouldn't be happy in a relationship with somebody else. When I started working on me, we quit working on the marriage."

It is apparent that Betsy's working on herself and the two of them working on the marriage ought to have proceeded simultaneously. I suggested that she and Hank return to their counselor for work on the marriage, for it appears that they had not gone nearly the full route in renegotiating the partnership, and that she did not really want to give up on it.

"I don't," she agreed. "Yet I wasn't getting anything out of it. He wants me to come home, but I'm afraid that things might be the same."

If Betsy goes home with the understanding that she and Hank are going to reinvent and revitalize the marriage, and they set about making the necessary emotional contact and revising their ways of relating, they can probably convert this unhappy relationship into one that will make both feel good about themselves and each other. Often, couples who are absolutely miserable are able to do this.

However, the two of them need to learn in marriage counseling how to go about this. They need to learn how to make emotional contact with one another and how to give themselves and the other person freedom to feel their own feelings. They need to learn how to renegotiate. There is a lot of interpersonal business to be learned sometimes. It doesn't take long, but it does have to be learned if a marriage is to be renegotiated successfully.

The potential for reinventing a rewarding partnership that I sensed in this marriage of Betsy and Hank seemed to be lacking in that of another caller, Ellen, mother of two. There did not seem to be sufficient positive feelings remaining between herself and her husband after their eleven years together.

"We have nothing in common," she said. "I don't think there's anything about me that he really likes. That's what he tells me. I can't understand why he sticks around. All these years I've fought against giving up. I think I still care for him, or I wouldn't have stuck it out this long, but romantically I don't want to be bothered, although I sort of put on an act. The way I am bothers him. But he doesn't look at himself to see why I am that way. He does just what he wants to do. He'll take off on a Saturday and I'll be home alone the whole day. When he comes home, he's had too much booze. I cannot be romantic, but I'm supposed to be. I think a lot of my problem is that he's done a lot of girl-chasing. I guess I've built up anger over the years, and maybe he has, too."

There is a possibility that two people who are so terribly angry and alienated might eventually reinvent a more rewarding relationship through marriage counseling or family therapy, where all the frustrations and angers that have been kept inside would come roaring out. But it does not seem a strong possibility in this particular case. If Ellen gets in touch with her real feelings toward her husband, she may find them intensely negative. Her statement, "I still care for him," is a standard pro-forma kind of thing. When you have lived with someone and had children with that person, to confess that your deep sentiments are unloving can be painful and guilt-producing. We are trained to withhold negative sentiments for fear of dreadful consequences. Ellen may be going through some justification of her marriage simply because she is terrified of a divorce. Often, people in a relationship such as this find in counseling that they are so disillusioned and disappointed that they cannot relate to the other in a way that provides any real possibility of a happy marriage. At that point they will seriously consider breaking up the relationship.

How to Reinvent a Marriage

If a partnership does have potential for renewal, the first step necessary to move toward that goal is to stop hurtful marital games. Marriage partners with considerable hostility and distrust cannot begin to build a more rewarding relationship without first ceasing habitual ways of interacting that create frustration, anger and feelings of being unloved in each other. These destructive patterns make a better relationship impossible.

Partners must also recognize that every human being has sensitivities. A couple may need a signal ("off limits" will do) that warns, "You're hitting me where I'm vulnerable. You're pushing a button that triggers inner pain in me—some anxiety or guilt or feeling of unworthiness. If you choose to do that, I am going to counterattack or withdraw or protect myself in some other way that is not going to feed positively into our relationship."

If two people truly want a significant, caring relationship, they must respect the other person's "off limits."

It isn't enough to stop negative habits, of course. To start a marriage cycling positively, two people must take down the emotional fences they set up around themselves that say, "You can come this far but no further," and risk revealing some of their inner feelings and inner attitudes to one another. They have to make a commitment that improving the relationship is worth risking, testing and trying, over and over again. The real differences must be fought through to at least partial resolution or compromise. Essentially, two persons have to commit themselves to being flexible, to learning and changing.

Some degree of problem-solving often comes about readily when real communication is opened up between partners. Usually, both persons in an impacted relationship have so concentrated on their own frustrations and dissatisfactions, and have been so fiercely determined to be heard, that they haven't actually listened to the other person. Typically, when a couple comes in for counseling, if I ask a husband to explain his wife's point of view on an issue, he suddenly discovers that beyond a few catch-phrases, he can't begin to represent significantly what she wants or is feeling—what she has frantically been trying to tell him. When I ask the wife to represent her husband's point of view, she discovers the same thing. Beyond what he has screamed and shouted over and over again, she knows nothing of his feelings, even one layer below the surface. "My God! Does she (or he) really feel that? I didn't understand that. I had no idea," a partner often exclaims when the desires and feelings of the other are finally clarified.

In this clarification process, a counselor amplifies or exaggerates what each partner says, so that the message comes through clearly. When this is done, partners are often not only surprised by what the other feels or wants, but are startled to really hear how harshly judgmental or hostile their own remarks to the other person are.

Frequently, one or both persons feel that upsetting behavior by the other is motivated by malice. "I think he really does love to hurt me," or, "I think she enjoys nagging and putting me down," one may say. But often, when both start to understand the other person's feelings and frame of reference, each recognizes that the upsetting behavior has been simply a self-protective response to the partner's fears and doubts about himself or herself.

This does not always happen, of course. A spouse may have developed a strong, unchangeable conviction that the other person is basically malicious and wants to injure. This is most often true when the person who behaves hostilely has such a deep wellspring of historical anger that the slightest provocation triggers uncontrolled lashing out, as in the case of wife-beaters and child-batterers—and husband-abusers, the women who talk a husband into an anxiety state at two in the morning. In such a relationship, there is nothing that can be done to revive the marriage.

In less severe instances, when a spouse who has seen a partner as malicious recognizes the upsetting behavior has actually been a self-protective response, typically each partner begins to see the other more as a vulnerable, needing, wanting human being. Then the hard, defensive shell of self-protectiveness that each has worn starts to melt. Feelings of tenderness and genuine concern for the other arise, with each wanting to give the other at least some of what is wanted.

Each thing that two people do for and with one another helps create feelings in the other of being loved and appreciated. The welling-up of these positive emotions in one person triggers behavior in this person that similarly reinforces positive feelings and sentiments in the other. A counselor attempts to amplify these positive feelings and translate them into a clear understanding that if both persons give, both persons will receive.

If the hostile games of a poor marriage are stopped and positive feelings and ways of behavior are established, both spouses perceive that it is no more difficult for a relationship to cycle positively than it was for it to cycle negatively. It is as easy to be affectionate, appreciative and responsive as it is to be angry, hurtful and injurious to the feelings and esteem of the other person.

However, when a punitive marital game has occurred over a long period of time, it can be difficult to stop it, even when both partners realize that the game is undesirable. Underlying these hurtful habits is the fact that we humans tend to go toward that which is familiar to us, even when it is self-defeating. We tend to repeat and repeat behavior. Every reservoir of underlying goodwill and every bit of self-awareness must be tapped to halt the hostile scenarios. Issues that must be dealt with in reinventing the relationship may trigger deep inner sensitivities. When one person feels that an issue is threatening sensitive feelings of self-protection or self-avoidance, there is a powerful impulse to strike out at the other in old, destructive ways.

Marriage Counseling is Sometimes Inadequate

Sometimes a marriage fails when a successful relationship could have been achieved through adequate counseling for individual partners separately on their own emotional issues. Lack of this kind of assistance is one of the weaknesses of the family-reconciliation counseling provided by some courts, which have not been very successful in bringing couples back together. Court-sponsored counselors are limited to a few sessions per marriage, and usually have no capacity to work with marriage partners individually. Sometimes six months or more of individual counseling is needed before the marriage can be worked on effectively. One or both persons may need to learn to let go of strongly entrenched behavior and fears derived from childhood in order to create a working partnership with another person. This appears to have been the case with the husband of twenty-six-year-old Judy, whose marriage failed despite counseling. With adequate family therapy in which her husband, Rod, would have learned about his style and why he behaves in a certain self-protective way, it might well have been saved.

"We came from different family backgrounds, and being so opposite attracted us when we first met," Judy said. "It was a 'let me show you my world and then we'll have our own' kind of thing. But we never were able to solve our problems. We went through conciliation court counseling and then we went to a private psychiatrist. But it seems that after you've lost that certain feeling, it is almost impossible to establish a good relationship with that person again. I thought he was a responsible person and he was not. I think the more I did, the easier it was for him to sit back and let me do everything. I reached the point where I started losing respect for him. When we were in counseling, he'd start doing things again and we'd start going places, but it was never lasting. When we tried to discuss our differences, I'd get very animated and exaggerated and he would say, 'If we're going to fight, I don't want to talk about it.' I finally got to the point where I said, 'What do I need with him?'"

When either partner is unwilling to fight, and this occurs often, it is difficult to work through a relationship. When I say fight, I don't mean in a destructive way, by putting down or punishing the other in hostile confrontation; I mean constructive fighting in which each person gives the other room to feel his or her own feelings, to express these feelings and then, together, begin to negotiate a reasonable compromise position on a lifestyle together.

For this, both persons need what might be called a creatively selfish approach. We often confuse negative selfishness—the attempt to manipulate or control other people—with positive self-orientation in which you honestly say, "I start with me. I start with what I want and how I am. I'll tell you as openly as I can what my inner feelings are. And if you do the same, we'll deal with each other more openly than if we pretend that we're super-generous people and end up being self-sacrificial."

Differences That Are Hard to Resolve

Some differences between partners can be extremely difficult for couples to work out. A difference in belief systems can be very upsetting. If one person feels strongly about a religion and the other is agnostic or atheistic, or has a different religion, the difference can be a source of continuing pain and anger when children come along. A difference in ethical systems, or in standards of honesty in personal or business dealings, can cause one spouse to identify the other as a bad person. There are many areas in which people offend one another. Differences in styles of expressing affection and in social styles can be tough to resolve, as can differences in sentiments and feelings toward parents. Families often become powerful influences in the problems between couples, especially if a young adult hasn't developed a comfortable way of relating to his or her own parents without being powerfully manipulated by feelings of obligation, anger or guilt.

Sometimes the differences between partners are so great and the issues so profound that an unrealistically large amount of goodwill and capacity to risk would be necessary to reinvent a marriage. At times the differences may amount to basic incompatibility. This may be the case in the seven-year marriage of twenty-five-year-old Joannie, who was troubled by a lack of intellectual stimulation from her twenty-seven-year-old husband when she called.

"My marriage is a case of 'can't live with him and can't live without him,'" she said. "When he's gone during the day, I miss him and look forward to his coming home. But as soon as I see him, I get very depressed. Sometimes I won't even say hello to him because I just get disgusted. I think the main thing is I've outgrown him. I know exactly what he's going to say, no matter what I say. Lots of times I just answer for him and he'll say, 'Huh?' I'll say, 'Yeah, that's what you were going to say.'

"We talk freely together, but I have to talk to him almost

like I'm talking to a child. I cannot explain things to him at my intellectual level. He doesn't want to learn anything more than he knew when he was in the eleventh grade. It's hard to talk to him as a person, as I talk to friends who are in college right now.

"But he's extra good to me and I really do love him. I would never want anything to happen to him and I want the best for him. And though a wave of depression sweeps over me when he comes home, if he would turn and leave, I would want him. How can I be that way?"

What I hear from Joannie is that she has a deep affection for her husband, but is not fulfilled or rewarded in the partnership, at least at the moment.

I suggested that she and her husband see a marriage counselor for a thorough evaluation of their points of compatibility and incompatibility. It is quite possible that her husband is of limited intelligence. It is almost equally possible that he has ample intelligence, but views himself as not being smart and hasn't developed it. It is important for the two of them to find out which is the case. If they are incompatible in intelligence, the probability of their maintaining a loving relationship for a lifetime is not very high. But if the incompatibility is merely the result of a behavior pattern, they can change their situation. They can involve themselves in adult education activities and discussion groups in order to create intellectual stimulation and excitement in their lives.

When an Unhappy Marriage Cannot Be Changed

If a marriage cannot be reinvented in a way that can be reasonably satisfactory to both people, my feeling is that the two people deserve another chance at life. I do not go along with the notion that love in the romantic sense is necessary for a happy marriage, or love in any sense, unless the definition includes tolerable friendship. I don't think intense physical attraction is necessary, nor do most marriage counselors. I think that two people can have a considerable range of differences in attitudes and behavior, and still have a reasonably satisfactory marriage.

But when, as often happens, the affection, loyalty and trust of a connubial relationship are so fractured that each relates to the other primarily by attempting to injure and demean, or takes refuge behind a wall of indifference, a partnership is in a pretty sad state. I think that people deserve better than that. I have seen hundreds of badly distressed marriages in which one or the other partner was not willing, psychologically, emotionally or attitudinally, to change the nature of the relationship.

Sometimes the original attraction and affection has so faded that it is not worth it to that person, or to both persons, to try to renew a marriage. An astonishing number of marriages are so agonizing during the first year that it is difficult for the two people to forgive one another. A powerful avoidance reaction similar to that created in behavior-modification aversive training (such as is sometimes used to train people to give up cigarette smoking) takes place that is difficult to counter.

A good many people who marry are not natural candidates for marriage. They don't want the involvement of an up-close relationship with a spouse, and should not have married in the first place. Some experts cite evidence that up to thirty percent of the adult population is in this category.

Some substantial minority of those who go to a marriage counselor basically don't like one another, or at least they don't like one another as spouses. They chose the wrong person for reasons that were meaningful when they were nineteen or twenty, but their partner is now very different emotionally, attitudinally and even physically from the kind of person they want to be with today.

This seemed basically the case with twenty-eight-year-old Mary, who described her marriage as "rotten" and tells about it here, although her reasons for marrying were hardly sound in the first place.

"I knew my husband for only one day before we married a year later," she said. "He was in the service and I felt sorry for him. I didn't want to send back his engagement ring. The marriage just kind of happened. I think this guy loves me, but I don't think there's anything left in the marriage for me. When I'm away from him with the kids or around other people, I feel happy. When he's around, I'm very moody. I don't want to leave him because I don't want to hurt him. He depends on me a lot. But I'm in such an emotional state now, I don't know.

"I have three kids who don't know exactly what to do with their father either, because he doesn't pay much attention to them. It has reached the point where my twelve-year-old son wants to live at the YMCA to get away from his dad. I'd like to take my kids and have a life of my own and not have to worry about whether he's going to get mad about something. But it's a hard decision. I've thought about marriage counseling, but this man doesn't even want me to go to a doctor. I haven't been to a doctor in years because I don't want to fight and hassle him anymore."

It is pretty clear that Mary's relationship and home life are grim. Her husband loves her in some dependent, needful way, but there are very few rewards in the marriage for her. When he's around, she's depressed. She feels pity for him and perhaps has some anxiety about going out in the world alone. But I hear no positive note of affirmation as a basis for continuing in this relationship.

Her future will probably be quite dismal if she remains in this situation. By the time her children have left home and she is in her mid-forties, it is likely that her feelings of powerlessness will have been reinforced to the point where she will have given up on herself and will be into some compulsive behavior. She may well be an alcoholic, a gambler or obese, or she will have major psychosomatic illnesses. She probably will also have had major stress-related surgery one or two times.

The situation will probably be as hurtful for her husband as it is for her, but in a different way, because he has a different personality and conditioning. It was Mary who called, so we don't know what he is feeling. But undoubtedly he, too, has several kinds of inner pain and guilt.

Chapter 12

Radical Alternatives for Reinventing a Marriage

Just as our lives have critical periods as we pass from one phase or age to another, a marriage has successive stages and periods of crisis in which divorce rates peak.

The very first year or two is a critical period for many couples, as romantic fantasy fades and adjustments are required in the transition from single life to being a married person. In the most successful marriages, the intense romantic idealization stage is supplanted by one in which partners become more real and available to one another, and actively learn about each other. But a great many couples never experience this mutual learning process, which is necessary to creating a close friendship. For thirty-five to forty percent of couples, the honeymoon is a partial or near-total disaster which is translated into virtual noncommunication from that point on. In other partnerships, one or both partners are traumatically upset in the first year by feelings of having lost freedom they were not psychologically prepared to lose.

After five, six or seven years (the period popularly recognized as the "seven-year itch"), many men and women come to see a marriage that started out as fun, as drudgery. Often a woman has had three or more children and views herself as a drone in the grimmest sense of the word. Her husband, whose financial commitments to family and home often seem enormous in comparison with his income at that stage in life, also feels heavily burdened. Each suffers stress and is inclined to blame the other for it.

Frequently, a critical marital period is linked to a particular transition point in life and the feelings associated with it, which act as a catalyst for focusing dissatisfaction and upset in a marriage. Beginning anxieties about facing middle age underlie the critical period that peaks after twelve to thirteen years, when most spouses are in their early or mid-thirties. At this time, concern about the quality of life one is going to have, and whether it will match one's aspirations, becomes paramount. Many persons put responsibility for these anxieties on the other person. They expect a spouse to make them happy and, not feeling happy, they blame the other.

Another period that often leads to marital embattlement occurs after about eighteen years, when a woman who has become less important as a mother and homemaker is experiencing the empty-nest syndrome. This is often followed by a period of crisis between twenty-four and twenty-eight years, when men are often experiencing panic associated with facing fifty. The tremendous feeling, which many have, of having missed something in life, particularly something sexual, is reflected in a high degree of extramarital involvement at this time. Marital strife again peaks around thirty-two years among people who have remained married until the kids are well out of the house, and finally face each other on a one-to-one basis and decide that they don't like each other.

In these periods of crisis, what had seemed tolerable (or even pretty much all right) earlier in a marriage, may become quite intolerable. Partners may then look at one another and say "You're not what I bargained for. This isn't what I want."

Once this kind of feeling begins, it increases rapidly. The sexual relationship, which may have been anywhere from moderately good to moderately bad, declines precipitously, as do other positive factors—warmth, closeness, affection, thoughtfulness, the degree to which partners can count on one another, the quality of social life, etc.

As this occurs, each partner feels more and more rejected and alone. Then childhood feelings of being deserted, abused or unloved well up to feed the process. The result is two embattled people with a great deal of pain and upset. Each identifies the other as the unloving, ungiving, unsupportive enemy, and wants to beat on the other.

Within twenty-four to thirty months after two people become so fiercely embattled, two-thirds divorce. Others, who have sufficient sentimental and emotional ties or moral and religious concerns that they won't give up the marriage despite its unhappy state, may eventually transform the relationship to a largely satisfactory one if they seek marriage counseling. But standard methods of marriage counseling often won't work when partners lack a strong sense of connectedness.

Typically, couples in this situation are people who have carried fears, doubts and negative expectations into the marriage. The man may have been angry at his mother and have a hostile view of all women. The wife may not only be the recipient of this hostility, but may have fears and doubts about men from her early years. Each one may have a negative self-image and blame the other person for not somehow making it right.

A common instance involves a woman who felt unattractive as a child and then had a few years of popularity in her late teens, when for the first time in her life she felt attractive, although deeper down in her feelings she still had an image of herself as the unattractive girl of her childhood. She has retained extra weight after each of several pregnancies, and is now habituated at one hundred and forty-five pounds and is again feeling unattractive. Because the one period of her life in which she felt good about herself was just before her marriage, she blames her husband for her unhappy state, associating him and the marriage with getting fat, being disapproved of, having to contend with the demands of kids, etc.

Her husband, also burdened by the demands of domesticity and feeling dissatisfied with himself for his own historical reasons, is also angry and blames his wife for the disappointing quality of his life. Each identifies the other as the culprit in their misery. So if the two go into marriage counseling, they each go with the idea that the counselor will straighten out the other.

The counselor will try the usual techniques for reconciliation: attempting to initiate active listening and problem solving, and to identify for both partners how they are responding to their own particular life crises or inner emotional business. But they may be unwilling to deal with the emotional problems of their own individual lives and face how much they are using the other person to avoid doing so.

Both have a strong vested interest in not working together on the marriage, because blaming the other person has become central to defending themselves from feeling responsible for the quality of their own lives. If they allow themselves to really hear and respond to the counselor, they will be forced to give up this crutch, and that can be very tough to do—sometimes exquisitely, agonizingly tough. Often partners simply will not do it in the usual counseling situation. So, with a whole constellation of problems between them, they cannot begin to solve any of them.

Such a couple can often be jarred out of old hostile habit patterns and the marriage renewed and reinvented satisfactorily, however, with what I call radical alternatives in marriage counseling.

The Radical Alternatives

There are three levels of radical methods available to a counselor working with such a couple, each more radical than the preceding one.

At the lowest level, a skilled marriage counselor attempts to break down the inflexible, self-righteous postures of the partners simply by shocking them into seeing what they are doing to each other and to the marriage. He discerns how each is using the relationship as a club against the other, takes the litany of indictments of the other person that each makes, and reviews these with the couple. In doing this, he extracts the pure essence of what each has charged, maximizing the charges for shock value. When faced with this version of what they have been saying to and about one another, each is startled and dismayed by the savagery and vitriol of his or her own attack on the other person and shrinks back from it. The counselor then declares that the marriage is doomed, the relationship finished, stating that both spouses have so battered it that it cannot be revived through normal means. This is a second shock to the two persons. For the very first time they are confronted in a very stark way with how they have collaborated hurtfully and destructively to create mutual pain in their relationship, and they are appalled.

Sometimes this in itself will have a strong enough effect so that both persons begin to hear each other and find in themselves a willingness to start a process of bringing the mutual battering to a halt so that healing can begin.

Then intimate communication that has never existed between them can be initiated, along with an active process of forgiving each other for the past and letting go of it. Warmth may then be created between them through touching, physical affection, etc. Each must learn to hear the other in a more tolerant and accepting kind of way, so that both can begin to have some hope of getting more from the relationship, and to believe that they can give to the other without injuring or betraying themselves.

In doing this, each has to give up something very powerful—the notion that the other person is responsible. So both badly need to gain a feeling that they are getting something out of relating in this new way—that through giving, they will get. As the relationship improves, a part of what they get is a sense of excitement over the discovery that they have more power and influence over their own lives than they had believed.

This first alternative may often fail because simply shocking two such embattled persons into seeing their own roles in a marriage breakdown may not be sufficient to start this marriage renewal process. In many cases, each is highly irritated and intolerant of the other, with hostile habit patterns so entrenched that they cannot halt the fighting.

With goodwill and capacity for communication so badly eroded, they cannot come out of any important emotional or intellectual exchange feeling good. Without creating some emotional space between them so that their hostility level can diminish, they are unable to get a positive process started.

The standard radical alternative in this case is a brief separation. This can be a constructive step toward reinventing the marriage if each partner has counseling during that time. It can give both parties the time and the aloneness for some positive processes to occur. A most important one that may get started is that the two people, who are accustomed to railing at each other for not giving them what they want in life, may begin to identify themselves as separate individuals and get in touch with the fact that loneliness, disappointment in life, feelings of depression or oppression, etc., occur in them quite separately from their partner. No longer able to use the other as a scapegoat for the negative feelings they experience, they may learn that these feelings come out of their own needs and fears as individuals. As a result, they may begin to see that the central cause of their unhappiness lies in their own individual ways of experiencing life, and start to let go of the notion of the other person as culprit.

A brief separation may also give two people time to miss some things that they enjoy in the other person and some of the things they are accustomed to having the other person do for them. If they start to seek friendship or love in the outside world, they are very likely to discover that their goals and values in a relationship are different from those of their young years before marriage, and may begin to discard some elements of their disappointment that love in marriage didn't meet their early romantic expectations.

A separation is most likely to be effective in bringing about such changes if it lasts at least sixty to ninety days. Separation for less than thirty days is likely to be worse than useless. Such a short separation arouses feelings of abandonment and of being abused or misused, which feed a sense of distrust between partners. It is not long enough for positive processes to occur, so it usually exacerbates problems without solving any.

For some embattled couples for whom reinventing a satisfying marriage is a possibility, even sixty to ninety days of separation is not sufficient time for the separation to contribute constructively to the relationship. Partners are often not able to adequately clarify and identify their own individuality in that time. They have too far to go to understand clearly that each person's life has its own separate unity, and that to the degree that they have blamed each other for the poor quality of their lives, they have failed to see where they are in their own separate lives and have failed to take responsibility for getting what they want in life.

A separation of two or three months also may not be sufficiently long for one or both partners to satisfy desires to live out youthful fantasies with social and sexual exploration. Frequently, such a separation is a period of frantic chasing for one or both. When they try to get back together, information about a partner's dating and sexual involvement has often reached the other person, causing profound upset and increasing anger.

As a way of dealing with the kind of relationship in which this unsatisfactory result is likely, I have developed a technique of separating marriage partners within the same household. This concept of marriage partners as roommates is now being used by many marriage counselors across the country.

In this kind of experience, you and your partner agree to set aside the marriage for a period of no less than six months and no more than nine months, but remain in the same household. Under the terms of the written contract you sign, you occupy separate bedrooms and give up all marital expectations and demands. Neither of you is responsible for providing the other with companionship, sexual pleasure, entertainment, etc. And neither of you is responsible for preparing the other's meals, doing the other's laundry, or providing anything else for the other. However, mutually acceptable financial arrangements for the six to nine months are set in the contract and cannot be changed, so that if either person has no direct income, the other no longer has monetary control.

Each of you must take responsibility for finding social life outside the marriage, and you are free to have whatever kind of relationships you desire. This does not mean that either or both of you will have extramarital affairs, but it does mean that extramarital affairs are a possible choice. If one of you has been involved with someone outside the marriage, this involvement can now be in the open. Neither of you is free to push an outside relationship in the other's face, however. Dates must be met away from the household and cannot be brought home, for it is unacceptable to use the roommate concept to brutalize or punish one another. But each of you is free to state without explanation or justification that you will be out on a given evening or away for a weekend.

Each of you is required to take individual responsibility for your relationships with your children, parents and other members of the extended family. You are no longer free to be buffered by the other person in those relationships.

If one of you wants to spend an evening with the other, whether to have dinner, watch television, go to a movie or have sex, you are required to ask for it by making a date two days in advance.

The purpose of this kind of arrangement is to totally fracture marital expectations and habitual ways of relating. It does this quite effectively. Often the new household arrangements alone knock the props out from under long-standing power struggles that may have been either explicit or implicit. The arrangement also gives you and your partner time to get deeply enough involved in new experiences and your own personal emotional business so that unconsciously, without even being aware of it, you both begin to forgive and forget things you have been blaming each other for with savage recriminations. After six to nine months, you have been through so much in the way of new experience that you may hardly remember what you were so angry about.

During this time, communication between the two of you is structured to prevent continuing hostile attacks on one another. You are required to have dinner together twice a month to share with one another how you have been and what you are feeling. You can get together more frequently if you choose, but this is discouraged during the first month, so that each of you has time to get a sense of personal aloneness and an awareness of responsibility for the quality of your own life.

In your meetings, you are not permitted to blame the other for *anything*. If one of you starts to indict your partner, that person has the right to say, "Halt! Off limits!" If that doesn't end the indictment, the meeting is over until the next required one.

What Happens Under a Roomates Contract

While the roommates concept is effective in breaking up habitual destructive ways of relating between two embattled spouses and in creating an environment in which the start of a constructive process of rebuilding the marriage is possible, the approach is useful only when two people have sufficient positive feelings for one another underneath the anger to be willing to go through a very painful period in order to fully try to reinvent the marriage.

When you go into this kind of experience, in the beginning you usually experience some loneliness. You soon see that if you want to have fun or any other social rewards, you must take the initiative in seeking them, and you start to internalize responsibility for the quality of your life, rather than projecting responsibility for your happiness on your spouse or others.

At first you may also have feelings of considerable relief in being free of the strains and constraints of marriage, and you may start dating experimentally. However, if your partner begins dating first, you will likely experience jealousy, anger and upset. Ironically, after a month or six weeks your roles are likely to be reversed, with your partner jealous and angry and you dating. Usually, each of you will cycle through these roles several times, although there may be periods when both of you are enjoying some elements of single life.

Each partner is required to develop a separate social life within three or four months that each can identify as pleasing and satisfactory. A woman may socialize mainly with other women and a man with other men if that is what they individually prefer, although I try to make sure there is some cross-gender dating by both persons, as I consider that useful to the learning experience. However, such dating need not have romantic or sexual involvement.

If you are a woman who cannot see yourself in that kind of role, I suggest as a start that you go to a movie with a woman friend, then to a lecture, a concert or the theater with a woman friend or two. After that, I might suggest that you and a woman friend or two visit a cafe where there is music you enjoy. Little by little you expand your activities, becoming more familiar and comfortable in new situations and relationships as you do so. In reaching out for the experiences and contacts you want, you are likely to discover that you have resources you may not have thought you had. You may have social skills and a capacity for warmth and friendliness that you hadn't developed in the late-adolescent years before your marriage. Within weeks you may be saying to yourself, "I'm a fairly attractive person. I'm doing okay out there. I've got three or four friends. There are people who want to be with me." Most probably, you will end up dating in some form, and will be terribly excited about it.

In the first three to six months, much of the anger and bitterness between you and your partner fades. Your tendencies to see each other as frustrating, unloving enemies begin to fall away because you no longer have the structure of marital expectations to sustain them. Historical anger that you have recycled (your "I'm mad at him because he wasn't there for me in the final months of my pregnancy," and his "I despise her for every time I wanted to make love and she turned her back on me") somehow start to fade out.

If you or your partner were overweight, you probably have started to lose the extra pounds as the anger that was translated into obesity diminishes. Other compulsive behavior, such as drinking and gambling, may also be reduced.

Through your social experiences with other persons and the feedback on your experiences in required twice-monthly sessions with your marriage counselor, you begin to know a great deal more about yourself. If you're a man who is angry at women, you discover that you carry that feeling into every relationship with a woman. If you're a woman with a sex-kitten routine (a "poor, powerless, helpless me" game), after you have used it with other males, you begin to see how you act that out. And conversely, if you're a woman who has been inclined to parent your husband, seeing him partly as if he were one of your kids, in new relationships your tendency to relate to a man in that fashion will be pointed out to you. ("Do you mother every man you have a relationship with?" you may be asked.)

If you have been married for more than a few years, you may have found that the value system you grew up with has changed a bit in terms of how men and women deal with one another, and in sexual mores. You may have found more honesty and open self-disclosure and begin to relate in new ways yourself.

As anger fades, you and your partner begin to have fresh views of one another as potential social, intellectual and sexual partners. At the twice-a-month dinners you share, you begin to listen in a more respectful way to your partner and feel you are being listened to in return. After five or six months in the experience, the two of you are talking together as friends on a level of intimate communication that neither of you would have believed possible earlier. This process is, of course, augmented in your visits with your marriage counselor.

By then, you begin to test for answers to the questions in your mind: Am I somebody important in your life? Do you have deeply caring feelings for me? After all of the hurt and disillusionment, is it possible that we can start again to create what we wanted with one another in the first place? Can we have fun together? Can we revitalize intimate conversation? Can we revitalize our sex life?

This testing process is the beginning of a whole new courtship. It may start with an evening together that has turned out to be the most exciting night the two of you have spent together in fifteen or eighteen years. Then one of you may propose a weekend together, which you are entitled to do with forty-eight hours' notice. Your new sense of friendship and camaraderie may now be spiced by renewed intensity of feelings of interest and excitement about the other person.

Shortly after that, your marriage counselor will reengage you in more intense counseling on your relationship with each other, with the objective of inventing a whole new marriage. You will work on intimate communication and on sensual and sexual renewal. You will work on a whole range of specific issues that have been the main battlegrounds of the relationship and are now areas of negotiation. You will talk about how you want to be loved—about the ways of being recognized and appreciated that give you a feeling of being loved. We all have a hierarchy of self-worth in terms of which we want to be recognized, and frequently two people are quite out of touch with what is an indication of love to the other person. At the end of all this, the odds are nearly two to one that you will reinvent a successful, satisfying marriage. Of the more than five hundred couples (on whom I have data) who have gone through the process of the roommates contract, sixty to sixty-five percent have done so. About twenty-five percent have opted for divorce because one or the other partner has fallen in love with somebody else or has decided a single state is preferable to being married. Ten percent have not been able to make a clear-cut decision at the end of the contract. These couples seem to fiddle around for a year or two, either with trial separations or partial renewal of their marriages, but in the end most of this group have divorced.

In comparison, only twenty-five to thirty percent of married couples who legally separate for six months or longer come back together and have a successful marriage. Similarly, only twenty-five to thirty percent of a control group of couples who were considered by myself and other counselors to be good candidates for the roommates concept, but instead went through extended separations of sixty days or more, renewed their marriages.

I do not recommend that two people experiment with this concept without the assistance of a marriage counselor or therapist, however. This kind of experience generates painful and upsetting feelings. It is important to be able to vent those feelings to someone who has a sense of what is going on between partners and can provide some knowledgeable feedback and reassurance. The process is one of accelerated emotional change that can provide an invaluable personal learning experience for each partner, whether the marriage is successfully reinvented or not. But without the help of a knowledgeable and experienced third person, a roommates experiment might be more destructive than helpful.

Chapter 13

Will History Repeat Itself?

Most people find divorce one of the more painful experiences of life. Even when there is a great sense of relief, breaking up a marriage that has lasted three years or more usually creates feelings of loss, guilt, anger and a general sense of failure.

Frequently, there is an enormous readjustment to single life. A woman usually experiences a severe shake-up in loss of dependency. Traditionally trained to see herself as incomplete without a man, and to view a husband, at least in part, as a protector, she suddenly faces the task of becoming an independent adult person. A man who moves to an apartment by himself, leaving his children with his wife, finds himself without a family and, typically, experiences great pain of loss even when the relationship has been a terrible one.

Social life becomes fragmented for both. Single persons don't fit in with others as they did when married. Friends often have conflicts of loyalty and tend to tune out both ex-partners. New kinds of social relationships have to be established, and new kinds of relationships with children.

Ending a marriage also generally has painful practical consequences. A substantial lowering of one's standard of living is usual; there is no way that a given income can do for two households what it previously did for one.

How people react to this constellation of distressing feelings and demands for readjustment varies greatly.

As painful as the experience is, the period of divorce is for many people a time of revitalization and renewal, when they create new and more fulfilling ways of living.

Unfortunately, almost as many people use divorce as an excuse to give up on life and sink into a morass of apathy and depression. Often they find the loneliness of divorce intolerable, and succumb to some compulsive behavior such as alcoholism or obesity. Others rush into another marriage, which sometimes turns out to be no better than the first, and often cycle from marriage to marriage.

Persons who choose a particular post-divorce direction usually share certain traits or ways of responding to life. Those who create a new and more fulfilling way of living typically are people with the will to survive, learn, adapt, change and grow, who go through a period of intense self-learning in the breakup of a marriage.

Those who have identified themselves as powerless, frightened and helpless tend to exaggerate those tendencies and sink into depression. Divorce reaffirms and reinforces their childhood feelings of unworthiness and unlovability.

Those who cycle from one marriage to another again and again usually have little understanding of themselves, of what they want out of life, or how to go about getting it. They gain little self-knowledge in the failure of a marriage. They attempt to avoid the pain and loneliness of divorce by rushing into another relationship, and don't allow themselves the time or make the effort necessary for self-learning and growth. Often they are quite dependent persons, unwilling to take responsibility for their own lives.

This was the case with twenty-four-year-old Jean, who was unhappy in her third marriage when she called. She was very confused about who she was, what she wanted and what choices would be good for her.

"My husband's older than I," she began her account. "I think I fell in love with him because my other husbands were the same age as I. They weren't mature enough. And I had always wanted an older man. I guess I wanted security, to be protected and taken care of. But he treats me like his daughter rather than his wife. He keeps giving me advice with authority like he's my father, not my husband. And he beats me as if I'm a little child. All his friends are his age or older, and when we go someplace, he says he feels I'm just a little kid compared to them. I never had a father, so I guess maybe that's what I was looking for, but I didn't want this. I think he's too old for me. And I think it complicates it that he's black and I'm white, although neither of us brings that up, even when we're fighting. It's just that I think it has something to do with it."

Combining differences in both age and race in a marriage puts extraordinary demands on both partners, as does any double set of areas of major difference—age and education, or education and socioeconomic level. The accommodations required are so great as to make a successful marriage extremely difficult.

To work out well, a black-white relationship needs a great deal of maturity, flexibility and willingness to give on the part of both partners. It requires a degree of inner strength and tolerance and capacity to deal with problems that I don't think Jean has working for her in the marriage.

For an older man–younger woman relationship to be successful, a man must have considerable willingness to give up nurturing and controlling, and provide maximum room for the woman's maturation and development as a person. In some such marriages, the man essentially seeks a daughter—someone he can dominate—rather than a wife, because he is afraid of women and not emotionally prepared to deal with one who is a full-fledged adult person with strength and confidence. When that happens and a young woman like Jean, who has sought a nice daddy to take care of her and be kind to her, finds she has an authoritarian, mean daddy, she acts out teenage rebellion. She tries to frustrate him, to drive him up the wall in many ways.

It seems likely that these two have identified these frustrating roles for themselves and are stuck in them. Jean has rationalized her marital difficulties as simply a matter of her husband's being too old and hasn't gained any understanding of her own role in her marriage failures. She seems destined to repeat this pattern indefinitely.

Self-Defeating Choices of a Partner

Although Jean may seem an extreme example, many people are similarly confused about themselves, and almost guarantee marriage failure by their choices of partners. Often they make the same kind of self-defeating choice over and over again.

For example, some men with a great need for warmth and affection repeatedly seek out women who present themselves very sexually. However, a woman who makes such a presentation often has a great deal of sexual anxiety and is frequently an inhibited, unrewarding sex partner. She may send out all kinds of messages that literally scream at a man, "You can get anything from me but warmth and affection." But such a man will be attracted again and again by this type of woman, who will deny him what he genuinely wants.

Sometimes a person from a cold family in which there was little affection and touching repeatedly marries someone from a warm, affectionate family, then feels uncomfortably pressured by the spouse's demands for physical affection and other warm responses that people with the childhood experience of a cold family usually can't easily give.

Some naturally quiet people marry and remarry lively ones who are loud and boisterous, then find that they can't stand them in marriage. They love the liveliness for a short term, but hate it over an extended period.

Persons who are cautious and careful with money are often attracted by those who spend it profligately. They find it momentarily exciting, but over a long period it drives them wild.

Many people who never had tenderness or supportiveness from parents will choose a spouse who acts out the role of an unloving, disapproving parent. Others, who had overprotective parents, tend to pick spouses who fill the role of the parent who put them down as weak, fearful and dependent childlike persons. Conversely, some people habitually pick the parent role in this kind of situation. This was the case with forty-eight-year-old Louise. She played the role of overprotective mother with the weak, dependent men she married. As soon as they gained some momentum of their own and rejected her manipulation and control, she rid herself of them. Here she talks about her relationships.

"I put my first husband through college. I worked at two jobs and bought a house and furnished it. When he graduated, he thought he was too smart for me, so I dumped him. I had many boyfriends after that, but I was afraid to marry. Then I married one who wanted to be in show business. I got him into show business. He was making good money and started putting me down, although I am a very attractive woman.

"What's the matter with these men? I helped them get started. But they couldn't stand it that I could buy things and meet people. Then they always wanted me back after the divorce. But when I got rid of them, it did not bother me for more than two weeks. After that I was happy.

"I am the type of woman that can really love a man and do anything for him. I am a strong woman. I can speak up for my rights like my father. My mother was like a mouse. She could never speak up. But the men I find are like a death for me. Younger men are always after me. I don't want to raise a child. I may think I love them, but two weeks later I don't care for them. I just go for beautiful eyes or hair. I prefer men who know better than I do."

Fiercely determined not to be like her weak mother, Louise is living her life responding to her love/hate of her father. She seeks out men whom she can temporarily dominate, rather than men who are strong, confident and worthy. The ones she finds are so humiliated by their dependent role, in which they feel that dignity and pride are denied them, that when they get into a position where they don't have to accept the domination, they want to get out of the relationship.

Apparently, Louise is somewhat tired of her role, but she doesn't know how else to be. The only possibility she has of allowing herself to respond to a man as strong as herself, one she could consider worthy and competent, is in changing her attitudes toward herself and becoming less afraid of men.

For a Better Life After Divorce

Most unhappily married people have little or no perception of the overall process that brought their marriage to its unhappy state. They can recount event after event in which they feel that they were mistreated by the other person, but are unaware of the roles each partner acted out or of the individual attitudes, emotional preconceptions and personal styles that were behind the roles.

Divorce is a time when you badly need to get a clear sense of these factors. If you learn the lessons in what really happened between you and your partner, the knowledge will be translated into self-knowledge. As you perceive what went on between the two of you in the marriage, you begin to see what you want and how you want to be. Then you can determine what experiences you want to expose yourself to in order to go from the pain and loneliness of divorce into a more positive experience of life. You have the capacity to shape your life in a way that will please you.

Learning the Lessons of the Marriage

The seeds of opportunity for the self-learning that will aid in revitalizing your life exist in any divorce situation. As a traumatic event that thrusts you into a new kind of life situation, divorce breaks up old ways of dealing with people and offers opportunities to see yourself and test yourself in new ways. A lot of old behavior patterns simply aren't appropriate in new situations.

Some people gain a fresh view of themselves as a series of accustomed behaviors change by happenstance. After separation from a partner, persons who have felt chronically angry and viewed themselves as irritable and irascible sometimes find themselves walking around humming and greeting people with a smile. They rediscover themselves as friendly, fun-loving, outgoing people who have been inhibited or undermined by the frustrations and anger in their marriages, or simply have adopted the behavior of passive, depressed partners.

Sometimes a person who has felt dead sexually begins to see persons of the opposite sex as attractive and potentially exciting. It becomes obvious that the reason for the earlier disinterest was that sex in the marriage had been a negative experience, perhaps because of a sexually inhibited partner. The person who has been without sexual desire may go through a period of sexual exploration and experimentation. In six months he or she may go from one end of the spectrum in sexual interest and desire to the other.

Sometimes considerable learning takes place when two partners are in the process of divorce. While they are working out a property settlement and talking about how they are going to relate to their children, suddenly out spills the backlog of hidden feelings and attitudes that they had never before been able to express to one another.

For some people, the fact that parents and friends express intense concern enables them to break open and pour out previously inhibited feelings and identify things they did not allow themselves to experience within the marriage.

However, most people need actively to seek to learn the lessons of the marriage. Some people do this in talking through the relationship over an extended period of time with an intuitive friend, minister, priest or rabbi. I recommend postmarital counseling to facilitate significant self-learning and aid in working through feelings about the marriage as well as the practical problems of readjustment in relations with children.

Repeating Past Mistakes

If you fail to learn the lessons of an unsuccessful marriage, not only may you repeat a poor choice of partner, but you are likely to repeat mistakes in relating that contributed to the breakdown of your marriage. In fact, you may be a poorer candidate for an intimate relationship than you were originally. Negative childhood attitudes and feelings that may have confused and distorted your view of your first marital relationship and caused you to behave in undesirable ways will have been reinforced with a new dimension of anger, frustration and self-doubt, and will be carried into any new relationship.

For example, a bad marriage commonly reinforces feelings of anger and distrust toward the opposite sex. When you start a marriage or any other close relationship with a subliminal anticipation that the person of the opposite sex is not going to treat you well, typically you create circumstances that will cause your partner not to treat you lovingly. Then you are convinced by this that you were right in the first place in distrusting the affection or kindness of the other person.

If you gain an awareness of these feelings, you can alleviate them by going through a process of opening them up and experiencing the pain, fear, frustrations and anger, or whatever form the feelings take. You can do this not only in counseling, but in groups of other divorced persons in which these kinds of feelings are discussed and acted out. Such groups are sponsored by Parents Without Partners, Young Single Parents, some colleges and other community organizations.

If you do not rid yourself of these feelings, you may anaesthetize or internalize them, but they will remain with you, a latent time bomb to infect and degrade the quality of any new relationship. You may avoid them for several years. But any crisis or period of cross-purposes between you and your new partner will break open the encapsulated anger and distrust. The feelings will flood the relationship, exploding a mini-crisis into a full-blown crisis of confidence between you and your partner. You then are likely to start demeaning, defeating and shortchanging one another. The conversation of twenty-five-year-old Elizabeth, who has divorced her husband, Bob, shows the devastating effect of such feelings. I would guess that Bob, who had been married previously, brought deep distrust of women into his first marriage, where it was reinforced, then carried these scars into marriage with Elizabeth. Discovery of his infertility triggered the release of the feelings into the relationship. There are many other situations in a marriage that might have done so, however.

"He was always good and kind to me and I loved him very much," Elizabeth said. "Then, about two years ago, he started accusing me of having relations with other men or planning to have them. He used to say that I was going out at lunchtime and having a ball. I think it started after he found out he couldn't have children. It was something that he had suspected for years. He is ten years older than I, and had been married before. We hadn't had any plans to have children and I accepted this. I don't think I'm suited to having children, so I felt this would solve the problem for us. We'd always had a fantastic sex life. But he started saying, 'You're going to go out with some guy to get pregnant.' I didn't think I had to defend myself constantly for something I didn't do. When I wouldn't fight back, he would say that showed he was right. I just couldn't take it anymore. I still care about him, but I just can't live with him.

"He keeps saying, 'You don't know what my life is like,' and, 'You're the only thing I ever cared about.' I don't think he could care about me and say the things he has. I told him that he needs to talk to someone professionally. He said there's nothing wrong with him, that it's me. I took so much of it that I got to thinking maybe it was my fault, so I had a long conversation with my doctor. But he said there's nothing wrong with me and to ask Bob to see somebody professionally. He wouldn't do that. I haven't known what else to do, so I've been trying to say, 'It's over. I still care about you and I still care what happens to you, but I don't want to be involved in your life anymore.' He keeps calling and saying, 'Do you want to go to dinner?' When I say no, he says, 'Oh, well, you have other plans. I don't want to ruin them.' I've said, 'Can't we at least be friends?' But he says, 'I don't want to be your friend. I care too much.' I say, 'You can't feel that way and say the things that you've said to me.' And yet I know that I still feel for him something very deep, and I'll probably always feel it for him.

"I decided to try to make a new life for myself, but I haven't been very successful at it. I've drawn myself into a shell. I'm afraid to go out and meet somebody because I'm so afraid I'll let somebody kick me in the teeth again. It's happened so many times."

These two are involved in a tragic event. Elizabeth still has important emotional ties with Bob, whose intense suspicion and anxiety betray some elements of serious psychological upset. Both will end up with deep anger and a reinforced distrust of the opposite sex, and will be very unhappy for a long time unless each learns the lessons in this marriage and gets in contact with these deep feelings. Their relationship came apart for reasons neither can make sense of because they're irrational reasons, emotional reasons. I suggested to Elizabeth that she and Bob dump the whole concept of blame in the situation and seek out a family therapist in order to gain an emotional understanding of the deep, intense feelings operating in them and between them. If, after that, both recognize that they cannot revitalize the marriage in a way that both can accept, at least they will be able to quit as friends.

The Need for Relearning Experiences

Reinforcement of negative attitudes from childhood is not the only way in which a bad marriage may train you to react to people important to you in ways that are destructive. You may have had experiences in marriage that have undermined your confidence in specific areas and need to relearn that everybody is not the way your partner was.

For instance, if your partner was sexually unresponsive, you will have a great deal of anxiety about your capacity to please another person sexually. You are likely to feel very vulnerable, become self-protective and carry a lot of sexual anxiety and insecurity into any new relationship.

You may have had a partner who withdrew when anything created frustration or anger, essentially saying, "I don't want to talk about it." If you have had that experience over and over again, you will have been conditioned to responding with anger, frustration and an immense sense of futility when confronted by differences with another partner, because you will expect your partner to withdraw. Even if your childhood experience conditioned you to feel that everything could be discussed, that people could get angry and still work things through, you will have partly lost the capacity to respond in that way and need to relearn it.

Sometimes, persons in an unhappy marriage lose the capacity to identify what they are actually feeling. When you are involved with someone who is important to you and you experience frustration over and over again, one way of diminishing the anger and pain is to tune out the experience as you would tune a radio so that it is not quite on the station. In a tuned-out state, you do not respond strongly to a wide variety of emotional stimuli and feelings. Many feelings become blended together with noise and static and are compressed into one emotional state that you simply lock into. It may be a state of glumness or passivity or angry confusion. Or it may be constant preoccupation with busy activity. In this state, you lack self-awareness and are unable to identify when you are angry and when you are pleased. You can't discriminate between momentary frustration and rage.

When this state has become habitual, you need a relearning experience in counseling or group therapy, where you will receive intense feedback concerning your experience and how you are using your personality.

Another reason why the self-learning process of therapy or counseling is highly desirable is that divorce brings you into intense contact with primitive fears of being alone, rejected and abandoned. Many men and women have experienced feeling abandoned at some time in childhood, and retain a special sensitivity to those feelings. It may have been caused by parents breaking up, or Daddy going off to war, or a parent being ill for an extended period of time. It is extremely desirable in the dissolution of a marriage not to reinforce these childhood feelings, which are a major factor in the depression and anxiety states of many people. These feelings can be minimized in counseling sessions in which a person clarifies and redefines personal purposes and objectives, gaining a feeling of going on to new opportunities and possibilities.

Relations With Children

If divorcing partners ventilate their anger and other feelings associated with the marriage in counseling sessions and learn what actually happened in their relationship, they can come out of a divorce feeling that they have the potential to be friends, or at least as cooperative and comfortable with one another as is desirable for children in the family.

Divorce need not be destructive or even hurtful to children if parents are reasonably friendly and understand the importance to youngsters that parents neither compete for the children nor attempt to lacerate each other's dignity or image in the eyes of the children. If both parents are supportive and loving and give children a clear sense that they will not be abandoned or deserted by either parent, divorce can be better for the young than living in an unhappy environment, subjected to stress and tension between parents, which creates a hurtful model of adult relationships.

However, children do get hurt when parents use them as weapons against each other. Their natural growth and development, their ego strength, their image of themselves in the world can be sadly undermined.

In the past, in the dissolution of a marriage it was generally assumed that there was a good person and a bad person. Courts attempted to establish guilt for the breakup, and property settlements were based on punishing one partner and rewarding the other. This almost inevitably created or heightened hostility and recriminations that are extremely undesirable for children. The evolution of the idea of irreconcilable differences as the basis for divorce has greatly diminished the punitive nature of marriage dissolution. Although no-fault divorce is presently the law of the land in only a handful of states, more and more courts and legislatures across the country are moving in this direction.

Letting go of a marriage without a great deal of post-divorce hostility is still difficult for many people, however. Often the process is complicated by a strong element of dependency. Many times there is mutual dependency in a marriage. Two people who resent and dislike one another will hold onto the relationship for dear life, fearing that if they let go they won't survive, although sometimes it is only after people have split up that they understand how dependent they were.

Dependency may have played a considerable part in the angry reaction of the husband of twenty-six-year-old Penny, when she decided on divorce.

"I always had to be the strong one in the family," she told me. "He felt his role was to work forty hours and bring in the money. I've had to take care of the children, spank them, make the decisions. I'm tired of it. I want to be a woman. I want to have someone take care of me. I've been in this marriage eleven years, and that's long enough. I want to get out of it now. I'm getting old. I'll be thirty in four years. I think we outgrew each other. What you want at fifteen and what you want at twenty-five are two different things. It was a strong sexual attraction when we were teenagers.

"My husband doesn't want the divorce and he's bitter and nasty. I want to be adult about it. Why can't people just say, 'Okay, we didn't make a go of it,' and let it go without ugliness and fighting? We can't even see each other without arguing. When he comes for the kids, he has to honk his horn.

"We went for marriage counseling before we broke up, but it became too painful for him and he stopped going."

Penny apparently has decided clearly that there is to be no reviving of this marriage, and wants a more graceful exit. It is highly desirable that she and her husband have some additional marriage counseling to work through the unfinished emotional business between them. If in counseling they clarify that neither is at fault or an inferior or bad person, but that they simply have grown apart, it might be possible for them to be friends after they are no longer married. This would be useful to both as well as to the children. Hostility between them will have some unfavorable effects on the children, no matter how the two of them try to be decent and fair. The children will sense the tension and the unresolved feelings. If Penny's husband refuses to go for additional counseling, it would be worthwhile for her to go alone for three to five sessions to ventilate her own anger and clarify the lessons of the marriage. She may then be far more tolerant of her ex-husband's dependency pain.

Improving the Odds for Success in a New Marriage

If you go through an adequate self-learning process during and after divorce, you may come to feel that being married is not congenial to your natural way of being. If you are a part of that segment of the population not suited to marriage, you are not likely to feel happy in any long-term commitment, and marrying again will probably reconstitute the same kind of painful experience as the first time.

You do not need to remarry to have a rewarding life. But whether or not remarriage is your goal, you must take responsibility for designing a fulfilling existence for yourself. You must reach out for the friendships and associations you want. You must test and explore new ways of being. In many ways you have to start all over again.

If you do choose to marry again, your chances for success

in a new partnership will be greatly improved if first you give yourself sufficient time as a single person. It is fairly rare that a marriage consummated in the emotional stress of a divorce holds together well. It takes time to disentangle from the stressful emotional experiences of an unsuccessful marriage if you are not to carry much of the anger, doubts, fears and guilts from it into a new relationship.

People differ tremendously, but, as a generalization, it takes about eighteen months to fully withdraw psychologically from a marriage of two to twelve years. After a marriage of fifteen to thirty years, two to three years of withdrawal may be needed. Usually, the longer the marriage, the longer the time needed for emotional decompression.

Thirty-six-year-old Jerry, whose conversation follows, would have liked to see the process speeded up in the case of the woman he speaks of, but this cannot be done with good results. Here he describes his dilemma.

"I've been going with a woman for almost ten months, and I love her very much. She says she loves me but she doesn't want to discuss marriage. She was married for eighteen years and it was pretty painful, I guess. Her divorce was final just last fall. She says she's just not ready to get married again, but she doesn't want to lose me. She says 'You're everything I want but I just don't feel I'm ready.' I've been divorced longer than she has, and I've reached the point where I'm ready to settle down. I feel we should either discuss marriage or be ready to part. I don't want to force her into anything, and I don't want to make a mistake by breaking it off too hastily. But from my point of view, if I'm the right person for her, she would know it."

If Jerry were to come into my office, I would suggest that he and the woman in his life give themselves six to nine additional months of nonexclusive dating in which they would not be obligated to one another. Even if they are enormously attracted to one another, it is desirable for them not to fence each other in prematurely. They should give the relationship time and space, and view it as a plant that must grow to a certain size before it blooms.

If he pressures her, she may marry him, but if she's not emotionally fully withdrawn from her first marriage—if she has not had some respite, relief and freedom from a painful breakup—she will remarry with a lot of anger deep inside.

Frequently, newly divorced persons need time as single persons not only to disentangle themselves psychologically from the painful experiences of their marriages, but to learn what they are like as separate individuals. In the last memory they have of themselves as single, they may have been eighteen or twenty years old. At the time of divorce they may be thirty-seven, forty-five or fifty. If this is your experience, you may need to explore, test and reinvent ways of being to discover what pleases you as an individual, what your idea of fun is, and what kind of a person would suit you in a long-term commitment. Younger people, in particular, often have special needs for considerable time between marriages to become acquainted with themselves as separate adult individuals. It is best if they remain single for two or three years to learn about themselves and further develop their adult personalities. If you have time to learn to enjoy life as a single person and then decide to marry again, it is likely that the second marriage will be a deeper, richer, more rewarding relationship.

Thirty-seven-year-old Jeannette, who was happy in her second marriage when she called, makes this point here. Her story is an excellent example of the best way to use a marriage breakdown.

"I was nineteen at the time of my first marriage," she began. "We were both in college and it wasn't until we got out that we started to realize we had very different ideas about how we wanted to spend the rest of our lives. We went to a marriage counselor, but I could see that the marriage was not going to succeed. We didn't particularly fight. I never cried. I don't think I ever laughed very much. It was a bitter divorce, but I think I learned a lot through marriage. Looking back now, he is almost like a stranger.

"At the time of the divorce, I was almost twenty-six. I had never lived by myself, or had any serious boyfriends before we were married. I felt I needed someone objective to talk with. I had good friends, but I wasn't sure they were objective. So I continued to see the counselor for quite some time. I was single for three years and I think I needed those years between marriages to learn about myself and meet all kinds of people. I remember going to the grocery store and discovering that I didn't know what kind of bread I liked. That's a trivial thing not to know about yourself. But there were so many things.

"When I finally met the man I'm married to now, it was a natural, comfortable thing. It wasn't like lightning struck, but he was someone I felt I knew. He's my best friend now."

Chapter 14

Live-in Arrangements

Of all the alternatives to traditional marriage that have been experimented with and talked about in recent years, the premarital live-in arrangement is the one that has taken hold and been adopted by large numbers of people.

Probably more than half of such arrangements are an exploratory kind of trial marriage to see if something more in the way of involvement and commitment is down the road. It is rare to find a person under thirty who in deep inner feelings does not want the closeness, stability, intensity and continuity in a relationship that adds up to marriage. But marriage is by no means always a consideration with live-in partners. People of all ages have adopted the lifestyle, and it apparently has different values for different people.

Some divorced persons see matrimony as a jail, and the live-in as a way of having a close relationship without hearing the clanging of prison gates. People in the latter part of life choose this arrangement to avoid complications with estates and adult children, or the loss of a woman's income through marriage. Some couples drift into a live-in quite casually and expect it to be temporary. In many situations, participants regard the live-in as a learning experience, a chance to test and explore how they are with another person, and often to explore nontraditional, equalitarian kinds of relationships in which roles are blurred. To teenagers it is a chance to learn about the opposite sex and about themselves in a connubial-type relationship. Divorced persons often see it as a way of learning the marriage potential of a relationship without risk of repeating the pain, embarrassment and sense of failure of another divorce.

This lifestyle has definite advantages for many people. It also has disadvantages that may be slight or great, depending on the persons involved. Some of these factors are dealt with by the two callers whose conversations follow.

"I'm fairly independent and I wasn't ready to give up my independence all at once just because of something like a wedding," said Marcia. "When you get married in the traditional way, suddenly you haven't anything of your own. The best part of living together is that you can combine your lives gradually. You can give up sections of your independence when you're ready to. I was thinking about the fact that I had my own money. I work and I had that security. The gradual adjustment wasn't as important to him, but fortunately he was willing to wait for me.

"There have been some uncomfortable social pressures, however. I've been more involved with them than he has. It was difficult for me at first with the families. My family resented the fact that I was an adult and could lead the life I wanted. But the most difficult problems have been with his side. He was married before, and his ex-wife has caused quite a bit of difficulty with his twelve-year-old son. She has called me names and told the boy things that are wrong and bad. He doesn't see us acting bad, but he hears about it. So he's confused. But I think that dealing with the problem, deciding how to handle his son and doing this in front of the boy, has brought us closer together. It's a good feeling to know that you can go through problems together and survive them even better than you thought you could."

For another caller, twenty-seven-year-old Molly, a live-in arrangement apparently was necessary for her to rid herself of an upsetting image of men as wife-beaters, which her first marriage had ingrained in her. Not being locked into the relationship, she was able to rebuild her confidence that she could be her own person, feel her own feelings and express them without being beaten.

"My first marriage was so bad I just had to find out if this one would work before getting legally tied into the relationship," she said. "My family opposed my living with a man outside of marriage, however. He is fifteen and a half years older than I am, and they felt that had a lot to do with it. And they wondered why someone my age would have any use for someone his age. He's just a couple of years younger than my mother. Then I turned up pregnant and that added more fuel to the fire.

"For quite some time he was asking for marriage, and I didn't want to get married. Later, when I decided I did want it, he didn't. So we split up. Two weeks later we were back together, and the next day we applied for a marriage license. A couple of weeks later we were married. That changed everything with my family. Now he's the greatest son-in-law that they could have. And we're very happy. Our daughter adds to that, of course. It's funny, but even when my parents disliked what I was doing, they still found extra time for her. She was never made the illegitimate grandchild. She was simply the grandchild and was special in everybody's heart."

The routine of "first he wants marriage and she doesn't; then she wants it and he doesn't (and vice versa)" is very common with live-in partners. Two people don't necessarily arrive at the same emotional place at the same time. This is sometimes a source of a great deal of unhappiness and pain, for the more involved partner frequently views the other's reluctance to marry as rejection. That can be an upsetting and destructive element in the relationship. But these two apparently came out all right.

The Advantages of Simply Living Together

The basic advantage for this couple or any other in living together without marriage is the open-endedness of the relationship. Live-ins don't generally feel any freer from the constraints of possessiveness that operate in a marriage than married people do, although they often think they are going to. When they decide to allow each other freedom to date outside the relationship, they often go through as much pain as young marrieds who decide to have an open marriage. But when their lifestyles do not commingle in a reasonably satisfactory way, or they find that they are growing apart, they do feel freer to end the relationship—not without some guilt, hurt and feelings of rejection, necessarily—but the end is likely to be much less upsetting than a divorce.

Another facet of feeling free to end a relationship is that you also feel freer to test and explore within it. Playing a part in this, of course, is the freedom from the pressures of society's expectations of a marriage.

Sometimes a live-in couple can communicate more openly on differences than can spouses in the early stages of a marriage when they are concerned about the expectations of relatives and others that they're going to be fabulously happy. If one feels angry and shortchanged, it can be easier to express this dissatisfaction with a blunt, "Right now I feel like walking out." If both become irritated to the point that they feel fed up with one another, they can separate for a short period with less intense feelings of desertion and rejection than are involved in the temporary breakup of a marriage, which creates consternation among family members and friends. This freedom to take a respite from the relationship can be of value when two people are in a process of transition from idealized romance to a state in which two admittedly imperfect human beings are trying to work things out.

You Don't Have to be Like Your Parents

For many young people, the most important value in testing and exploring in a live-in relationship that works out well is the unlearning of parental models of what it is to be a man and a woman in a close male-female relationship. Because a live-in arrangement is open-ended, it does not carry the obligations and responsibilities associated with marriage, and this historical conditioning is not likely to play as important a part in it. Not having a preconceived image of the live-in situation and being free to leave it, you do not fall into parent roles as readily. In an extended live-in experience, you may be able to disentangle yourself from these historical associations and recognize that you are not an extension of your parent and are not stuck with your parent's behavior in marriage.

A Live-in Has Disadvantages

Not being locked into a relationship often enables two people to take life less seriously and have fun together without heavy feelings of responsibility and obligation. But there is another side to open-endedness. It causes partners to feel less secure with one another and can create painful feelings in a person who has a powerful need to be loved in secure terms.

Frequently, one or the other person has difficulty saying "I want" because of fear of total rejection and a breakup of the relationship if the other person says a strong no. When partners are testing the marriage potential of a relationship, this kind of anxiety can inhibit openness almost as much as it is likely to be inhibited in the first year or two of marriage.

In some live-in arrangements, openness is inhibited for other reasons. Partners may have chosen this type of relationship because they fear intimacy or are afraid to commit themselves to a deeply sentimental, long-term partnership. They fear not finding the trust and security they would like, so they make a virtue of not making a commitment, and idealize distance.

Another problem with which many young live-in partners must cope is parental opposition to their lifestyle. Opposition may cause them to draw closer together for a time, like allies under attack, but it can also cause a great deal of discomfort. When a live-in arrangement badly offends against parental moral or religious beliefs and lasts for an extended period of time before marriage, it is often difficult and awkward for partners to relate to their own families even after they are married. It is not uncommon for parents to remain resentful and unforgiving, never fully accepting their son-in-law or daughter-in-law, and not even forgiving their own progeny.

It's Not for Everyone

The live-in experience is a considerably more negative one, however, when cohabitation without marriage transgresses against a young partner's own moral or religious beliefs. There are still a substantial number of young people who are raised to feel that sex is immoral outside of marriage. When young people underestimate the strength of early training and, under the influence of less tradition-oriented peers, go into live-in arrangements, their experience can be painful and destructive.

If your religious or moral beliefs identify some part of what you are doing as wrong, anxiety and guilt feelings become a part of the experience. These feelings are not only distressing, but can distort what you might learn in the relationship and can pollute relationships with those who are important to you. You may have such a degree of guilt that you go through a self-rejective or self-punitive experience, or have an angry hostile relationship with somebody you really care for—the person you are living with, perhaps, or parents from whom you really want loving affection. Ultimately, you may associate intimacy with another person with guilt and anguish. This can create a lot of confusion about love and sex and caring feelings in you, which can lessen the probability of your having the capacity for a close, loving relationship in marriage later.

The story of thirty-four-year-old Hilda, who felt deeply humiliated and demeaned by a long-term live-in arrangement, shows how upsetting and destructive negative feelings about this lifestyle can be in a relationship.

"I lived with Mike for ten years and had four children before we got married two years ago," she said. "He was still married to his first wife. It was, 'I'll get a divorce next year,' year after year. Finally I left him and he got his divorce. In a way, I married him kind of out of spite. I felt he owed me something and he owed my children. I felt that my name should be on the record as his wife. It's a security. I believed in marriage all those years, and I felt he was getting the benefits and I was getting nothing. He had nothing to lose and I did. I probably missed many chances of marrying a much better husband.

"He isn't the best husband. We have our differences. But I don't let it bother me. I have my own life to live and he lives his.

"I can't blame him all the way. I went into it with open arms. But it wasn't what I wanted. He never threw up to me that I wasn't his wife, though. He treated me like his wife, with all the respect, and took care of me like a wife. He can't really accept the thing himself. He doesn't like to talk about it."

Hilda and Mike had a very bad experience in living together without marriage. It would have been far, far better for both of them to have decided on marriage or no marriage at a very early point and to have moved one way or the other. The message I hear from Hilda is that she felt too dependent and needful after a year or two in the relationship to stand up for herself and force Mike to clarify his feelings about marriage and come to a decision. By the time she did stand up for herself, she hated him as the agent of her humiliation. She can't forgive him because she can't forgive herself for her own behavior in not standing up for herself when her negative feelings first became troublesome. Unless these two go into family therapy where she can ventilate this anger and they can work their feelings through, there is not much possibility of this becoming a close and happy relationship.

To Have a Good Live-in Experience

Hilda's experience is a powerful illustration of the importance of having ongoing communication between partners about feelings. Each person should know where the other one is emotionally. Attitudes, feelings and even motivations for being in the arrangement often change as a relationship evolves.

It is equally important before going into a live-in arrangement to be open about feelings and attitudes. You should try to define your purposes clearly with one another, and as far as possible identify the kinds of useful learning you can achieve within the arrangement. A major pitfall in a live-in involvement is the possibility that participants may have very different motives for being in a relationship and never communicate these motives to one another.

In some relationships, motives are deliberately concealed by one partner who is an exploiter. In that kind of situation, the other partner may have a profoundly negative experience. Sometimes a woman who thinks of a wife as a drudge or workhorse goes into a live-in arrangement because she wants to be financially taken care of without the responsibilities or obligations of contributing to the relationship as a fully participating partner. Often the situation is reversed. A woman who makes a substantial financial contribution and has hopes of developing a relationship that will lead to a permanent commitment is simply a sex partner and someone to do household chores in the secret agenda of the man.

A large number of people drift into live-in arrangements without making a clear choice of the relationship and without identifying their expectations of one another. They not only do not talk about their expectations, but do not individually think through their own desires.

It is highly desirable that two people actively choose the relationship rather than drift into one in this way. If you make a conscious decision to live with someone, you are more likely to bring up and work through questions that should be discussed. Is it to be a sexually exclusive arrangement? Are you testing its marriage potential? What will the consequences be as regards friends and families? What kind of relationship will you have with any children involved? What will be the financial arrangements? If both persons have jobs and share expenses, finances can usually be worked out without complications. But when one is to stay home as a housekeeper, mother or surrogate mother, the issue is more complicated and particularly needs to be dealt with. There is a need for legal standards for financial protection of long-term live-in partners, and the courts are now dealing with this matter. In any live-in arrangement that goes beyond a year, I feel that both partners should discuss and make honorable arrangements for the security of each in case things between them should go sour. I have seen situations in which a man or a woman with no money of his or her own has lived with another person for three or four years, then had a tremendous blowup. The partner who has owned the house or held the lease on the apartment has ordered the other out of the home that night, or used a threat of eviction to force submission. A person who gets into that kind of position is at the very least short-sighted, and at worst self-punitive and self-defeating. However, usually both get hurt.

If you recognize openly that each of you is bringing into a live-in arrangement all the circumstances of your life—obligations, associations and feelings—and discuss them, you begin to build a foundation for the relationship, a basis for trust, loyalty and affection as it evolves and matures.

When you don't bring these things forward and deal with them, a great deal of emotional thrashing about can occur later, with disillusionment, anger and rejection as the likely outcome.

The experience of thirty-nine-year-old Ruth shows the pain and anger that problems and issues not openly faced and negotiated can cause. She and Brad had drifted into a live-in arrangement without discussing what kind of a relationship they wanted seven and a half years before she called. The arrangement had evolved into what amounted to a spousal partnership, yet they were still not openly facing differences between them that were very upsetting to Ruth.

"He has an awful lot of problems and I guess I must, too, to put up with him," she began her account of their situation. "He's a free-lance commercial artist, and sometimes his work drives him up the wall. When he has a business problem he can't work out, he sits and broods for weeks. Then one day I'll go home, and he'll have moved out bag and baggage. He does it about once a year. The first couple of times, it shattered me. He runs home to his brother and stays two weeks to a month. When he gets his work squared away, he comes back home. His moving out doesn't mean anything to him, but I have a terrible amount of bitterness built up inside of me because of these occurrences, although usually I am able to accept people as they are.

"Yet I feel I can't leave him. I care for him too much. Our relationship is just like we're married. And I hate to go through the whole business all over again of building a relationship with someone else. I'm a special kind of person. I don't drink. I don't smoke. I like outdoor living. He has all these oddities that I have. So I don't feel like I could start all over again. When he's gone, I'm miserable. I feel that I have to learn to accept him as he is. When we first met, I kept trying to change him. I know the proper attitude is to just let him go wherever he wants to go. But somehow I need to get rid of this resentment."

Brad's running away from home when he is under stress undoubtedly creates tremendous feelings of being deserted in Ruth, making her feel that rather than being his primary resource, basically she is not. She needs to let him know how terribly upsetting this is to her, and negotiate some surcease from this kind of treatment. She has the right to identify her feelings, needs and desires to him and renegotiate upsetting elements in the relationship, just as he has the right to identify his emotional needs and desires and seek what he wants, for these two constitute a family. After so many years together, they have an emotional marriage and each one affects the other in deeply meaningful ways.

Apparently, Ruth has very insecure feelings about her own lovability and self-worth that make it extremely hard for her to ask for what she wants, which is a loving, caring commitment with someone who will not desert her. Instead of demanding that she acts as a self-sacrificing mother substitute for him. That is not using herself well.

She can't change Brad's tendency toward intense frustration and depression. But he can change it if he engages in some learning about himself and his self-defeating patterns of behavior, whether these have to do with taking on some jobs that are too difficult for him or whatever. These two really need family therapy to get a clearer sense of what they are doing and how they are doing it, to one another and to themselves.

Pitfalls for the Recently Divorced

Quite frequently, problems arise in live-in arrangements because one partner has not psychologically terminated involvement with, and emotional feelings toward, a previous partner. After the breakup of a marriage, many persons who are feeling a lot of pain over the loss of intimacy and loss of the routine of having the company of another person, frantically search around for someone to fill the gap in their lives and quickly jump into a live-in arrangement. Often the result is a disaster.

Typically, when you have just ended a spousal relationship, you haven't rid yourself of anger and disappointment. You haven't a clear understanding of what happened between you and the other person, and you aren't yet comfortable with your feelings. When you jump into a new relationship without giving yourself time to disengage emotionally from the old one, not only are you likely to pick someone not suitable, but you carry a lot of the old negative emotional feelings and ways of responding into your new relationship, just as you would into a new marriage. After a fairly short period of time you are likely to transfer some of your angry feelings toward your past spouse to your new partner and begin to repeat your earlier experiences, sometimes in a worse way. You need to be a separate, single individual for a while.

Thirty-four-year-old Alex, whose live-in partner, Fran, called the program, is an example of a man who has not given himself adequate time alone after breaking up his marriage. After living with Fran for two years, he still needs time by himself to go through the pain of the dissolution of the marriage and the loss of being in the household with his children. Here, Fran describes the upset this is causing in their relationship.

"We are not married because he is still married, but I feel that his relationship with his wife is completely over. She is dating and they both realize they're going to get a divorce. But they have two children, four and six, and every Saturday morning, sometimes before I get up, he is over there for ten or twelve hours. I have never met the children and they have no idea where he lives. In the last couple of weeks, his wife has been working for the first time. He's been on vacation and has been spending every day at her house taking care of the kids, instead of sending them to the day-care center where they will go when he has to go back to work.

"I wondered what you think of a man keeping his children away from me and his new way of life. It's our only problem. A couple of months ago it came to a head. I couldn't stand it any longer and we discussed it for three days. We almost broke up. But he didn't want that. Later he told me he had decided that he had been wrong in his thinking and that he has to start changing things. But that was two months ago and nothing has changed. It's hard for me to weigh the situation, because I don't know him as a father. I haven't seen him as one. I only know him as my lover. He thinks that his wife will remarry, but the thought of another father coming in bothers him. He went to a psychologist who told him he should be thankful that the other man would be willing to come in and love his children."

What anyone "should feel," and what he or she does feel, may be very different. Alex feels what he feels. But if he has that much guilt and anguish and compartmentalization of feelings before he and Fran are married, she had best find out what lies under the tip of the iceberg in terms of feelings, for this problem may be deeper and broader than she suggests, and may threaten their relationship. At the least, Alex is a deeply troubled man.

The general experience of fathers who are divorced and feel close to their children is that they can maintain a loving relationship with them while integrating them into their lives with new women friends or a future wife. Quite often, a stepmother is able to achieve a very close and loving relationship with her husband's children.

The Impact of a Live-in on Children

Many divorced persons who have had painful experiences in marriage feel a strong need to explore how they relate to another person in a live-in arrangement before contemplating marriage, and often it takes quite a long time in the situation before they feel really secure. So, more and more frequently, children have parents who have live-in partners. Often the children are a part of the household of the parent with the live-in arrangement. There is no single answer to how living in this situation will affect children, but the arrangement is not *necessarily* bad for them. It depends on the attitudes of both of the child's natural parents, as well as the feelings between the live-in and his or her partner. Often an ex-spouse with some jealousy or historical anger will strike out at the other parent to the children, not recognizing how destructive and hurtful this is for them. The situation may be especially escalated in the case of a live-in arrangement if the lifestyle is offensive to the ex-spouse's beliefs. But if a child is not to be victimized by a parental power struggle over what is right and what is wrong on this or any other issue, parents need to have a great deal of tolerance for the attitudes and value system of the other person.

How a live-in arrangement will affect a child also depends on whether or not the live-in partner is a warm, loving person who is open to affectionate relationships with children, and what sort of ties the children have with the natural parent who is not in the household. If either partner, especially the woman, feels emotionally embarrassed by the arrangement, that is likely to affect a child negatively. The attitudes and responses of the extended family, neighbors, etc., also may play a part. If a live-in arrangement creates severe stress in the extended family, children pick that up and respond by feeling that they have to choose sides—with mommy against grandma, say. This can create a great deal of anguish, guilt and anger in a child.

But in general, a child who has the experience of a fairly stable, emotionally pleasurable and happy household that includes a natural parent and a live-in parent substitute is better off than a child who is living with one parent alone, especially if that parent is feeling lonely and shortchanged by life.

Most children are very flexible and adaptable. Young children, in particular, are usually open to being loved and to giving love in a relationship very quickly. Basically they are looking for warmth, affection and positive reinforcement from loving persons. They will identify almost any situation as normal, provided they feel safe, comfortable and loved.

There are exceptions, of course. Angry, emotionally upset children who feel embattled by life, or by parents or parent substitutes, will not have this adaptability. Accommodation by an older child is also much more complex.

It can be particularly difficult for a teenage girl, for she typically has some feelings of sexual competition with her mother for male attention, whether this competition is explicit or quite low-key. If she lives with a mother who has a live-in partner, she may have an inclination to compete with her mother for the attentions of the man. If she lives with her father, and another woman moves not only into the house but into her father's bed, that can be very upsetting to her. She's in a competitive situation in which she cannot win, at least not in any healthy way.

An older boy also may have problems. If his father has a live-in partner, he probably has a natural loyalty to his mother and is likely to feel that he ought to resent the woman. Even if his father marries again, he may have some prejudgment that his stepmother is not good enough, but this feeling is likely to be stronger in a live-in situation, which lacks full social approval and supportiveness. It is likely to require considerable trust and understanding between father and son to create a climate in which a twelve-year-old will be willing to give the woman a fair chance. However, by the time this boy is sixteen, he may be battling to free himself from control or smothering by his mother. At that point he may seek out a close friendship with his father's live-in partner as a way of offsetting his feeling of embattlement with his mother.

Sometimes at this age, girls as well as boys reverse the common situation in this way and see a father's live-in partner as something like a young aunt, who is less judgmental and less controlling than their mother.

Here, twenty-four-year-old Sandy discusses her concern about the effects of a live-in arrangement on her four-year-old daughter.

"The man I'm going with has asked me to move in and then possibly get married," she said. "I have a four-year-old daughter who is in great condition emotionally right now, and I worry about what might happen to her if I move in with Kurt and it doesn't work.

"In the last two years I've tried to let my daughter participate in all my decisions. I feel she has a right to, because she is part of my family. The other night, Kurt and I asked her what she thought about us living with him. Kurt likes children and is very good with them, but she is very jealous of anybody who tries to have close contact with me, and she proceeded to tell us about her other family with her daddy and myself.

"She'd rather be with Kurt and me on Sundays than with her dad. She'd rather be with me alone, but when it comes time for her to go with her dad and she knows I am doing something on that day with Kurt or someone else, she would rather be with me and whomever. But for some reason she always brings up her dad when she sees me getting close to somebody else."

Whether or not Sandy and Kurt go into a live-in arrangement as a test of whether or not they should marry is a decision that they ought to make without bringing a child into emotional collaboration on it. It involves feelings and issues a child is not prepared to deal with. Their decision should take Sandy's daughter into account, but not as a participant in making the decision.

If a surrogate father is brought into the household, the child will go through a major adjustment. If he leaves after she has developed a significant relationship with him, she will have some feelings of desertion or rejection. How strong these will be will depend in part on the strength of her relationship with her natural father. But if Sandy becomes overly committed to her daughter's desire to have her mother to herself, Sandy will become angry with her. Her anger will be a greater threat to her daughter's security,stability and well-being than would the possibility of the loss of Kurt if the relationship falls through.

When there is real caring between the adults in a live-in arrangement and the partnership lasts a fair amount of time— a year or two or more—the situation is not likely to hurt a child unacceptably. The effects would be similar were the adults to marry and be divorced.

However, a live-in arrangement that comes about without a significant caring relationship between partners is very undesirable for a child, who picks up feelings in the home. Such pairings are likely to be short-lived, and a parent may go from one live-in to another repeatedly. This can give a child an emotionally damaging model of human existence. The child gets the impression that relationships are transient and that people use one another and throw one another away—or that people use one another in ways that are not kind or caring, and relationships end up with people feeling used and angry.

Parents with children in the home owe it to the children and to themselves not to have a parade of live-in partners passing through the home. They owe it to the children and to themselves to work through any relationship to the point where it is a very important relationship. One should have a live-in arrangement only if it is truly acceptable to oneself emotionally, psychologically and socially.

Elinor, a mother who is exercising that kind of care in her life, expresses her views here.

"When you're divorced, there's a void that can't be filled just by going to bed with a man for the night. I believe that every divorced person has this void," she told me. "And I think that nine out of ten times when a woman goes to live with a man, it's because she cannot make it on her own, either psychologically or financially. But I am not going to go out and live with a man just to fill that need. I have a six-year-old daughter and I do not feel that it is psychologically right for me to bring a man into our home and then have him leave. Little girls have a way of putting their mothers on pedestals, and I would hate to fall off and break my neck in her eyes.

"I have had about three offers to live-in since my divorce two years ago. I intend to do it when the right time comes, but in the case of each of these men, I had second thoughts about it. I felt that if I had second thoughts, I didn't really love the man. If I had loved him, I would have gone right into it without thinking.

"Actually, I know I haven't met the right man because each day I enjoy meeting new people—women as well as men. And I say to myself in the morning, 'This is a great day and I wonder whom I will meet today.' I've met many intelligent people and I've had nice relationships as far as dating."

When Live-in Partners Marry

Many live-in partners eventually marry. How these marriages work out varies greatly. Unfortunately, couples often decide on marriage even after it has become apparent that the relationship is not a desirable one. An astonishing number of young persons who go into this supposedly open-ended arrangement cannot allow themselves to break it up. They try a live-in because they want a learning experience and peer group approval. But when it comes down to the nitty-gritty of the situation, their moral training—that in order to cohabit you should be married—grabs them. Or perhaps one is especially sensitive to rejection and feels unable to say, "I don't want to marry you and I don't want to live with you anymore." Time and again, I have had young people tell me, "We lived together six months (or a year or more) and it was going downhill. We knew it was not a good choice for either of us. But about the time we should have broken up, one of us said, 'Let's get married.' And we did."

Not all marriages of partners who have been comfortable in a live-in arrangement work out well either. Marriage may change a relationship for the better or for the worse. There is always some change, the essential one being that the whole weight of social consensus and law superimposes obligations and responsibilities on the relationship, which has been optional up to now. Depending on the attitudes and psychological conditioning of the individuals involved, this may affect the relationship anywhere from slightly to profoundly.

Some people who have cohabited comfortably are intensely distressed by marriage almost immediately. Feelings of being burdened and historical images of parents being punitive to one another come down on them, and suddenly, behavior in a spouse that was anything from tolerable to appealing in the prior live-in situation generates anger because it is associated with the insensitive, controlling or avoiding behavior of one or the other parent.

Often this happens because a live-in arrangement has been too short and both partners have been acting out roles they think the other person will like, as is common in the romantic-fantasy period of a relationship. But sometimes it happens to longer-term live-ins as well.

However, people who have not had a good model of a marriage in their parents, but during a year or two of living together have learned that they can relate in different and better ways, find that marriage is an affirmative experience that confirms and reinforces the positive things the two have created in the relationship. The commitment to long-term involvement and the sense of security, trust and partnership that marriage brings add a new dimension of warmth and appreciation. For many people there is also a relief in having family, religious and social sanction for cohabiting. Marriage is guilt-free and they feel much more comfortable.

Live-in partners who are testing the marriage potential in a relationship ought to explore and experiment in relating to one another in a way that is a fairly close simulation of how they want to be during the first years of marriage. They should consciously use the live-in experience to learn about themselves, because conflicts and angers that are held in abeyance in the live-in are likely to be exacerbated by marriage.

This will almost certainly be the experience of nineteen-year-old Carrie and twenty-three-year-old Greg, who called the radio program a week before their marriage after a year and a half of living together. They apparently had no idea of how to achieve a real partnership, and were flip-flopping back and forth from one to the other taking the dominant or subordinate role in the relationship. They will expect marriage to make them loving and trusting partners and will be quickly disillusioned. Instead of eliminating distrust and the implicit hostility toward the opposite sex already operating in their relationship, marriage will exaggerate these feelings that come out of historical associations.

Here, Greg describes the hostile control-and-counter-control game these two are playing.

"Sometimes I let her have her way too much. I wait on her hand and foot the way she wants and she spends all the money she wants and does anything she wants. Then she starts taking advantage and I kind of start laying the law down. I tell her, 'This has got to stop.' And she eases off. Then she lets me go astray too much and then she pulls me back."

This hostile game is a way of saying, "I'm using you and you're using me and I'm going to get mad but I'm going to inhibit it and you're going to get mad and you're going to do the same thing." It may seem fairly light and carefree to them now, but when they marry, the relationship is no longer optional and the behavior is no longer behavior that they can choose to engage in or not. Then it is likely to become a heavy and angry struggle for power, as a lot of feelings that are submerged come out.

A Summing-up

There is considerable evidence that many young partners who live together learn a good deal in the experience. Typically, much of the mythology and unrealistic expectations of the young, related to love and sexuality, fall away. For a young person who has not had a sibling of the opposite sex within an age range that provides a community of interests, the opportunity to experience a contemporary of the opposite sex at close range provides a very important kind of learning. The live-in also provides learning about the give-and-take necessary in relating to another person up close and learning about oneself in a connubial-type relationship. The seven basic areas of difference between people that cause trouble in a marriage also come up in a live-in situation: attitudes about sex; the use of money, religion and other belief systems; intellectual companionship; the quality and character of social life; relationships with extended families; and the problems of raising children or whether partners want children.

To many people with strong, traditional family values and a strong sense of traditional morality, this lifestyle is upsetting or even abhorrent. But social attitudes are changing rapidly. Many parents who, a mere five years ago, would have been horrified by the idea of their children—especially their daughters—having a live-in arrangement are no longer overly upset by it. Influenced by the extremely high failure rate of teenage marriage, many now tend to view the arrangement as a developmental step.

It seems likely that in another decade it will be more generally recognized that marriage ought to be the end-point of testing a relationship rather than a beginning, that divorce is too hurtful to have it otherwise.

By then, the number of parents who see the live-in arrangement as a desirable experience is likely to increase, and trial marriage will probably be the norm for segments of the population.

So far, the success rate for marriages of persons who have lived together before marrying is only about ten percent greater than that of other couples. But as more and more young people feel they can live with one another without feeling guilty and embattled, they may use the experience more constructively, making better marital choices based on greater self-knowledge and greater knowledge of the other person. We may then begin to see the first significant decline in the divorce rate.

Chapter 15

Improving Your Chances for a Successful Marriage

Will marriage survive? Now that the national divorce rate approaches fifty percent and new styles of relationships are being experimented with by greater and greater numbers of people, it seems likely that alternative lifestyles will play a significant role in the future. But it also seems likely that traditional marriage will survive. The impulse to pair—the desire to find another person with whom you can have a close, important and enduring relationship—is deeply built into the psyches of most people. However, we may see more variety in marital patterns in the future as more and more people recognize their freedom to design their own individual lifestyles. We may see some kind of legalization of the live-in situation and some legitimatizing of trial marriage, which teenage marriage has, in effect, become. We may see some form of renewable-term marriage, in which couples do a serious reassessment of their marriages at set intervals of several years and actively work on marriage remediation if the relationship is neither really good nor really bad.

We may also see more close, loving twosomes in marriage in the future than we have in the past. There are trends in society increasing the likelihood that a greater percentage of future marriages will be happy, rewarding partnerships.

Despite the lasting quality of the marriages of past generations, traditional marriage has not been particularly successful as a way for two people to relate to one another. Studies that go back fifty years tell us that two out of three marriages produce more hurt, pain and frustration than joy and reward. Only about fifteen or twenty percent of married couples have the kind of loving and intimacy that we idealize in the marriage situation."

Today, the narrowing of differences between men and women is creating a climate that, over time, will improve the potential for fulfilling marriage. Two people who experience themselves as worthy, strong, lovable individuals are most likely to have rewarding marital relationships. Feeling themselves to be people of value, they have no need to diminish their partners or to demand continual reassurance and approval. Rather, they are giving persons, ready to express appreciation of the strengths and attributes of each other because it is pleasurable to give. A disparity of power between partners is probably the most frequent central issue undermining a marriage. Equality of confidence, pride in self, and social and occupational recognition are the best insurance for a happy marriage.

Another reassuring aspect of the marriage scene today is that people are marrying later in life. Serious problems in early marriage are so common as to be considered almost inevitable. Eighty percent of the nineteen-year-olds in California who marry are divorced within seven years—and eventually, ninety-one percent of them. There is an estimated eighty percent failure rate in these young marriages in the rest of the country.

Statistically, the probability of a fulfilling marriage rises dramatically when one is a little older. By then, in the experience of living, you may have acted out some of the painful issues of your childhood. The extra years also give you a chance to evolve your personal style and be clear about what you are, what you like, how you want to treat someone and how you want to be treated. At eighteen or nineteen, your style as an individual is largely an amalgam of that of the other people in your life and of your heroes and heroines, past and present. Your personality goes through rapid modification during your twenties as your own unique, adult self emerges. There is no way you can know at eighteen or nineteen what kind of person you will be at thirty.

A young woman in her late teens usually responds to a male in terms of the images and values that are important to her contemporaries. In her mid-twenties she is likely to look for her own special characteristics in a man. A young man at twenty may be enormously concerned with the color of a woman's hair, her bustline or the shape of her legs, but by the time he is twenty-six or twenty-seven, he also is likely to be more concerned about other qualities.

Adding to the problems for early marriages is the fact that during the period of growth in which our unique adult self is emerging, our inner feelings can be confusing and obscure. To let another person know what you are feeling is doubly difficult at this time. When both marriage partners are in this growth process, it can be extremely hard for them to make emotional contact. Very often, both soon see the other as unloving or unlovable, and develop deep anger over feelings of isolation or rejection. When you add this disappointment to the initial expectations of great romantic love, you have a volatile mixture.

Statistically, the best chance for a good marriage occurs when the woman is twenty-five to twenty-seven years of age, and the man is between twenty-nine and thirty-two.

The Decline of Romantic Fantasy

Contributing to the improved outlook for marriage is a decline in the overindulgence of the past in the notion of romantic love as a basis for marriage. As we moved away from the nineteenth-century concept of parental choice of marriage partners to the idea of individual choice, there was a surge of enthusiasm for romantic love as the appropriate guide in this choice. The popularity of this concept put pressure on youngsters to pair off prematurely, curtailing their freedom to explore and experiment with a variety of people, thus limiting the choice of partners. In the worst instances, young people went steady at fifteen and sixteen, then married at nineteen, with neither partner having had any experience with another person.

This unrealistic emphasis on romantic love seems to be on the wane. Young people in their mid-twenties and older seem to be gaining awareness that love, in the sense of the intense, overwhelming sexual attraction of romantic fantasy, is not necessary to a successful marriage and is sometimes a poor guide to one. They appear to be much more realistic than their forebears about taking into account practical issues of compatibility—religious, ethnic and socioeconomic values, etc.

At least part of this new realism is due to the sophistication of the young generation. Youngsters are now exposed, through motion pictures and television and in literature aimed at teenagers and young adults, to a much broader experience of the character and quality of family relations and emotional life than ever before. The realism of many of these dramatic and literary presentations today provides a view of possible alternatives to one's own limited direct experience.

An additional factor in creating this more realistic assessment of potential marital partners has been the spreading custom of premarital cohabitation, which is essentially trial marriage. And those young people who do not experience a live-in affair still hear a great deal about them from their contemporaries. This greater realism in the choice of marital partners should considerably diminish the emotional and sexual mismatching that has characterized many marriages.

Marital Mismatches

In such an important relationship, we do a good deal of accommodating and adjusting, and people do change. But we also remain somewhat true to the original nature of our own individual personalities—the psychological and biological styles generated in the early years of life.

If you start marriage with a considerable mismatch of attitudes and social, emotional or sexual styles, it may never be possible to bridge the gap in a way that makes the relationship truly fulfilling. By the time you recognize these differences, it is difficult and painful to admit a mismatch.

Here, thirty-nine-year-old Leslie talks about recognizing after seventeen years of marriage that she isn't the right woman for her husband "in terms of personality."

"It's taken me a long time to accept and verbalize this fact," she said. "I am an aggressive, driving person. I have other pursuits besides raising five children—like getting a master's degree in teaching and training the mentally retarded while managing to keep my household together. My husband wanted me to stay home and take care of the kids.

"Until recently, I didn't realize how much I'd changed over these last fifteen years. I had thought marriage was a place to grow in, and I felt as if I had not been growing. Against resistance, I have grown. But there was always this wall of resistance from my husband. He has given in to my pursuing my goals with reluctance in each successive growth period. This was a frustrating experience for me.

"I feel better for having admitted that we're mismatched to myself and to him. The threatening elements have been reduced. Now I feel there is nothing to fear. I don't have to try any longer. But I'm not sure where I go from here. I know I don't want a divorce or anything like that. He's a very capable husband in most respects. But I would like to use this information constructively for better understanding and communication. I have announced that I will not pursue anything else educationally, because I feel it would be a disaster. Self-denial doesn't come easily when you're a person with a fair amount of drive. I feel very smothered. But I think I'm resigned."

There is pain and anger behind Leslie's resignation. She and her husband need to talk about their different attitudes and feelings and expectations. A number of them haven't been resolved, and perhaps never will be. They have some breaking through to do on the issue of Leslie's getting some encouragement within the relationship, if she is to continue in it.

Useful Aids in Achieving Marital Happiness

There would be fewer mismatches and less marital conflict if couples would seriously attempt to discover their differing views and attitudes before marriage.

We make a substantial investment when we go into marriage. We invest our feelings, our deep sentimental and romantic images, our desire to love and be loved, as well as our time, energy, earning capacity, child-rearing potential, companionship, etc. Yet most young couples planning marriage do not deal with the large range of practical issues they will inevitably confront in the relationship, such as the issue of parenthood and attitudes toward work, material possessions, social life, sensual and sexual contact, and extended family. What may seem like insignificant details during the period of intense romantic fantasy often become very distressing differences later.

As lifestyles proliferate in our changing society, and traditional marital roles and expectations are modified or dropped by increasing numbers of people, the potential for differences between two people is greater than ever before.

If two people want to increase substantially the probability of a successful marriage, they will seek some outside influence to prod themselves into clarifying their attitudes and genuinely getting acquainted.

The "State of Your Union" Questionnaire, which follows this chapter, is one tool that can serve this purpose. If two people go through it together in a very open way, answering questions fully, it will provide a basis for a great deal of intimate communication. Not only can this clarify expectations and differences, but it can also illuminate the elements in the relationship that are romantic fantasy, and identify the ways in which each person fights for (or avoids) what each wants in the relationship.

Participation in lecture-discussion groups on marriage or reading relevant books can also be helpful in triggering useful discussions. Premarital counseling and psychological group work are, of course, very effective in giving prospective partners a clearer profile of where they stand with one another.

That increasing numbers of people are becoming aware of the need to clarify expectations before marriage can be seen in the growing popularity of premarital contracts. Basically, the contract is a mechanism for communication. Partners put down on paper what each expects from marriage, defining all aspects of these expectations, from money and children to emotional needs. To develop such a contract fully, you have to communicate. I have found marital contracts useful for clarifying expectations and attitudes, not only with young people in premarital counseling (who often startle each other with their divergent views), but also with older persons remarrying and with persons who have separated and are in marital and emotional crisis.

The "State of Your Union" Questionnaire can also be useful to the already married in opening the kind of communication that is needed for partners to gain insight into their relationships and negotiate troubling differences.

A number of other kinds of assistance for couples seeking to improve their marriages are also available today. Schools, churches and other organizations offer innumerable courses designed to help.

The marriage encounter weekend, which many religious organizations sponsor, is valuable to many couples who have marriages that are going reasonably well. In this experience, they gain fresh perceptions of their relationships and of the inner lives and feelings of each other. They also acquire useful insights into the ways of relating of other couples. Participants are often astonished by what they see happening in their own marriages, and become aware of possibilities for bettering their partnerships. The excitement generated by this awareness is enhanced by sharing the experience with others who feel the same way. This excitement adds to one's will to go through the process of partially reinventing the marriage.

Marriage counseling and family therapy, group and individual psychotherapy, and the many workshops on personal relationships and personal growth that have evolved out of modern psychotherapeutic thinking also can be extremely helpful, and for some couples, that kind of professional support is essential if a marriage is to become rewarding. The whole concept of the inherent capacity for personal emotional growth that underlies modern psychotherapy has significant implications for marriage, because it provides the means of altering the crippling emotional legacies that families hand down from generation to generation.

No marriage or any other important and continuing relationship between two human beings ever becomes totally free of conflict or some degree of negative feelings. But in most spousal partnerships, positive feelings can be expanded and negative ones decreased, in some cases dramatically. Partners can learn to recognize the hurtful ways they relate to one another and learn new and positive ones. They can learn how to develop close emotional contact, and how to fight constructively to work out differences. They can learn to create the kind of loving, caring, giving and taking partnership, capable of absorbing the stress of life, that is marriage at its best.

"The State of Your Union"
Questionnaire

Relationships can range from ideal to disastrous. Have a little fun—and learn some interesting things about your own relationship by scoring yourself on this "State of Your Union" questionnaire.

Its primary value is as a tool for beginning to talk with your partner about those aspects of your relationship that are not likely to be examined frequently.

The first two sections of the questionnaire deal directly with attitudes that affect our ability to create intimacy and a satisfactory sexual relationship.

The next two sections cover areas in which differences between partners are most likely to create problems; lifestyle, attitudes toward extended family, and the uses of money.

The last section should be particularly useful to couples trying to decide whether or not to have children. However, it may also help parents to recognize facets of themselves that lead to difficulties in child-rearing, and aid divorcing couples in child-custody decisions.

Each of you should work through the questions on your own, without consulting the other. Be as honest as you can; don't put down an answer because you know *intellectually* that it is probably the preferred attitude. Use your real feelings as a guide.

Score yourself according to the method given at the beginning of "Answers to the Questionnaire" (p. 238). Your score in each section can give you an assessment of your position in your relationship.

After each of you has scored him or herself, take some time together to discuss the questionnaire, item by item. If each of you has been honest, you will have a great deal to talk about, and you will learn a great deal about your partner and your relationship.

In answering the questions, mark the "Yes" column if your answer would be "much of the time," "usually," or "to a considerable degree." Mark the "No" column for answers like "not generally true," "not often," or "no, to a considerable degree."

If your answer lies somewhere between yes and no, then mark the "M" column. ("M" could stand for "moderately".)

Section 1

How Open to Intimate Communication Are You?

Questions	Yes	M	No

1. Do you and your partner discuss inner life feelings?
   (If you do this a good deal, a mark under "Yes" is appropriate. If you rarely or never do it, mark "No". If you do it, but infrequently, mark "M".) ___ ___ ___
2. Do you feel you have personal rights that are inherent in the dignity of your self? ___ ___ ___
3. Are you really free to exercise your personal rights (Question 2) within your relationship? ___ ___ ___
4. Have you as strong a sense of yourself *in* your relationship as you had as a single person? ___ ___ ___
5. Can you tolerate a sense of aloneness or separateness? ___ ___ ___
6. Do you experience a clear sense of your own self-worth? ___ ___ ___
7. Have you a high degree of hidden anger toward the opposite sex? ___ ___ ___
8. Do you have feelings of suspicion about the opposite sex? ___ ___ ___

	Yes	M	No

9. Do you feel intimidated by (or less important than) persons of the opposite sex?

10. Do you have a strong sense of male and female roles—a sense that men are supposed to behave one way and women another?

11. Do you try to maintain an image with other people, including your partner? An image of tough courage, perhaps? Or martyrdom? Or sizzling sexuality?

12. Is importance in your relationship based on sex roles?

13. Does one person consistently act out a parent role in the relationship? Does the man act as "daddy" to a "little girl"? Does the woman mother the man?

14. Does one of you do most of the reaching out to the other for closeness, taking most of the risk of self-disclosure?

15. Do you see yourself as a complicated person? Do you have conflicting sets of feelings? Complex motivations?

16. If you disagree with your partner, do you feel there is something *wrong* with him or her?

17. Do both of you tend to hear one another in a tolerant and accepting way?

18. Do both of you feel free to initiate negotiations around an issue?

19. Are you both respectful of each other's way of being? Is it all right with you for your partner to be different from you?

20. Is it all right for you and your partner to feel and express anger and upset in the relationship?

	Yes	M	No
21. Do you habitually hide pain in your relationship?	—	—	—
22. In earlier relationships (in childhood, youth, and other love relationships), did you deal with pain by hiding it?	—	—	—

Section 2

Your Sexual Relationship

Question	Yes	M	No
1. Do you consider yourself knowledgeable about sexual anatomy and responses?	—	—	—
2. Are you uncomfortable with nudity—your own or your partner's?	—	—	—
3. Can you laugh, play and horse around as part of your sexual experience?	—	—	—
4. Is sex important and enjoyable to you?	—	—	—
5. Are you pleased with the frequency of your sexual activity?	—	—	—
6. Are you usually pleased with your orgasmic reaction?	—	—	—
7. Do you feel there is sufficient touching, caressing and tenderness in your sex life?	—	—	—
8. Can you talk freely with your partner about your sexual relationship?	—	—	—

		Yes	M	No
9.	Can you ask for what you want in sex with your partner?	___	___	___
10.	When something delightful happens in sex, can you verbalize this to your partner?	___	___	___
11.	When something disappointing happens during sex, can you verbalize this to your partner?	___	___	___
12.	Are the feelings of warm affection and recognition as being special to your partner missing in your lovemaking?	___	___	___
13.	Do you feel really comfortable initiating sex?	___	___	___
14.	Do you feel really comfortable having your partner initiate sex?	___	___	___
15.	Do you initiate sex about half the time?	___	___	___
16.	Are you unable to tell your partner when you aren't in the mood for sex?	___	___	___
17.	Do you permit sex when you don't really want it?	___	___	___
18.	Were your parents good examples of loving sexuality? Did they convey a sense of being pleased and comfortable with their sexuality?	___	___	___
19.	Is it difficult for you and your partner to expose and resolve differences in your sexual attitudes?	___	___	___
20.	Can you and your partner share sexual fantasies?	___	___	___
21.	Do you plan to experiment further in the variety of sexual activities with your partner?	___	___	___

Section 3

Lifestyle and Familial Attitudes

Question	Yes	M	No
1. Do you enjoy the same type of people that your partner does?	—	—	—
2. Do you enjoy the same type of social activity that your partner enjoys?	—	—	—
3. Do you like the same sports, games, and outdoor life that your partner does?	—	—	—
4. Are your ideas of happy cultural experiences the same as your partner's? Do you like the same plays? Music? Art?	—	—	—
5. Are vacations together highly enjoyable?	—	—	—
6. Do you like the way your partner looks?	—	—	—
7. Does your partner's taste in clothes appeal to you?	—	—	—
8. Can you genuinely admire your partner's accomplishments?	—	—	—
9. Do you feel completely comfortable in your partner's presence?	—	—	—
10. Are you more ambitious, more goal-oriented than your partner?	—	—	—
11. Do you procrastinate?	—	—	—
12. Do you tend to be chronically late?	—	—	—
13. Does your partner have habits that upset you?	—	—	—
14. Do you like and enjoy your parents now?	—	—	—

	Yes	M	No

15. Do you like and enjoy your partner's parents?
16. Do you like and enjoy your siblings?
17. Do you like and enjoy your partner's siblings?
18. Do you generally enjoy your extended family—aunts, uncles, cousins, in-laws?
19. Do you and your partner quarrel about family?
20. Do you think you see traits of a disliked relative in your partner's personality?
21. Is your partner kinder and more helpful to friends and neighbors than to you or your children?

Section 4

The Uses of Money

Question	Yes	M	No

1. Do you regard your personal income as yours, instead of as the income of the relationship?
2. Do you regard your partner's income as jointly owned?
3. Does one person control the money available for discretionary expenditure?

	Yes	M	No

4. Do you view money as power in the relationship?
5. Do you and your partner each have some separate money that you can spend freely?
6. If one person in the household handles the bookkeeping, is that okay with the other?
7. Are you afraid of handling money? Afraid you will spend it extravagantly, or be unable to accurately calculate a budget or bank balance?
8. Do you spend compulsively, buy expensive items on impulse, or constantly shop?
9. Do you spend money when you are angry?
10. Do you fritter away money on little things?
11. Do you feel guilty when you spend money?
12. Do you deny yourself, but spend freely on your children? Your home? Your car?
13. Can you spend money *only* on the house? The car? A boat? Or any other *single* area of life?
14. Can you accept gifts comfortably?
15. Do you need gifts for reassurance of love?
16. Do you and your partner agree on a savings program?
17. Do you have long-term monetary goals, such as retirement with dignity, or children's education? Have you a program to fulfill these goals?
18. Are your business affairs arranged in a way that would be wise in case of the death of either spouse?

		Yes	M	No
19.	Is money *too* important a factor in your life?	___	___	___
20.	Is money not taken seriously enough in your life?	___	___	___
21.	Do you quarrel about money?	___	___	___

Section 5

Are You Suited for Parenthood?

Question	Yes	M	No
1. Do you enjoy or have a pleasant response to children?	___	___	___
2. Are children necessary to your concept of family?	___	___	___
3. Do you feel "yearnings" when you see a six-month-old infant?	___	___	___
4. Do you enjoy touching and being touched?	___	___	___
5. Are you a nurturing kind of person? Did you enjoy babysitting as a youngster? Did you like caring for pets, or a younger sibling?	___	___	___
6. Would you say you're relaxed, rather than high-strung?	___	___	___
7. Are you tolerant of the noise and excitement of small children?	___	___	___
8. Do you have good control over your temper?	___	___	___
9. Will having children interfere with your career?	___	___	___
10. Are you a very jealous person?	___	___	___
11. Is privacy necessary to your well-being?	___	___	___

		Yes	M	No
12.	Are you an extremely neat, fastidious person?	—	—	—
13.	Is travel, or variety in your place of residence, very important to you?	—	—	—
14.	Do you view the world as a dangerous place?	—	—	—
15.	Are you a controlling person? Do you need to control the world around you?	—	—	—

Answers to the Questionnaire

The answers given here are the preferred ones, derived from norms based on a sampling of well over two hundred couples. Every time your answer agrees with the preferred one, give yourself three points. If your answer is exactly opposite to the preferred one, give yourself one point. Each "M" answer gets two points. Add up your points in each section and compare the totals with the norm.

Section 1
Intimate Communication

1. *Yes.* To reveal to a partner the inner pain, conflicts, hopes and joys of one's inner life is the essence of intimate communication. It involves taking the risk of lowering the self-protective barriers we normally erect between ourselves and other people.

2–6. *Yes.* These questions are all associated with feeling yourself to be an autonomous, worthy person, relating to a relatively equal partner. If you view yourself in this way, you relate to your partner from a position of strength. You are not a child; your need to be liked, taken care of or approved of by others does not govern your actions. You are unlikely to be inhibited by fear of disapproval in revealing your feelings. The sense of separateness and aloneness, which is a part of the feeling of autonomy, makes you aware that you must communicate your feelings if a partner is to know and understand them.

7–9. *No.* Each of these attitudes toward the opposite sex, held by large numbers of people, inhibits our willingness to be self-disclosing to a partner. Becoming aware of these feelings, which come from early life experiences, and sharing this awareness with a partner, can be the beginning of intimate communication.

10. *No.* Most of us cannot fill a particular role comfortably all of the time. A strong sense that men are supposed to be one way in their feelings, and women another, often inhibits self-disclosure between partners. When a person feels in conflict with his or her image of gender identity or role, the natural impulse is to defend oneself by keeping this inner pain locked inside.

11. *No.* This question also has to do with both gender identity and self-image. When we can't be the way we want to be, we have inner pain that is difficult to disclose.

12. *No.* Feelings that one sex is more important than the other come from familial, social and subcultural conditioning. We have a tendency to hide these attitudes; this can create conflict. Intimate communication can help to dispel this conflict.

13. *No.* Occasional playful "daddying" and "mommying" can be rewarding mutual nurturing that may enrich a partnership. But habitually dealing with one another in parent-child roles is destructive.

14. *No.* If only one person habitually takes risks for closeness, he or she tends to withdraw gradually, waiting to be met or matched by risks of the other partner. This creates a climate where intimate communication withers and dies.

15. *Yes.* We all have complex feelings, thoughts, motivations and ways of getting what we want. If you see yourself as a simple person, you are avoiding recognizing the subtleties of your own inner life.

16. *No.*
17–20. *Yes.* These five questions indicate the degree of tolerance of differences between you and your partner. High tolerance for difference is desirable, rather than rigid feelings that there is only one correct way to deal with life. It shows an ability to accept the fact that you have differing realities based on different life experiences. Diversity between partners exists, and tolerance and respect for it must also exist if intimate communication is to be achieved.

21–22. *No.* Hiding pain, anger or upset is avoidance of the self-disclosure necessary to intimate communication.

Maximum score—66
Excellent score—60–66
Good score—54–59
Requires attention—53 or less.

Section 2
Your Sexual Relationship

1. *Yes.* The more knowledgeable you are about the anatomy, physiology and sexual responses of your partner, the more likely you are to have a good sexual relationship. However knowledgeable we think we are, though, it is always good to periodically update and refresh our understanding of these areas by reading, lectures, classes, or whatever will be useful to individuals.

2. *No.* Being comfortable with nudity in your intimate relationships makes an important contribution to good sexual life.

3. *Yes.* Playfulness is an important dimension of sexual spontaneity. It is the natural human response to sex in primitive societies, where people have not been inhibited by social, cultural or religious proscriptions.

4–7. *Yes.* A "no" answer by either partner to any of these four questions indicates some disappointment or disillusionment in sex. Not dealing with the problem can lead to a partner's withdrawal from sex—or at least from warm, positive sexual involvement. Or it may create anger, which will be expressed in other areas. It might even lead to infidelity.

8–11. *Yes.* If you can each talk freely about sex with your partner, asking for what you want and commenting in a matter-of-fact way—without indictment—when something delights or disappoints you, the potential for a rich sexual life is enhanced.

12.   *No*. Many women, and a lesser number of men, complain that a partner's lovemaking, however knowledgeable or varied it may be, seems mechanical. This kind of disappointment has to do with a desire for recognition as someone who is loved. Sufficient attention and affection, given in a way that is meaningful, is lacking before, during and after lovemaking. Feeling such a lack triggers inner anger, which begins to erode mutual pleasure in the sexual experience.

13–15.   *Yes*. Many of us have fears of rejection and experience a great deal of embarrassment in asking the other person to participate in something we want.

16–17.   *No*. Some people feel anxious or guilty about turning down a partner's request for sex, and accept a sexual initiative when they don't really want to. If a person does this with any frequency, sexual feelings will begin to erode in a way that will have a destructive effect on the relationship. A male making love to his partner only because he feels she expects it is inviting partial impotence. For a female, it is much the same; her capacity to be sexually aroused will be undermined.

18.   *Yes*. If your parents were good love/sex models, you are likely to be pleased and comfortable with your own sexuality. If not, you need to fight to overcome negative attitudes you acquired from them.

19.   *No*. Partners often hide from one another the offense and upset they experience over differences in sexual attitudes. The hidden anger that results erodes good feelings, warmth and spontaneity in sex. Sharing the knowledge that these differences exist can be a first step to finding a middle ground where both can be comfortable.

20.   *Yes*. Sharing of fantasies leads to enhancement of the sexual relationship.

21.   *Yes*. For many people, a lack of variety in sex causes boredom. A "yes" answer indicates that you intend to avoid letting your sexual experiences together become a routine.

Maximum score—63
Excellent score—54–63
Good score—46–53
Requires attention—45 or less.

Section 3
Lifestyle and Familial Attitudes

1–4. *Yes.* It's certainly not necessary for partners to have *strong* "yes" answers in all areas. But the more you enjoy in common, the more likely you are to view your partnership as a friendly companionship.

5. *Yes.* The ability to enjoy vacationing together indicates intellectual and emotional companionship and warmth of feelings.

6–8. *Yes.* Positive feelings toward your partner's attributes have less to do with objective reality than with good feelings toward him or her.

9. *Yes.* If you often feel uncomfortable with your partner, you may be receiving messages that he or she does not like some natural part of your personality (boisterousness or whining, perhaps). The situation ought to be discussed, and adjustments made to allow both of you more comfort within the relationship.

10. *No.* When only one person is striving for goal-achievement, the other often becomes angry and resentful about relinquishing time and attention. The achievement of the goal may seem more important to the ambitious person than the goal of happy marriage.

11–13. *No.* Lateness, procrastination and annoying habits are ways of triggering behaviors and feelings associated with childhood anger. They are ways of getting back at parents, and the partner in the relationship is seen in a parental role. Watch out. These behaviors tend to feed a cycle of anger and frustration that can seriously undermine a relationship.

14–18. *Yes*.

19. *No*. There *are* persons in good relationships who can give opposite answers, but in general, friendly feelings toward extended family is one of the best predictors of positive attitudes in a relationship.

20. *No*. This is a way of expressing anger toward the partner.

21. *No*. The person who is kind to friends and neighbors at the expense of his/her partner and/or children has been termed "street angel—house devil." It is not uncommon for persons raised in an unhappy home to be uncomfortable with affection, warmth and emotional intimacy within a relationship.

Maximum score—63
Excellent score—55–63
Good score—46–54
Requires attention—45 or less.

Section 4
The Uses of Money

1. *No*.
2. *Yes*.
3–4. *No*. Money is symbolic of adult authority in our society. When one person controls the finances, authority and power tend to be held by one person (as in a patriarchy or matriarchy) rather than by relational partners. When money is viewed as jointly earned and controlled, no matter whose name is on the paycheck, partners are likely to have a more positive set of attitudes toward one another.

5. *Yes*. While joint control of decisions on budgets and major expenditures is desirable, each partner needs some small amount of money for independent use. It is degrading to one's dignity as a person not to have any resources that can be used autonomously.

6.   *Yes*. Delegation of bookkeeping to one person is necessary for efficiency. If the way you are handling this is *not okay* with both of you, then you need to discuss and deal with this problem.

7.   *No*. Handling money is symbolic of coping with the world. Being afraid of it is an indication of fear in other areas.

8.   *No*. Compulsive buying, impulse buying and constantly shopping all indicate a childlike view of money. The child inside of us takes control in the area of money when be behave in any of these ways. Shopping constantly, while partly a way of filling time, is partly comparable to constantly visiting the toy store. Spending compulsively is a way of trying to tell yourself that you have more money than you really do. All these behaviors are ways of avoiding other life problems. Like any other compulsion, spending can get out of hand, becoming a threat to financial stability.

9–10. *No*. Here, too, your inner child is taking over.

11–12. *No*. These questions relate to self-denial. A self-denying, self-sacrificial approach to life virtually always ends up with anger and depression.

13.   *No*. If you spend money in an unbalanced way, putting inordinant amounts into one area of life, others will obviously be shortchanged. If spending reflects an interest not equally shared by both partners, the non-spending partner can easily become resentful and angry.

14.   *Yes*. Not being able to accept gifts comfortably and graciously has to do with feelings of unworthiness. This frequently leads to misunderstanding and anger between partners.

15.   *No*. Needing gifts for reassurance of love also relates to feelings of unworthiness.

16–17 *Yes*. Not having long-term monetary goals and an appropriate savings program often leads to problems in later years. When partners realize they face retirement with very limited resources, they also face the possibility of recriminations and a higher level of irritability.

18.   *Yes.* Attention to such arrangements indicates thoughtful concern for each other's well-being.

19–20.   *No.* Either extreme, whether money seems too important or too trivial a factor in life, creates discomfort and divisiveness. Partners need to discuss how to diminish the anxieties and discomforts that exist.

21.   *No.* Quarrels over money that arise when people have widely divergent attitudes toward its use can be fierce. However, this is frequently a way of acting out conflicts in other areas of the relationship. Often the struggle is really over power or dominance, but money serves as a concrete focal point.

Maximum score—63
Excellent score—56–63
Good score—50–55
Requires attention—49 or less.

Section 5
Are You Suited for Parenthood?

1–3.   *Yes.* These are obvious indicators of inclinations toward parenthood as an appropriate choice.

4.   *Yes.* Enjoying touching is extremely important to positive parenting during infancy and early childhood—and it's a desirable attribute for parents of children of *any* age.

5.   *Yes.* If you have low nurturance factors in your personality, you're not likely to be comfortable with or tolerant of the demands and circumstances of parenting.

6–8.   *Yes.* Negative answers here indicate that you should consider very carefully before opting for parenthood.

9.   *No.* Which is more important to you? Be sure of the answer before you commit yourself.

10.   *No.* If you're a jealous person, you'll tend to be jealous of your spouse's closeness with the children. You may be

jealous of your children's love for your spouse. Since children often play one parent off against the other, jealousy is detrimental to good parenting.

11. *No*. Remember, children are noisy and invade parental privacy. When they are very young, they need constant parental attention. Be sure you're willing to share that much of your life.

12. *No*. Children won't be able to maintain your standards of order. Will you be able to tolerate it?

13. *No*. This attitude is at odds with children's need for stability, continuity and semipermanence.

14. *No*. Your fears might undermine a child's confidence, ego strength and feelings of security.

15. *No*. Children invite being controlled because they need to be directed, influenced and protected. However, too much control inhibits their development. If you have a need to control the people around you, you will have to keep a tight reign on this tendency if you want to avoid over-controlling your children.

Maximum score—45
Excellent score—40–45
Good score—35–39
Requires thorough examination—34 or less.

About the Author

Dr. Norton F. Kristy is co-founder of The Center for Counseling and Psychotherapy in Santa Monica, California. He is licensed as both a clinical psychologist and marriage and family counselor. Dr. Kristy is former professor of psychology at the University of Illinois, UCLA, and Colorado College. For many years, he was Senior Research Scientist in Psychology at the Rand Corporation. Dr. Kristy, who has been involved in public and commercial radio and television for over thirty years, has also been a pioneer and innovator in bringing psychological counseling to radio talk shows. During the 1970s, he was syndicated nationally on the Bill Ballance radio show.